Writing Literature Reviews

A Guide for Students of the Social and Behavioral Sciences

THIRD EDITION

Jose L. Galvan

California State University, Los Angeles

 Pyrczak Publishing

P.O. Box 250430 • Glendale, CA 91225

Although the author and publisher have made every effort to ensure the accuracy and completeness of information contained in this book, we assume no responsibility for errors, inaccuracies, omissions, or any inconsistency herein. Any slights of people, places, or organizations are unintentional.

Project Director: Monica Lopez.

Editorial assistance provided by Cheryl Alcorn, Randall R. Bruce, Karen M. Disner, Brenda Koplin, Erica Simmons, and Sharon Young.

Cover design by Robert Kibler and Larry Nichols.

Printed in the United States of America by Malloy, Inc.

"Pyrczak Publishing" is an imprint of Fred Pyrczak, Publisher, A California Corporation.

ISBN 1-884585-66-3

Contents

Model Literature Reviews for Discussion and Evaluation

Continued →

Detailed Contents

Notes:

Introduction to the Third Edition

The purpose of this book is to provide students with a practical guide to the complex process of writing literature reviews in the social and behavioral sciences. The primary focus is on reviewing original research published in academic journals and on its relationship to theoretical literature. However, most of the guidelines presented here can also be applied to reviews of other kinds of source materials.

Audience for This Book

This book was written for students who are required to write literature reviews as term papers in content-area classes in the social and behavioral sciences. Often, their previous training has not prepared them to search databases for reports of original research and related theoretical literature, analyze these particular types of literature, and synthesize them into a cohesive narrative. Instead, they are often taught how to use secondary sources such as encyclopedias, reports in the mass media, and books that synthesize the work of others. In addition, they are usually not taught the conventions for writing papers in the social and behavioral sciences. This book is designed to fill this gap by giving students detailed, step-by-step guidance on how to write comprehensive reviews of primary source materials.

Students who are beginning to work on their theses and dissertations will also benefit from this book if they have not previously received comprehensive instruction on how to prepare critical analyses of published research and the theories on which it is based. Undertaking a thesis or dissertation is stressful. This book should serve as a source of calm and logic as students begin to work on their literature review chapter.

Finally, individuals who are preparing to write literature reviews for possible publication in journals as well as those who need to include literature reviews in grant proposals will find this book helpful.

Unique Features

The following features make this book unique among textbooks designed to teach analytical writing:

- The book's focus is on writing critical reviews of original research.
- It guides students through a systematic, multistep writing process.
- The steps and guidelines are organized sequentially and are illustrated with examples from a wide range of academic journals.
- Each chapter is designed to help students develop a set of specific products that will contribute toward a competent literature review.

Notes to the Instructor

Many colleges and universities have adopted "writing-across-the-curriculum" programs, in which all students are required to write papers in all courses. While the goals of such programs are admirable, many instructors are pressed for time to cover just the traditional content of their courses and have little time to teach writing. Such instructors will find this book useful because the explicit steps in the writing process are illustrated with examples throughout, which make it possible for students to use it largely on their own. In addition, many professors "naturally" write well but have given little thought to and have no training in *how to teach writing*. Used as a supplement, this book solves that dilemma by providing a detailed guide to the writing process.

Much of what most of us know about writing was learned through what Kamhi-Stein (1997) calls the "one-shot writing assignment" (p. 52).[1] This is where the instructor gives an assignment at the beginning of the term, using the writing prompt, "Write a paper about *<specific topic>*." Conceptually, we tend to view this type of assignment as a single task, even though students may go through several discrete steps in the process of completing it. In fact, when writing papers that involve library research, the quality of the finished product depends in large measure on the care with which we undertake each of these steps.

In this book, the activities at the end of each chapter are designed to guide students through these various steps or stages of the writing process. These activities can be recast as a series of tasks that can easily be incorporated into the syllabus of a survey course in a specific discipline as a multistep writing assignment. Thus, this book has two complementary audiences: (a) instructors who may want to incorporate this multistep writing approach into their course syllabus and (b) students, working independently, who may need help in planning and implementing the various stages involved in completing a major writing assignment, such as the literature review chapter of a thesis or dissertation.

About the Third Edition

Many of the examples have been updated throughout this new edition. Also, two new chapters have been added: Chapter 6 (Analyzing Qualitative Research Literature) and Chapter 7 (Building Tables to Summarize Literature). In addition, this edition contains a larger number of model literature reviews than the previous edition. These model literature reviews can serve as the basis for classroom discussions and as source material for end-of-chapter activities for Chapters 1, 8, 9, and 10.

Acknowledgments

I thank my supervisor, Dr. Theodore J. Crovello, for allowing me to schedule days off when I need them and for encouraging me to find ways to continue to pursue my professional and academic interests, even while working as an academic administrator.

I am also indebted to my editor, Dr. Fred Pyrczak, for suggesting the topic for this book and for his generous assistance with the research design content of Chapters 1 and 5. In addition, I am indebted to my colleagues on the faculty of California State University, Los Angeles, especially Drs. Marguerite Ann Snow and Lia D. Kamhi-Stein, whose work on the multistep writing approach inspired this book's organization. All three of these individuals offered countless helpful suggestions, most of which are now part of the final manuscript. Errors and omissions, of course, remain my responsibility.

---

[1] Kamhi-Stein, L. D. (1997). Redesigning the writing assignment in general education courses. *College ESL, 7*, 49–61.

Feedback

I welcome your feedback and am especially interested in receiving suggestions that can be used to improve the next edition of this book. You can write to me care of the publisher using the address on the title page of this book or by e-mailing messages to me via Info@Pyrczak.com.

Jose L. Galvan
Los Angeles, California

DEDICATION

For my daughter, Melisa,
a wonderfully creative and independent writer.

Notes:

Chapter 1

Writing Reviews of Academic Literature: An Overview

This book is a guide to the specialized requirements of writing a literature review in the social and behavioral sciences. In it, you will be learning how to write a review of the literature using primary (original) sources of information in the social and behavioral sciences. By far, the most common primary sources are reports of empirical research published in academic journals. This chapter begins with a brief overview of this type of source. It is followed by brief descriptions of four other types of material found in journals: (1) theoretical articles, (2) literature review articles, (3) anecdotal reports, and (4) reports on professional practices and standards. These are followed by an overview of the writing process you will be using as you write your review. This overview includes a brief summary of the rest of the book.

An Introduction to Reviewing Primary Sources

Why Focus on Empirical Research Reports?

The focus of this book is on *original* reports of research found in academic journals. They are *original* because they are the first published accounts of research. As such, they are *primary sources* of information, providing detailed reports on the methodology used in the research and detailed descriptions and discussions of the findings. In contrast, research summaries reported in textbooks, popular magazines, and newspapers as well as on television and radio are usually *secondary sources*, which typically provide only global descriptions of results with few details on the methodology used to obtain them. As scholars, you will want to emphasize primary sources when you review the literature on a particular topic. In fact, your instructor may require you to cite primary sources exclusively in your written reviews of literature.

Journals in the social and behavioral sciences abound with original reports of *empirical research*. The term *empirical* refers to *observation* while the term *empirical research* refers to *systematic observation*. Research is systematic when researchers plan in advance whom to observe, for what characteristics to observe, how to observe, and so on. While empirical research is the foundation of any science, one could reasonably argue that all empirical research is inherently flawed, hence the results obtained with research should be interpreted with caution. For instance, listed below are three major issues that arise in almost all empirical studies and the problems they pose for reviewers of research.

- *Issue 1: Sampling.* Most researchers study only a sample of individuals and infer that the results apply to some larger group (often called the population). Furthermore, most researchers use samples with some kind of bias that makes them unrepresentative of the populations of interest. For instance, suppose a professor conducted research using only students in his or her introductory psychology class, or suppose a researcher mailed a questionnaire and obtained only a 40% return. Clearly, these samples might not be representative of the populations of interest.

> Problem: A reviewer needs to consider the possibility of errors in sampling when interpreting the results of a study. Deciding how much trust to put in the results of a study based on a flawed sample is a highly subjective judgment.

- *Issue 2: Measurement.* Almost all instruments used for measurement in empirical research should be presumed to be flawed to some extent. For instance, suppose a researcher uses a self-report questionnaire to measure the incidence of marijuana use on a campus. Even if respondents are assured that their responses are confidential and anonymous, some might not want to reveal their illegal behavior. On the other hand, others might be tempted to brag about doing something illegal even if they seldom or never do it. So what are the alternatives? One is to conduct personal interviews, but this measurement technique also calls for revelation of an illegal activity. Another alternative is a covert observation, but this technique might be unethical. On the other hand, if the observation is not covert, participants might change their behavior because they know they are being observed. As you can see, there is no perfect solution.

> Problem: A reviewer needs to consider the possibility of measurement error. Ask yourself whether the method of measurement seems sound. Did the researcher use more than one method of measurement? If so, do the various methods yield consistent results?

- *Issue 3: Problem identification.* Researchers usually examine only a part of a problem—often just a very small part. Here is an example: Suppose a researcher wants to study the use of rewards in the classroom and its effects on creativity. At first, this sounds manageable as a research problem until one considers that there are many kinds of rewards—many kinds and levels of praise, many types of prized objects that might be given, and so on. Another issue is that there are many different ways in which creativity can be expressed. For instance, creativity is expressed differently in the visual arts, in dance, and in music. Additional forms of creativity can be expressed in the physical sciences, in oral expression, written communication, and so on. No researcher has the resources to examine all of these. Instead, he or she will probably have to select only one or two types of rewards and only one or two manifestations of creativity and examine them in a limited number of classrooms.

> Problem: A reviewer needs to synthesize the various research reports on narrowly defined problems in a given area, looking for consistencies and discrepancies from report to report while keeping in mind that each researcher defined his or her problem in a somewhat different way from the others. Because empirical research provides only approximations and degrees of evidence on research problems that are necessarily limited in scope, creating a synthesis is like trying to put together a jigsaw puzzle for which most of the pieces are missing and many of the available pieces are not fully formed.

Considering the three issues presented above, you might be tempted to conclude that reviewing original reports of empirical research is difficult. Undoubtedly, it sometimes is. However, if you pick a topic of interest to you and thoroughly read the research on that topic, you will soon become immersed in a fascinating project. On the vast majority of topics in the social and behavioral sciences, there are at least minor disagreements about the interpretation of the available research data, and often there are major disagreements. Hence, you may soon find yourself acting like a juror, deliberating about which researchers seem to have the most cohesive and logical arguments, which ones have the strongest evidence, and so on. This can be a fascinating activity.

You also might incorrectly conclude that only students who have intensively studied research methods and statistics can make sense of original research reports. While such a background undoubtedly is very helpful, this book was written with the assumption that any intelligent, careful reader can make sense out of a body of empirical research if he or she reads carefully and extensively on the topic selected for review. Authors of reports of original research do not just present statistics in isolation. Instead, they usually provide discussions of previous research on their research topic, definitions of basic concepts, descriptions of relevant theories, their reasons for approaching their research in the way they did, as well as interpretations of the results moderated by acknowledgments of the limitations of their methodology. Thus, a skilled author of a report on original empirical research will guide you through the material and make it comprehensible to you even if you do not understand all the research jargon and statistics included in the research report.

One final consideration: It is essential that you carefully and thoroughly read all the research articles that you cite in your literature review. Reading only the brief abstracts (summaries) at the beginning of research articles may mislead you because of the lack of detail and therefore cause you to mislead the readers of your literature review. Thus, it is your ethical responsibility to read each cited reference in its entirety.

Another Kind of Primary Source: Theoretical Articles

Not every journal article is a report of original research. For instance, some articles are written for the explicit purpose of critiquing an existing theory or to propose a new one. Remember, a *theory* is a general explanation of why variables work together, how they are related to each other, and especially how they influence each other. As a unified set of constructs, a theory helps to explain how seemingly unrelated empirical observations tie together and make sense. Here is a brief example:

> Consider the *relational theory of loneliness*.[1] Among other things, this theory distinguishes between *emotional loneliness* (utter loneliness created by the lack of a close emotional attachment to another person) and *social loneliness* (feelings of isolation and loneliness created by the absence of a close social network). This theory has important implications for many areas of social and behavioral research. For instance, this theory predicts that someone who is in bereavement due to the death of a spouse with whom they had a close *emotional* attachment will experience utter loneliness that cannot be moderated through *social* support.

---

[1] This example is based on material in Stroebe, W., Stroebe, M., Abakoumkin, G., & Schut, H. (1996). The role of loneliness and social support in adjustment to loss: A test of attachment versus stress theory. *Journal of Personality and Social Psychology, 70,* 1241–1249. The relational theory of loneliness is based on and is an extension of "attachment theory." For a detailed discussion see: Atkinson, L., & Goldberg, S. (2004). *Attachment issues in psychopathology and intervention.* Mahwah, NJ: Erlbaum Associates.

Notice two things about the example given above. First, the prediction based on the theory runs counter to this commonsense notion: that those who are lonely due to the loss of a significant other will feel less lonely with the social support of family and friends. However, the theory suggests that this notion is only partially true at best. Specifically, it suggests that family and friends will be able to lessen *social loneliness* but be ineffective in lessening the more deeply felt and potentially devastating *emotional loneliness*. Note that it is not uncommon for a theory to lead to predictions that run counter to common sense. In fact, this is a hallmark of theories that make important contributions to understanding human affairs and our physical world.

Second, the relational theory of loneliness can be tested with empirical research. A researcher can study those who have lost significant others, asking them about how lonely they feel and the types and strength of social support they receive. To be useful, a theory should be testable with empirical methods, which helps the scientific community determine the extent of its validity.

Your job in reviewing literature will be made easier if you identify the major theories that apply to your topic of interest. Writers of empirical research reports often identify underlying theories and discuss whether their results are consistent with them. Following up on the leads they give you in their references to the theoretical literature will provide you with a framework for thinking about the bits and pieces of evidence you find in various reports about specific and often quite narrow research projects that are published in academic journals. In fact, you might choose to build your literature review around one or more theories. In other words, a topic for a literature review might be to review the research relating to a theory.

It is important to note that a literature review that contributes to a better understanding of one or more theories has the potential to make an important contribution to the writer's field because theories often have broad implications for many areas of concern in human affairs.

Literature Review Articles

Journals often carry literature review articles,[2] that is, articles that review the literature on specific topics—much like the literature review that you will be writing while using this book. Most journals that publish review articles set high standards for accepting such articles. Not only should they be well-written analytical narratives that bring readers up-to-date on what is known about a given topic, but they should also provide fresh insights that advance knowledge. These insights may take many forms. Some major ones are: (1) resolving conflicts among studies that previously seemed to contradict each other, (2) identifying new ways to interpret research results on a topic, and (3) laying out a path for future research that has the potential to advance the field significantly. As a result, going through the process of preparing a literature review is not an easy way to get published in a journal. In fact, when you begin reviewing the literature on a topic, there is no guarantee that you will arrive at the level of insight that will pass the scrutiny of a journal's editorial board. However, if you follow the guidelines outlined in this book,

---

[2] Some journals also carry book reviews, test reviews, and reviews of other products and services. These will not be considered in this book. Hence, the term "review article" in this book refers only to a *literature review* article.

which emphasize analyzing and synthesizing literature (i.e., casting a critical eye on it; pulling it apart, sometimes into pieces and bits; and putting them back together in a new form), you stand a better chance than the average academic writer of producing a review suitable for publication.

It is worth noting that sometimes students are discouraged when they find that their topic has recently been reviewed in an academic journal. They may believe that if the topic was already reviewed, they should select a different topic. This is not necessarily a wise decision. Instead, these students should usually feel fortunate to have the advantage of considering someone else's labor and insights, that is, someone on whose work they can build or with whom they can agree or disagree. Writing is an individual process, so two people reviewing the same body of literature are likely to produce distinctly different but potentially equally worthy reviews.[3]

Anecdotal Reports

As you review the literature on a specific topic, you may encounter articles that are built on anecdotal accounts of personal experiences. An anecdote is a description of an experience that happened to be noticed (as opposed to an observation that is based on research, in which there was considerable planning regarding whom and what to observe as well as when to observe a particular phenomenon in order to gather the best information). Anecdotal accounts are most common in journals aimed at practicing professionals such as clinical psychologists, social workers, and teachers. For example, a teacher might write a journal article describing his or her experiences with a severely underachieving student who bloomed academically while in his or her classroom. Other teachers may find this interesting and worth reading as a source of potential ideas, but as a contribution to science, such anecdotes are seriously deficient. Without control and comparison, we do not know to what extent this teacher has contributed to the student's progress, if at all. Perhaps the student would have bloomed without the teacher's efforts because of improved conditions at home or because of a prescription drug for hyperactivity prescribed by a physician without the teacher's knowledge. Given these limitations, anecdotal reports should be used very sparingly in literature reviews, and when they are cited, they should be clearly labeled as being anecdotal.

Reports on Professional Practices and Standards

Some journals aimed at practicing professionals publish reports on practices and standards, such as newly adopted curriculum standards for mathematics instruction in a state or proposed legislation to allow clinical psychologists to prescribe drugs. When these types of issues are relevant to a topic being reviewed, they may merit discussion in a literature review.

---

[3] Keep in mind that empirical knowledge is an ever-evolving process—not a set of facts. Nothing is proven by empirical research; rather, research is used to arrive at varying degrees of confidence. Thus, researchers may differ in their *interpretations*, even if they review the same literature on a given topic.

The Writing Process

Now that we have considered the major types of materials you will be reviewing (i.e., reports of empirical research, theoretical articles, literature review articles, articles based on anecdotal evidence, and reports on professional practices and standards), we will briefly consider the process you will follow in this book.

An important, but often overlooked, distinction is made in this book between *conducting* a literature review (i.e., locating literature, reading it, and mentally analyzing it) and *writing* a literature review. Needless to say, one must first locate, read, and analyze literature before a review can be written. Furthermore, writing a literature review involves a series of steps. In the field of composition and rhetoric, these steps collectively are referred to as the writing process. They include (1) planning, (2) organizing, (3) drafting, (4) editing, and (5) redrafting. More specifically, the process involves defining a topic and selecting the literature for review (planning); analyzing, synthesizing, and evaluating the articles being reviewed (organizing); writing a first draft of the review (drafting); checking the draft for completeness, cohesion, and correctness (editing); and rewriting the draft (redrafting). The process is much like the one you may have followed in your freshman English class when you were asked to write an analytical essay. The organization of this book follows these steps in the writing process.

Writing for a Specific Purpose

The first order of business is to consider your reasons for writing a literature review. Reviews of empirical research can serve several purposes. They can constitute the essence of a research paper in a class, which can vary in length and complexity depending on the professor's criteria for the paper. In a research report in a journal, the literature review is often brief and to the point, usually focusing on providing the rationale for specific research questions or hypotheses explored in the research. In contrast, the literature review in a thesis or dissertation is usually meant to establish that the writer has a thorough command of the literature on the topic being studied, typically resulting in a relatively long literature review. Obviously, these different purposes will result in literature reviews that vary in length and style. Chapter 2 (Considerations in Writing Reviews for Specific Purposes) describes the differences in these three kinds of reviews.

Planning to Write

The first two tasks in planning to write a review of empirical research are defining the topic and locating relevant research articles. These steps are interrelated because the topic you specify will determine the specific literature you identify, and oftentimes the results of your literature search will guide you in defining the topic. Sometimes your instructor will assign a specific topic for a term paper; other times, the choice will be left up to you. The process of defining the topic is the first step covered in Chapter 3 (Selecting a Topic and Identifying Literature for Review).

The remainder of Chapter 3 deals with the process of *selecting relevant journal articles*. Research libraries are not what they used to be. While searching the library's stacks may prove fruitful for you, it can be a hit-or-miss experience because a library's holdings will vary greatly depending on resources, availability, and even vandalism. A better option is to search computerized databases and Internet resources. Reference librarians can help you get started, or you can sign up for a workshop on how to use electronic resources. In this book, you will learn some of the basic steps involved in searching databases. However, keep in mind that each database has its own unique features. It is beyond the scope of this book to describe all these differences in detail.

After you have located an adequate collection of articles concerning your topic, you should read and analyze them. This step is called the *analysis*, which involves reading an article and taking notes. In other words, as you read, you separate the author's prose into its parts or elements. Because you will be analyzing a number of articles, you will need to prepare a systematic collection of notes. Part of the analysis process is sifting the elements on which you made notes, retaining the pertinent ones, and discarding those you do not need. This step is the subject of Chapter 4 (General Guidelines for Analyzing Literature).

It is sometimes necessary to read and analyze the literature from a more specialized perspective. For instance, if your literature review is part of a research study you are planning to conduct, you will want to pay special attention to Chapter 5 (Analyzing Quantitative Research Literature) and Chapter 6 (Analyzing Qualitative Research Literature). These chapters provide a brief overview of more technical issues in analyzing these types of research.

Organizing Your Notes and Your Thoughts

Having followed the above steps, you should begin creating a synthesis, which involves putting the parts from your notes back together into a new whole. Think of it like this: Each of the articles you will have read constitutes its own whole. In your research notes, you will have written down parts or elements from each article. Then, you will put these notes back together in the form of a new organizational framework. After creating the new framework, you will evaluate the contents. In other words, you need to describe your evaluation of the quality and importance of the research you have cited. These steps are covered in Chapter 8 (Synthesizing Literature Prior to Writing a Review). At this point, you may want to build one or more tables to summarize the results of previous research. Chapter 7 shows how to do this.

Drafting, Editing, and Redrafting

Next, you should write your first draft. Based on your audience, decide whether you will write in a formal or less formal *voice*. An effective writer is aware of the reader's expectations. A term paper written for a professor who is knowledgeable in a particular field is different from a literature review in a thesis, which may be read by readers who are curious but not necessarily knowledgeable about a topic. A literature review in a thesis is different from a literature review in an article intended for publication in a journal or in a research paper written for a class. You should also identify the major subtopics and determine the patterns that have emerged from your notes, such as trends, similarities, contrasts, and generalizations. These steps are covered in Chapter 9 (Guidelines for Writing a First Draft).

Next, you should make sure that your argument is clear, logical, and well-supported, and that your draft is free of errors. Chapter 10 (Guidelines for Developing a Coherent Essay) will help you make sure that your argument makes sense to you and your readers. Chapter 11 (Guidelines on Style, Mechanics, and Language Usage) describes the first steps in making sure that your review is free of errors.

The final two chapters of the book coincide with the last two steps in the writing process: editing and redrafting. These steps are iterative (i.e., they are meant to be repeated). It is not uncommon for a professional writer to rewrite three or more drafts, each time producing a refined new draft. Chapter 12 (Incorporating Feedback and Refining the First Draft) provides guidelines on how to approach this stage in the writing process. Finally, Chapter 13 (Comprehensive Self-Editing Checklist for Refining the Final Draft) gives a detailed checklist for use in editing your own manuscript for style and correctness. Formal academic writing requires that you prepare a manuscript as free of errors as possible, and this checklist will help you accomplish that goal.

Activities for Chapter 1

1. Locate an original report of empirical research in your field, read it, and respond to the following questions. (How to locate journal articles on specific topics is covered in considerable detail later in this book. At this point, simply locate one in your general field of study. Your reference librarian or instructor can help you identify specific journals in your field that are available in your college library. Scan the tables of contents for a research article on a topic of interest and make a photocopy to bring to class with your answers.) Note that your instructor may want to assign a particular research article for this activity.

   A. Are there any obvious sampling problems? Explain. (Do not just read the section under the subheading "Sample" because researchers sometimes provide additional information about the sample throughout their reports, especially in the introduction, where they might point out how their sample is different from those used by other researchers, or near the end, where they might discuss the limitations of the sample in relation to the results.)

   B. Are there any obvious measurement problems? Explain.

   C. Has the researcher examined only a narrowly defined problem? Is it too narrow? Explain.

   D. Did you notice any other flaws? Explain.

   E. Overall, do you think the research makes an important contribution to advancing knowledge? Explain.

2. Read the first sample literature review (Review A) near the end of this book, and respond to the following questions. Note that you will want to read this review again after you have learned more about the process of writing a literature review. The questions below ask only for your first, general impressions. Later, you will be able to critique the review in more detail.

   A. Have the reviewers clearly identified the topic of the review? Have they indicated its delimitations? (For example, is it limited to a certain period of time? Does it deal only with certain aspects of the problem?)

   B. Have the reviewers written a cohesive essay that guides you through the literature from subtopic to subtopic? Explain.

   C. Have the reviewers interpreted and critiqued the literature, *or* have they merely summarized it?

   D. Overall, do you think the reviewers make an important contribution to knowledge through their synthesis of the literature? Explain.

Notes:

Chapter 2

Considerations in Writing Reviews for Specific Purposes

Although the guidelines given in this book apply to any literature review, you will want to vary your approach to the writing task depending on your purpose for writing a review. This chapter focuses on the three most common purposes for writing a critical review of research and the audience for each type: (1) writing a literature review as a term paper for a class, (2) as a chapter for a thesis or dissertation, and (3) as part of an introduction to a journal article.

Writing a Literature Review As a Term Paper for a Class

Writing a literature review as a term paper assignment for a class can be somewhat frustrating because the task involves (1) selecting a topic in a field that may be new to you, (2) identifying and locating an appropriate number of research articles using databases that you may not be familiar with, and (3) writing and editing a well-developed essay, all in about three to four months. To compound matters, most instructors will expect you to prepare your review of literature outside of class with minimal guidance from them. Of course, they will also expect your literature review to be thoroughly researched and well-written. This book will help you accomplish that.

With these difficulties in mind, it is necessary for you to plan your term paper project carefully. First, you should make sure you understand the assignment and know as much as possible about your instructor's expectations near the beginning of the semester. Thus, you should not hesitate to raise questions in class regarding the assignment. Keep in mind that if something is not clear to you, it may be unclear to other students who will benefit by hearing the answers to your questions.[1] Second, you will need to pace yourself as you undertake the writing process. Make sure that you allow sufficient time to follow the steps outlined in this book, including selecting a topic; reading and evaluating the relevant research articles; synthesizing and organizing your notes; writing, revising, and redrafting your paper; and editing it for correctness and adherence to the required style manual.[2] It is helpful to map out the weeks of your school term and lay out a timeline. The following is a suggested timeline for a 15-week semester.

---

[1] Idiosyncratic questions that other students may not find of interest generally should be raised with the instructor outside of class, perhaps during office hours. Examples are: You are planning to go to graduate school and want to write a more extensive paper than required by the professor, or you have written a literature review for a previous class and would prefer to expand on it rather than write a new review.

[2] The dominant style manual in the social and behavioral sciences is the *Publication Manual of the American Psychological Association*. It is available for purchase from most college and university bookstores, or it can be purchased online at www.apa.org.

Example 2.0.1

Stage 1.   Preliminary library search and selection of topic
                Complete by the end of Week 3
Stage 2.   Reading list and preliminary paper outline
                Complete by the end of Week 6
Stage 3.   First draft of paper
                Complete by the end of Week 12
Stage 4.   Revised final draft of paper
                Complete by the end of Week 15

Individual instructor's expectations regarding length of a written review and the number of references cited may vary widely. For term papers written for introductory survey courses, instructors may require only a short review—perhaps as short as a few double-spaced, typewritten pages with a minimum of five to ten references. For such a review, you will need to be highly selective in identifying and citing references—usually selecting those that are the most important and/or most current. For upper-division courses, instructors may require longer reviews with more references. Finally, for graduate-level classes in your academic major, your instructor may place no restrictions on length or number of references, expecting you to review as many research reports as needed to write a comprehensive literature review on your topic.

Given the limited time frame for writing a literature review as a term paper, your topic should usually be narrow. Look for an area that is well-defined, especially if you are new to a field. A good way to select a topic is to examine the subheadings within the chapters in your textbook. For instance, an educational psychology textbook might have a chapter on creativity with subsections on definitions of creativity, the measurement of creativity, and fostering creativity in the classroom. As an example, suppose you are especially interested in fostering creativity in the classroom. Reading this section, you might find that your textbook author mentions that there is some controversy on the effects of competition on promoting creativity (i.e., Can teachers foster creativity by offering rewards for its expression?). This sounds like a fairly narrow topic that you might start with as a tentative subject. As you search for journal articles on this topic,[3] you may find that there are more articles on it than you need for the term project assignment. If so, you can narrow the topic further by specifying that your review will deal with competition and creativity only in (1) elementary school samples and (2) the fine arts.

If you are not given a choice of topics and are assigned a topic by your instructor, begin your search for literature as soon as possible and report to him or her any difficulties you encounter, such as finding that there is too little research on the assigned topic (perhaps the topic can be broadened or your instructor can point you to additional sources your literature search did not identify) or there is too much research (perhaps the topic can be narrowed or your instructor can help you identify other delimiters such as reviewing only recent articles).

One of the consequences of having a short time frame for preparing a literature review as a term paper is that opportunities for feedback on your early drafts will be limited, so you will be responsible for doing much of the editing yourself. When you lay out

---

[3] Searching electronic databases with an emphasis on how to narrow the search is discussed in detail in the next chapter.

your timeline, leave time to consult with your instructor about your first draft, even if this has to be done during an office visit. Finally, you should use the self-editing guide at the end of this book to help you eliminate some common problems before you turn in your paper.

Writing a Literature Review Chapter for a Thesis or Dissertation

The review chapter for a thesis or dissertation is the most complex of the literature review types covered in this book because you will be expected to prepare the initial literature review as part of your research proposal, well before you begin your actual research. Conducting a literature review is one of the steps you will follow in the process of defining the research questions for your study, so you will probably have to redefine your topic and revise your research questions several times along the way.

Students writing a literature review chapter frequently ask, "How many research articles must I cite?" In addition, they ask, "How long should I make the review?" Some students are frustrated when they learn that there are no preset minimums either on the number of research articles to review or on the length of a review chapter. Often, standards regarding this matter will vary, depending on the nature of the topic and the amount of literature on it.

You should establish two main goals for your literature review. First, attempt to provide a *comprehensive* and *up-to-date* review of the topic. Second, try to demonstrate that you have a thorough command of the field you are studying. Keep in mind that the literature review will provide the basic rationale for your research, and the extent to which you accomplish these goals will contribute in large measure to how well your project will be received. Note that these goals reflect the seriousness of the task you have undertaken, which is to contribute to the body of knowledge in your field. Several traditions that have evolved through the years reflect how seriously academic departments view the writing of a thesis or dissertation. They include the defense of the research proposal, the defense of the finished thesis or dissertation, and the careful scrutiny given the final document by the university's librarian prior to its acceptance as a permanent addition to the library's holdings.

Some students procrastinate when it comes to writing a literature review chapter for a thesis or dissertation. After all, usually there are no set timelines. Therefore, it is important for you to set deadlines for yourself. Some students find it useful to plan an informal timeline in collaboration with the committee chair, perhaps by setting deadlines for completing the various steps involved in the overall process. The guidelines described in this book will be helpful in this regard. You should adopt a regular pattern of consulting with the professors on your committee to ensure that you remain focused and on track.

Finally, the level of accuracy expected in a thesis or dissertation project is quite high. This will require that you edit your writing to a level that far exceeds what may be expected in a term paper assignment. Not only must your writing conform to the particular style manual used in your field, but it should also be free of mechanical errors. The guidelines in Chapter 11 and the self-editing checklist in Chapter 13 will help you accomplish this. Make sure that you allow enough time to set your draft aside for at least a few days prior to editing your writing, and expect to use the self-editing guide several times before you give your adviser a draft of the review.

Writing a Literature Review for a Research Article

The literature review section of a research article published in a journal is the most straightforward of the three types of reviews covered in this book. These literature reviews are usually shorter and more focused than other types because their major purpose is to provide the background and rationale for specific and often very narrow research projects.

On the other hand, these reviews undergo a level of scrutiny that may exceed even that for a review for a thesis or dissertation. Research article submissions for refereed journals are routinely evaluated by two or three of the leading scholars in the area in which the research was conducted. This means that the literature review should reflect not only the current state of research on the topic, but it should also be error free. Here again, the self-editing checklist from Chapter 13 should be carefully applied.

Frequently, an author will write a journal article a year or more after the research was conducted. This often happens when students decide to write shorter, article-length versions of their theses or dissertations. If this applies to you, search through the latest issues of the journals in your field to make sure that your literature review cites the very latest work published on your topic.

Although there is some variation among journals, the literature review in a research article for a journal is usually expected to be combined with the introduction. In other words, the introduction to the research is an essay that introduces readers to both the topic and purpose of the research while providing an overview of the relevant literature. Therefore, the emphasis of the review should be on establishing the scientific context in which a particular study was conducted and how it contributes to the field; it should help demonstrate the rationale for the original research reported in the article. As such, it is typically much more narrow and focused than a literature review chapter for a thesis or dissertation.

Activities for Chapter 2

1. What is your purpose for writing a literature review?
   A. As a term paper for a class.
   B. As a chapter for a thesis or dissertation.
   C. As part of the introduction to a research article.
   D. Other: _____

2. If you are writing a literature review as a term paper, has your instructor assigned a specific topic to review? If yes, write the topic here. Also, write any questions you need to ask your instructor.

3. If you are writing a literature review as a term paper and your instructor has not assigned a specific topic, briefly describe two or three possible topics here. (If you are at a loss, examine your textbooks for ideas.)

4. If you are writing a literature review for a thesis or dissertation, write the topic here.

5. If you are writing a literature review for a thesis or dissertation, what is your timeline for completing the first draft? Share your timeline with your instructor for feedback.

6. If you are writing a literature review for a research article that might be published in a journal, name your research purpose or hypothesis. After you have read the literature on your topic, revise your purpose or hypothesis, if necessary, in light of the literature. (Remember that a research purpose or hypothesis should flow directly and logically from the literature reviewed.)

7. If you are writing a literature review for a thesis or dissertation, read the literature review chapters in at least three of the theses or dissertations approved by your committee chair. These are usually housed in the university library. Then, make an appointment with your committee chair to discuss his or her expectations for your review. Make notes here on what you learned about your chair's expectations for your literature review chapter.

Notes:

Chapter 3

Selecting a Topic and Identifying Literature for Review

"Where should I begin?" This may be the most commonly asked question by students preparing to write a literature review. While there is no easy answer, this chapter was designed to illustrate the process used by many professional writers and researchers for getting started. Keep in mind that writing is an individual process, so the procedures described here are intended to be used as a road map rather than as a prescription. By working through this chapter, you will be able to develop two important products that will help you begin writing an effective literature review: a written description of your topic and a working draft of your reading list.

Obviously, the first step in any kind of academic writing is to decide what you will write about, but the specific path you follow in working through this step will vary depending on your purpose for writing a literature review. The previous chapter described the three most common reasons for writing literature reviews.

In any of these types of literature reviews, you usually should narrowly define your topic. Example 3.0.1 presents a topic that is much too general. In fact, it is the title of a survey course taught at many major universities and represents a very extensive body of literature.

Example 3.0.1

General Topic: Child Language Acquisition

Obviously, the topic in Example 3.0.1 will have to be narrowed down considerably before it can be used as the basis for a literature review of manageable length. The steps that follow will guide you through a process that will result in better alternatives to this example.

✓ Step 1: Search an appropriate database.

Before you select a database and search it, you need to at least select a general topic. Suppose you select the topic in Example 3.0.1: Child Language Acquisition, which is very general and will yield more references than you can possibly use (as you will see below). Nevertheless, it is usually suitable to start with a general topic, see how much literature there is on it, and then narrow the topic to a more manageable one—a process that you will learn about in this chapter.

A general search using the topic in Example 3.0.1 will yield many thousands of records. Therefore, you should specify a set of parameters that will give you a focused result. For instance, you can limit your search to journal articles, which is recommended, or you can specify a limited range of publication dates, perhaps going back only five to seven years. A sample search conducted in the *Educational Resource Information Center* (*ERIC*) database using the general topic in Example 3.0.1: Child Language Acquisition yielded the results in Example 3.1.1, which are presented here in the order of the steps followed:

Example 3.1.1

Step	Number of Records
Search with descriptor *language acquisition*:	6,985
Limit search to journal articles AND to publication dates of 2002 to present:	429
Further limit the search to *language acquisition* AND *child language*:	128

How the search in Example 3.1.1 was conducted:

1. Accessed the *ERIC* database at www.eric.ed.gov
2. Clicked on "Advanced Search."
3. In the first field for "Keywords (all fields)," entered *language acquisition*.
4. For "Publication Type," clicked on the box for "All," which removed the checkmark, and then clicked on the box for "Journal Articles."
5. For "Publication Date," clicked on "pre-1966" for the "From" field and clicked on "2004" for the "To" field.
6. Clicked on "Search," which yielded **6,985 records** to journal articles as shown in Example 3.1.1 above.
7. Clicked on "Back to Search."
8. Changed "Publication Date" to "2002" for the "From" field.
9. Clicked on "Search," which yielded **429 records** for journal articles as shown in Example 3.1.1 above.
10. Clicked on "Back to Search."
11. Left *language acquisition* in the first field for Keywords, and added *child language* in the second field for Keywords.
12. Clicked on "Search," which yielded **128 records** for journal articles as shown in Example 3.1.1 above.

Note that for each article that is identified by the database, you will be given an abstract (i.e., brief summary). Appendix A contains the 128 titles and abstracts obtained by using the procedures described above. Note that the *ERIC* database was used in this example because its holdings are comprehensive and encompass several disciplines with an emphasis on education. Other databases, such as *PsycINFO* and *Sociological Abstracts*, would produce results that focus on other disciplines.[1]

---

[1] Unlike *ERIC*, the *PsycINFO* and *Sociological Abstracts* databases are available by subscription only. Most academic libraries maintain subscriptions that allow students and faculty access free of charge.

✔ Step 2: Shorten your reference list if it is too long.

Example 3.2.1 presents five possible revised topics based on the sample *ERIC* search. In this example, the revised topics illustrate the reclassification of the articles in Appendix A according to major areas of study that can be discerned from a review of the titles and abstracts of the articles. Depending on the specific nature of your course and on the academic department in which it is offered, you can now narrow your topic area by selecting one of the topics in Example 3.2.1. These classifications are given merely to illustrate the process. In fact, Appendix A can be reclassified into numerous other categories. Also, you will note that some of the articles appear in more than one category. For instance, reference number 13 has been classified as belonging to two categories: (1) Role of Parents in Child Language Acquisition and (2) Acquisition of Two Languages. Also, note that not all articles need to be classified. For instance, you might notice a number of articles that were conducted with non-English-speaking children and exclude them from further analysis if your primary interest is in English-language acquisition.

Example 3.2.1

Possible topic areas, with reference numbers from Appendix A: Sample ERIC Search; article numbers in bold deal with autism.

Language Acquisition by Children with Special Needs
  Sample reference numbers: **5**, 12, 31, **42**, **43**, 46, 47, 48, **49**, 55, **57**, 83, 84, 91, **93**, 96, 97, 98, 99, **101**, **113**, 116, **120**
Role of Parents in Child Language Acquisition
  Sample reference numbers: 4, 13, 16, 23, 32, 67, 68, 90, 115
Acquisition of Two Languages (Bilingual)
  Sample reference numbers: 13, 18, 19, 20, 21, 22, 27, 30, 52, 69
Acquisition of Grammatical Structures and Categories
  Sample reference numbers: 26, 88, 102, 105, 107, 112, 118, 121, 122, 128
Language Acquisition by Very Young Children
  Sample reference numbers: 1, 10, 40, 53, 64, 77, 79, 81, 125

After classifying the records for journal articles as shown in Example 3.2.1, examine them carefully for subsets that might serve as a topic for your literature review. For instance, nine of the articles for Language Acquisition by Children with Special Needs deal with children with autism. These article numbers are shown in bold in the example above. If nine articles are not sufficient for your purposes, go to Step 3 below.

✔ Step 3: Increase the size of your reference list, if necessary.

If you do not have enough references for your literature review, you can, of course, search back further than the year 2002. Searching for historical literature is discussed below in Step 14.

If you are using *ERIC*, you might also find additional references by clicking on "Details" for an *ERIC* record and then clicking on the link (i.e., underlined words) that have the author(s) name(s). For instance, for the first *ERIC* record in Appendix A, clicking on the author's name provided 13 additional references written by the same author, including books, teacher guides, and journal articles. Because academic scholars tend to conduct research and write on a given topic over an extended period of time, these references are often quite relevant to the topic at hand (i.e., Language Acquisition by Very Young Children).

In addition, when examining an *ERIC* journal article record, you can click on "Details" and then examine the list of "Descriptors" for that article. The descriptors for record Number 1 in Appendix A are shown in Example 3.3.1. These are related topics. By clicking on one, you will conduct a search of articles on these topics, potentially increasing the size of your reference list by identifying additional related articles.

Example 3.3.1

Descriptors associated with the record for the first article in Appendix A:

Caregiver Role; Cognitive Development; Early Childhood Education; Early Experience; Emotional Intelligence; Infants; Language Acquisition; Motor Development; Parent Role; Social Development; Thinking Skills; Toddlers; Visual Perception; Vocabulary

It is also possible to search *ERIC* for documents such as papers presented at conventions, curriculum guides, and theses and dissertations, which can be used to supplement the journal articles already identified. To locate these additional sources that might provide additional references, near the beginning of the *ERIC* search, leave "All" checked (see the box on page 18 in this book) and then conduct another search. Note that for a report to be published in a journal, it usually must pass the scrutiny of one or more editors and editorial consultants or reviewers with special knowledge of the area. This is *not* the case, however, for many of the other types of documents included in the *ERIC* database. Also, note that *ERIC* does not attempt to judge the soundness or quality of the information in the documents. Thus, some nonjournal documents may be less valid than journal articles as sources of information.

✔ Step 4:   Consider searching for unpublished studies.

Searching for unpublished studies is another way to increase the size of your reference list (see Step 3). In addition, you may want to search for published studies not published in journals[2] because some of these studies may be potentially important. A potentially important study may not be published in a journal for the following reasons:

1. Some studies of potential importance are never even submitted to journals for possible publication. For instance, theses and dissertations tend to be too long to publish "as is" in an academic journal and must undergo an extensive rewriting for publication. Many authors of theses and dissertations do not undertake this rewriting process. In addition, some researchers may become discouraged when the results of their studies are not consistent with their hypotheses. Instead of writing up such studies for submission to a journal, they may move on to conduct research in what they consider more fruitful areas or with alternative research methods.

---

[2] Studies not published in journals are commonly referred to as "unpublished studies" even though they may be available in print form in certain academic libraries.

2. Some journal editors and expert reviewers may be biased against studies that show no significant difference or that fail to confirm the research hypotheses posed by the researchers.

One way to locate unpublished studies is to contact authors of published studies to ask them if they are aware of any unpublished studies on your topic.[3] For instance, they may have conducted studies that they decided not to submit for publication or they may know of students or colleagues who have done this. A second way is to search electronic databases via the Internet. How this was done by one team of researchers is illustrated in Example 3.4.1.

Example 3.4.1[4]

Description of how a search for unpublished studies was conducted:

We attempted to include unpublished studies by searching the resources suggested by the Centre for Reviews and Dissemination (2001) and the Cochrane Non-Randomised Studies Methods Group (2004).

1. We searched for reports, discussion papers, and so forth in (1) the System for Information on Grey Literature (http://arc.uk.ovid.com/webspirs/login.ws), (2) the National Technical Information Service (http://www.ntis.gov/search/), and (3) the British Library Public Catalogue (http://blpc.bl.uk/).

2. We searched for dissertations and theses in (1) the Cumulative Index to Nursing and Allied Health (http://www.cinahl.com/) and (2) ProQuest Digital Dissertations (http://wwwlib.umi.com/dissertations/gateway).

3. We searched all of the birth cohorts included in the National Research Register (http://www.update-software.com/national/) and checked for eligible studies.

4. We searched for conference proceedings in (1) ISI Proceedings (http://portalt.wok.mimas.ac.uk/portal.cgi?DestApp=ISIP&Func=Frame) and (2) zetoc (http://zetoc.mimas.ac.uk/zetoc/).

✔ Step 5: Write the first draft of your topic statement.

Now that you have identified appropriate references, you can reexamine the list of articles you have generated and choose a more specific topic for your literature review.[5] The first draft of your topic statement should attempt to name the area you will investigate. Think of this statement as a descriptive phrase rather than as a paper or chapter title. Example 3.5.1 presents two topic statements: one for a literature review in the area of linguistics and the other in psychology. Note that these first drafts are still very general.

---

[3] Contact information such as a physical address or e-mail address is usually provided either as a footnote on the first page of a research article or near the end of an article—just before or after the reference list.

[4] Shenkin, S. D., Starr, J. M., & Deary, I. J. (2004). Birth weight and cognitive ability in childhood: A systematic review. *Psychological Bulletin*, *130*, 989–1013.

[5] At this point, it is premature for you to decide on a *final topic*. You should do this only after reading some of the articles you have located.

Example 3.5.1

Psychology:
Language Acquisition by Children with Autism

Linguistics:
Acquisition of Grammatical Structures and Categories

Each of the topics in Example 3.5.1 could be further narrowed by restricting it to a particular group such as "very young children" (e.g., Language Acquisition by *Very Young Children* with Autism).

✔ Step 6: Familiarize yourself with on-line databases.

All university libraries now subscribe to electronic databases. The manual searches of the past have given way to computerized searches. Therefore, it is important to familiarize yourself with your campus library's computer resources. If you are new to on-line databases, you should attend a workshop or class to learn how to use these services as well as carefully read any handouts concerning your university's database resources. As noted earlier, this book shows you only some general approaches to databases—not all the specific features of any of them.

✔ Step 7: Identify the relevant databases in your field of study.

Every academic field has developed its own database services, which are used by its students and scholars. Early in your search, you should identify the databases specific to your field of study. In addition to the information you receive in the library, you should ask your adviser or instructor about the preferred databases in your major. Then, you can find out where they are available and whether they can be accessed from your home or dormitory.

Table 1 illustrates the range of database resources available through California State University, Los Angeles (CSU, Los Angeles) library, as an example. This list is by no means exhaustive; in fact, larger research libraries will have many more research services than are listed in this table. If you are a student at a small university, it is recommended that you investigate whether your university's library maintains cooperative arrangements with larger institutions in your area.

Table 1
Summary of Selected Library Databases

Database	Subject Areas	Database Statistics
Basic Biosis	Life Science	300,000 records from 350 journals 1994–present, updated monthly
CINAHL	Nursing, Allied Health, Biomedical and Consumer Health	352,000 records from 900 journals 1982–present, updated quarterly
Dissertation Abstracts	Complete range of academic subjects	1,566,000 records 1861–present, updated monthly

(*continued*)→

Table 1 (*continued*)

ERIC	Education and related fields	956,000 records from journals, books, theses, and unpublished reports 1966–present, updated monthly
LLBA	Linguistics and Language Behavior Abstracts	250,000 records from journals, books, dissertations, book reviews, and other media 1973–present, updated quarterly
Medline	Nursing, Public Health, Pharmacy, Sports Medicine, Psychiatry, Dentistry, and Veterinary Medicine	9,305,000 records, including articles from 3,500 journals published internationally 1985–present, updated monthly
MLA	Literature, Language, Linguistics, and Folklore	1,308,000 records from 4,000 U.S. and international journals 1963–present, updated monthly
NCJRS	Corrections, Drugs and Crime, Juvenile Justice, Law Enforcement, Statistics, and Victims	140,000 records, including journal articles, government documents, and unpublished reports 1970–present, updated periodically
PAIS International	Social Sciences, emphasis on contemporary social, economic, and political issues, and on public policy	451,000 records from journals 1972–present, updated monthly
PsycINFO	Psychology and related fields. For full-text articles use PsycARTICLES.	1,249,000 records from 1,300 journals 1887–present, updated monthly
Social Sciences Abstracts	Sociology, Psychology, Anthropology, Geography, Economics, Political Science, and Law	562,000 records from 400 journals 1983–present, updated monthly
Social Work Abstracts	Social Work and related fields	30,000 records from journals 1977–present, updated quarterly
Sociological Abstracts	Sociology, Social Work, and other social sciences	519,000 records from 3,000 journals 1963–present, updated bimonthly
Sport Discus	Sports Medicine, Physical Education, Exercise, Physiology, Biomechanics, Psychology, Training, Coaching, and Nutrition	344,000 records 1970–present, updated quarterly

✔ Step 8: Familiarize yourself with the organization of the database.

The on-line databases described in Table 1 contain abstracts of several kinds of documents, including journal articles, books, conference presentations, project reports, and government documents. As you know from Chapter 1, this book focuses on reviewing articles in academic journals. For each of the thousands of journal articles in these databases, there is a single *record* with specific information about the article. In other words, each item on the list of titles you derive from your search of a database will be linked to an expanded description organized according to a set of categories of information. For instance, each of these records contains a number of *fields*, which include the article's title, author, source journal, publication date, abstract, and list of descriptors (i.e., terms and phrases that describe the article's contents). You can narrow the scope of a search by manipulating one or more of these fields. Publication date, source journal, and author are often used to narrow a search, but the most common method of searching a database is by specifying one or more descriptors. This method is covered next.

✓ Step 9: Begin with a general descriptor, and then limit the output.

Unless you have had previous knowledge of a particular topic, you should begin a search with a general descriptor from the database's thesaurus. If a thesaurus is not available, use a label or phrase that describes the topic you are investigating. If this procedure results in too many references, you can limit the search by adding additional descriptors using *and*. For instance, if you search for "social" *and* "phobia," you will get only articles that mention *both* of these terms. Here is an example: Searching the major database in psychology, *PsycINFO*, from 2000 to the present yields 773 documents (mainly journal articles) relating to "phobia." A search for "social" *and* "phobia" for the same time period yields 484 documents. Finally, a search for "children," *and* "social," *and* "phobia" yields only 70 documents.

Another effective technique for limiting the number of documents retrieved from an electronic database is to limit the search to descriptors that appear in only the title and/or abstract (summary of the article), restrictions that are permitted in *PsycINFO* and some other databases. Using these restrictions will help to eliminate articles in which the descriptor is mentioned only in passing in the body of the article because an article dealing primarily with phobias would almost certainly mention the term in one of these important places. (Note that in an unrestricted search, the contents of entire documents are searched.) A search of *PsycINFO* restricting the search for "phobia" in only the titles and abstracts from 2000 to the present yields a total of 671 documents, which is about a hundred fewer than the 773 retrieved in an unrestricted search. With the additional restriction that "phobia" appears in *both* the title and abstract, 251 articles were obtained, which is considerably less than the original 773.

✓ Step 10: Redefine your topic more narrowly.

Selecting a reasonably narrow topic is essential if you are to defend your selection of a topic and write an effective review on it. Topics that are too broad will stretch your limits of energy and time—especially if you are writing a review for a term project in a one-semester class. A review of a topic that is too broad very likely will lead to a review that is superficial, jumps from area to area within the topic, and fails to demonstrate to your reader that you have thoroughly mastered the literature on the topic. Thus, at this point, you should consider redefining your topic more narrowly.

Example 3.10.1 presents a topic that is problematic in that it is much too broadly defined. Even though the writer has limited the review to English-speaking children as old as four years, it is still quite broad. Apparently, the writer has chosen to consider studies of children acquiring both the sound and the grammatical systems. If so, the finished review will either be a book-length manuscript (or two) or a shorter manuscript that presents a superficial treatment of the literature on this broad topic.

Example 3.10.1
A topic that is too broad for most purposes:

This paper deals with child language acquisition. I will review the literature that deals with how children learn to speak in a naturalistic setting, starting with the earliest sounds and progressing to fully formed sentences. I will limit myself to English-speaking children, aged birth to four years.

Example 3.10.2 is an improved version of the topic in Example 3.10.1. Note that the writer has narrowed the focus of the review to a specific aspect of language. The writer has stated clearly that the review has two main goals: (1) to catalog the range of verbal features that have been studied and (2) to describe what is known about the route children follow in acquiring them. Even though it is very likely that this topic will be modified several more times based on a careful reading of the studies found, it is sufficiently focused to provide the writer with a suitable initial statement of the topic for his or her literature review.

Example 3.10.2
An improved, more specific version of Example 3.10.1:

This paper describes what is known about how children acquire the ability to describe time and to make references to time, including the use of verbs and other features contained in the verb phrase. I will attempt, first, to describe the range of verb phrase features that have been studied, and second, to describe the path children follow as they develop greater linguistic competence with reference to time.

✔ Step 11: Start with the most current research, and work backwards.

The most effective way to begin a search in a field that is new to you is to start with the most current journal articles. If you judge a recently published article to be relevant to your topic, the article's reference list or bibliography will provide useful clues about how to pursue your review of the literature. For Appendix A, for instance, a good strategy would be to obtain articles relevant to your research topic, photocopy the reference lists at the end of each one, compare those lists against the contents of Appendix A, and make strategic decisions about rounding out your reading list. Keep in mind two important criteria for developing your reading list: The reading list should (1) represent the extent of knowledge about the topic and (2) provide a proper context for your own research if you are writing a literature review as part of an introduction to a research study you will be conducting.

✔ Step 12: Search for theoretical articles on your topic.

As you learned in Chapter 1, theoretical articles that relate directly to your topic should be included in your literature review. However, a typical search of the literature in the social and behavioral sciences will yield primarily original reports of empirical research because these types of documents dominate academic journals. If you have difficulty locating theoretical articles on your topic, include "theory" as one of your descriptors. A search of the *PsycINFO* database using the descriptors "social" *and* "phobia" *and* "theory" yielded 50 documents, including the one in Example 3.12.1, which would clearly be useful for someone planning to write about theories relating to social phobia.

Example 3.12.1

An article obtained by using the term "theory" in the search:

Chen, Y. P., Ehlers, A., Clark, D. M., & Mansell, W. (2002). Patients with generalized social phobia direct their attention away from faces. *Behaviour Research & Therapy*, 40, 677–687. [*Abstract*: This experiment tested whether patients with social phobia direct their attention to or away from faces with a range of emotional expressions. A modified dot probe paradigm measured whether [subjects] attended more to faces or to household objects. Twenty [subjects] with social phobia (mean age 35.2 yrs) were faster in identifying the probe when it occurred in the location of the household objects, regardless of whether the facial expressions were positive, neutral, or negative. In contrast, 20 controls (mean age 36.1 yrs) did not exhibit an attentional preference. The results are in line with *theories* of social phobia that emphasize the role of reduced processing of external social cues in maintaining social anxiety.]

It is important to note that writers of empirical research reports will often discuss the relationship of their studies to related theoretical literature and of course provide references to this literature. You should follow up these leads by looking up the references.

✓ Step 13: Look for "review" articles.

A corollary to the search technique described in the previous step is to use the descriptor "review" as a search term when searching for review articles. Previously published review articles are very useful in planning a new literature review because they are helpful in identifying the breadth and scope of the literature in a field of study. They usually will include a much more comprehensive reference list than is typical in a research article.

Note that some journals publish only literature reviews, some emphasize original reports of empirical research but occasionally will publish literature review articles by leading researchers in a field, while other journals have editorial policies that prohibit publishing reviews. If you know the names of journals in your field that publish reviews, you might specify their names in a database search.[6] Because this will restrict your search to just those journals, this should be a separate search from your main one.

A search of *PsycINFO* using "substance abuse" *and* "treatment" as a Keyword (descriptor) in any field *and* "review" as a descriptor in the *title only* identified 49 potentially useful articles that contain reviews on the treatment of substance abusers. Two are shown in Example 3.13.1.

---

[6] In psychology, for example, *Psychological Bulletin* is an important journal devoted to literature reviews. A premier review journal in education is the *Review of Educational Research*.

Example 3.13.1

Two articles obtained by using "review" in the search:

Hopfer, C. J., Khuri, E., Crowley, T. J., & Hooks, S. (2002). Adolescent heroin use: A review of the descriptive and treatment literature. *Journal of Substance Abuse Treatment, 23,* 231–237.

Leri, F., Bruneau, J., & Stewart, J. (2003). Understanding polydrug use: Review of heroin and cocaine co-use. *Addiction, 98,* 7–22.

✔ Step 14:   Identify the landmark or classic studies and theorists.

Finally, it is important to identify the landmark studies and theorists on your topic (i.e., those of *historical importance* in developing an understanding of a topic or problem). Unfortunately, some students believe that this is an optional nicety. However, without at least a passing knowledge of landmark studies, you will not understand the present context for your chosen topic. If you are writing a thesis or dissertation, in which fairly exhaustive reviews are expected, a failure to reference the landmark studies might be regarded as a serious flaw.

It is not always easy to identify historically important studies at the very beginning of a literature search. However, authors of some journal articles explicitly note these, as is done in Example 3.14.1.

Example 3.14.1[7]

Excerpt from a research article that identifies a landmark theorist and related studies:

A significant contribution of Rogers is that he was the first to attempt to demystify the nature of psychotherapy by making sessions open to public scrutiny. In the 1940s, he published verbatim transcripts of therapeutic encounters. For more than 50 years, investigators such as Porter (1943), Snyder (1945), and, more recently, Brodley (1994), using these transcripts, have measured how therapists actually behave with clients. Regarding this issue, Gill (personal communication, August 28, 1991) wrote, "I also think Rogers deserves a great deal of credit for being the first person to present verbatim sessions. Since him, a number of people have plucked up the courage to do so but he was the first." (p. 311)

While reading the articles you selected, you will often notice that certain authors' names are mentioned repeatedly. For instance, if you read extensively on how social factors affect learning, you will find that Albert Bandura's social learning theory is cited by numerous authors of research articles. At this point, you would want to search the database again using Bandura's first and last names as one of the descriptors for two reasons: (1) to locate material he has written on his theory (keep in mind that you want it from the *original source* and not just someone else's paraphrase of the theory) and (2) to try to locate any early studies that he may have conducted that led him to the theory or that he

---

[7] Kahn, E., & Rachman, A. W. (2000). Carl Rogers and Heinz Kohut: A historical perspective. *Psychoanalytic Psychology, 17,* 294–312.

originally presented to lend credence to the theory. Keep in mind that people who present theories very often conduct research and publish it in support of their theories. Their early studies that helped establish their theories are the ones that are most likely to be considered "landmark" or "classic." Note that when you conduct such a search of the database for this purpose, you should *not* restrict the search to only articles published in recent years. Searching all years of the *PsycINFO* database while restricting the search to articles with the name "Albert Bandura" as the author of the article, *and* "social" in the title of the article, *and* "learning" in all fields yields relevant documents, including an early one, which is shown in Example 3.14.2.

Example 3.14.2

An early study by a leading researcher and theoretician:

Bandura, A. (1969). Social learning of moral judgments. *Journal of Personality and Social Psychology*, *11*, 275–279.

Finally, consult the relevant college textbooks. Textbook authors often briefly trace the history of thought on important topics and may well mention what they believe to be the classic studies.

Activities for Chapter 3

1. First, become familiar with the electronic databases in your field. (See Table 1 earlier in this chapter for a partial list of available databases.) You can do so either by attending a workshop in your university library or by reading the documentation and practicing on your own. Note that many libraries now allow you to search their databases on-line from your home, but you will probably need to use a university computer account to do so. Once you are familiar with the databases, select one database to complete the rest of this exercise.

2. If your instructor has assigned a term paper on a specific topic, search the database using a simple phrase that describes this topic. If you are working on your own, select an area that interests you, and search the database using a simple phrase that describes your area of interest. How many citations to the literature did the search produce?

3. Retrieve two or three records from your search and locate the lists of descriptors. Compare the three lists and note the areas of commonality as well as differences.

   • Write down the exact wording of three descriptors that relate to your intended topic. Choose descriptors that reflect your personal interest in the topic.

- Compared to the simple phrase you used when you started, do you think these descriptors are more specific *or* more general? Why?

4. Now use the descriptors you just located to modify the search.
   - First, modify the search to select more records.
   - Then, modify the search to select fewer records.
   - If you used the connector AND, did it result in more *or* fewer sources? Why do you think this happened?
   - If you used the connector OR, did it result in more *or* fewer sources? Why do you think this happened?

5. If necessary, narrow the search further until you have between 50 and 150 sources, and print out the search results.
   - Carefully scan the printed list to identify several possible subcategories.
   - Compare the new categories to your original topic.
   - Redefine your topic more narrowly, and identify the articles that pertain to your new topic. Prepare a list of the references for these articles.

Notes:

Chapter 4

General Guidelines for Analyzing Literature

Now that you have identified the preliminary set of articles for your review, you should begin the process of analyzing them *prior to* beginning to write your review. This chapter is designed to help you through this process. The end result will be two important products: (1) a working draft of your reference list and (2) a set of note cards that will contain specific, detailed information about each article, both of which you will need before you begin to write.

✔ Guideline 1: Scan the articles to get an overview of each one.

Obviously, you read the titles of the articles when you selected them, and you probably also read the abstracts (i.e., summaries) that most journals include near the beginning of each article. Next, you should read the first few paragraphs of each article, where the author usually provides a general introduction to his or her problem area. This will give you a feel for the author's writing style as well as his or her general perspectives on the research problem. Then, jump to the last paragraph before the heading "Method," which is usually the first major heading in the text of a research article. This is the paragraph in which it is traditional for researchers to state their specific hypotheses, research questions, or research purposes. Next, scan the rest of the article, noting all headings and subheadings. Scan the text in each subsection, but do not allow yourself to get caught up in the details or any points that seem difficult or confusing. Your purpose at this point is to get only an overview.

Note that by following this guideline, you will be *pre-reading*, which is a technique widely recommended by reading specialists as the first step in reading a technical report. Because pre-reading gives you an overview of the purpose and contents of a report, it helps you keep your eye on the big picture as you subsequently work through the details of a research report from beginning to end. The information you gain by pre-reading will also help you group the articles into categories, as suggested in the next guideline.

Example 4.1.1 shows in bold a typical set of major headings for a short research report in a journal.

Example 4.1.1

Title [followed by researchers' names and their institutional affiliations]
Abstract [a summary of the complete report]
[An introduction in which related literature is reviewed follows the abstract; typically, there is *no* heading called "Introduction."]

Method
  Participants [or Subjects]
  Measures [or Measurement, Observation, or Instrumentation]
Results
Discussion [or Discussion, Conclusions, and Implications]

Longer articles will often contain additional headings such as *Assumptions*, *Definitions*, *Experimental Treatments*, *Limitations*, and so on. Scanning each of these sections will help prepare you to navigate when you begin to read the article in detail from beginning to end.

The last heading in a research article is usually called "Discussion" or "Discussion and Conclusions." Researchers often reiterate or summarize their research purposes, research methods, and major findings in the first few paragraphs under this heading. Reading this section of a report on research will help you when you read the results section in detail, which can be difficult if it contains numerous statistics.

✔ Guideline 2: Based on your overview (see Guideline 1), group the articles by categories.

Sort the articles you have amassed into stacks that correspond roughly to the categories of studies you will describe. You may choose to organize them in any number of ways, but the most common practice is to first organize them by topics and subtopics and then in chronological order within each subtopic. Example 4.2.1 shows a possible grouping of articles into categories and subcategories for a review of research literature on the relationship between stress and parameters of the immune system in humans.

Example 4.2.1[1]

I. Conceptualizing Stress (Definitions)
    A. Acute Time-Limited Stressors
    B. Brief Naturalistic Stressors
    C. Stressful Event Sequences
    D. Chronic Stressors
II. Overview of the Immune System
    A. Components of the Immune System
    B. Immune Assays
III. Pathways Between Stress and the Immune System
IV. Models of Stress, the Immune System, and Health
 V. Who Is Vulnerable to Stress-Induced Immune Changes

Example 4.2.2 shows a possible grouping of articles into categories and subcategories for a review of research literature on the relationship between parenting style and child outcomes among Chinese and immigrant Chinese families.

---

[1] Based on Segerstrom, S. C., & Miller, G. E. (2004). Psychological stress and the human immune system: A meta-analytic study of 30 years of inquiry. *Psychological Bulletin, 130,* 601–630.

Example 4.2.2[2]

I. Conceptualization of Parenting Styles
   A. Research on Western Populations
   B. Cross-Cultural Studies
II. Parenting Style and Child Outcomes in Chinese Families
   A. Parental Control
   B. Parental Warmth
III. Confucianism and Its Impact on the Chinese Family

Organizing the articles into categories will facilitate your analysis if you read all the articles in each category or subcategory at about the same time. For instance, it will be easier to synthesize the literature on the effects of parental warmth (see point II-B in Example 4.2.2) if all the articles on this topic are read together, starting with the most recent one.

✔ Guideline 3:   Organize yourself before reading the articles.

It is important to organize yourself prior to beginning a detailed reading of the articles. You will need a computer, a pack of note cards to write your comments on, and several packs of self-adhesive flags that you can use to identify noteworthy comments. You can use different colored self-stick flags to mark different subtopics, different research methods, a review article or landmark study, or anything else that should be noted or might help you organize your review. If you are using a computer, you can use different colors of highlighting (available on modern word processing programs) instead of colored flags on note cards.

✔ Guideline 4:   Use a consistent format in your notes.

After you have organized the articles, you should begin to read them. As you read, summarize the important points and write them on the note cards. Develop a format for recording your notes about the articles you will be reading, and use this same format consistently. Building consistency into your notes at this stage in the process will pay off later when you start to write the review. As has been noted, you will encounter considerable variation across studies, and your notes should be consistent and detailed enough for you to be able to describe both differences and similarities across them. Example 4.4.1 illustrates the recommended format for recording your notes. Remember to note the page numbers whenever you copy an author's words verbatim; direct quotations should always be accompanied by page numbers, and it will save you considerable time later in the process if you already have the page numbers noted. Make sure to double-check your quotes for accuracy.

---

[2] Based on Lim, S.-L., & Lim, B. K. (2003). Parenting style and child outcomes in Chinese and immigrant Chinese families: Current findings and cross-cultural considerations in conceptualization and research. *Marriage & Family Review, 35*, 21–43.

Example 4.4.1

Author('s)(s') Last Name(s), Initial(s)
Title of Article
Publication Year
Name of Journal/Volume Number/Page Numbers

Notes (*responding to the following questions*):
1. What is the main point of this article?
2. Describe the methodology used. (Include numbers of participants, controls, treatments, etc.)
3. Describe the findings.
4. What, if anything, is notable about this article? (Is it a landmark study? Does it have flaws? Is it an experimental study? Is it qualitative or quantitative? and so on.)
5. Note specific details you find especially relevant to the topic of your review. (Make this as long as necessary.)

The points in Example 4.4.1 are given as examples to guide you through this process. In an actual case, you may choose to disregard one or more of them, or you may decide that others are more appropriate. You may need to create several note cards per source. For example, you might have a card for each article on the main point of the article, another one on the research methodology used, and so on.

It may also be helpful to use a separate card on which you make note of questions or concerns you have as you read a particular article, or on which you note any conclusions you may reach about the validity of the research. These notes can later be incorporated into your paper, perhaps in your discussion or conclusion, and using a separate card for this will save you valuable time later. These cards will also be quite helpful if you decide to build tables that summarize groups of studies for presentation in your literature review. Guidelines for building such tables are presented in Chapter 7.

For each article, one card should contain the complete bibliographic details, while the other cards on the article should be coded with just part of the bibliographic information such as the first author's last name, a key word from the title of the article, and the year of publication.

✓ Guideline 5: Look for explicit definitions of key terms in the literature.

It should not surprise you that different researchers sometimes define key terms in different ways. If there are major differences of opinion on how the variables you will be writing about should be defined, you will want to make notes on the definitions. In fact, if several different definitions are offered, you might find it helpful to prepare a separate set of cards containing just the definitions.

To see the importance of how terms are defined, consider definitions of *justice programs* and *entertainment-based justice programs* in Example 4.5.1. It excludes programs that are more than one hour long and ones that are based on real events from the study. Another researcher who uses a definition without these exclusions might obtain different results. As a reviewer, you will want to note such differences in definitions because they may help explain discrepant results from study to study.

Example 4.5.1[3]

Considered a particular "genre," or general category of TV entertainment (Gitlin, 1979), "justice" programs (sometimes called police dramas, crime dramas, legal shows, or lawyer shows) were defined as half-hour or one-hour television programs that focus on some aspect of the criminal justice system, such as law enforcement, criminal prosecution, courts, or corrections. Furthermore, entertainment-based justice programs were defined as fictional; that is, characters and events are fictional, they do not portray real-life characters or actual events. Using these…definitions, the researcher discovered 13 entertainment-based justice programs being broadcast…which included: *NYPD Blue.…* (p. 18).

Make special note of authoritative definitions (i.e., definitions offered by experts), which you can quote or summarize. For instance, the authors of Example 4.5.2 cite a definition used by a professional association in their literature review.

Example 4.5.2[4]

The American Massage Therapy Association (2003) defines *massage therapy* as manual soft tissue manipulation, including holding, causing movement, and/or applying pressure to the body.

Keep separate note cards with definitions of related terms. For instance, consider Example 4.5.3 in which the broader term "jealousy" is defined separately from the narrower term "romantic jealousy," which are distinguished from the definition of *envy*. Note that while the literature review in which Example 4.5.3 appears was published in 2005, older definitions are offered. There is nothing inherently wrong with citing older definitions if they are still considered to be valid.

Example 4.5.3[5]

Jealousy is defined as "a complex of thoughts, emotions, and actions that follows loss or threat to self-esteem and/or the existence or quality of the romantic relationship" (White, 1980, p. 222). *Romantic jealousy* is a set of thoughts, emotions, and responses following a perceived threat to a romantic relationship by a rival (Guerrero & Andersen, 1998b; Teismann & Mosher, 1978). Jealousy occurs when a person desires to protect a relationship with someone perceived as already pos-

---

[3] Soulliere, D. M. (2003). Prime-time murder: Presentations of murder on popular television justice programs. *Journal of Criminal Justice and Popular Culture, 10,* 12–38.
[4] Dryden, T., Baskwill, A., & Preyde, M. (2004). Massage therapy for the orthopaedic patient: A review. *Orthopaedic Nursing, 23,* 327–332.
[5] Fleischmann, A. A., Spitzberg, B. H., Andersen, P. A., & Roesch, S. C. (2005). Tickling the monster: Jealousy induction in relationships. *Journal of Social and Personal Relationships, 22,* 49–73.

sessed, in contrast to *envy*, which involves the desire for something or someone not currently possessed (Guerrero & Andersen, 1998b).

Note that it is usually a good idea to present definitions of key terms near the beginning of a literature review.

✔ Guideline 6: Look for key statistics to use near the beginning of your literature review.

Keep a separate set of note cards with key statistics that you might want to cite near the beginning of your literature review. Example 4.6.1 shows the first sentence of a literature review on the economic adaptation of immigrants and refugees. Note that citing a specific percentage is a much stronger beginning than a general statement, such as "Many individuals in the United States are foreign-born," would be.

Example 4.6.1[6]

About 10% of the United States population is foreign-born, a proportion that is expected to grow in the future (Doyle, 1999; U.S. Bureau of the Census, 2001). One of the issues....

Citing statistics at the beginning of a literature review is optional, with some topics lending themselves more to the technique than others. However, if you plan to start with a reference to quantities (e.g., *Some* adolescents....; *Frequently*, voters prefer....), it is desirable to provide a specific estimate if it is available. For many topics in the social and behavioral sciences, relevant statistics can be found on-line at www.census.gov.

✔ Guideline 7: Pay special attention to review articles on your topic.

If you find literature review articles (i.e., articles that consist solely of a literature review that are not just an introduction to a report of original research) on your topic or a closely related topic, read them carefully and make notes that will allow you to summarize them in your literature review. This was done by the authors of Example 4.7.1 in which they briefly summarized a previous review near the beginning of their own review.

Example 4.7.1[7]

A recent review of five national college drinking surveys (O'Malley & Johnston, 2002) summarized the major findings and trends that have accumulated over the past 20 years: more than two-thirds of college students drink alcohol, 40% are considered binge drinkers (i.e., consume five or more drinks at one sitting within the past 2 weeks), and rates of alcohol use have not changed substantially since the 1950s.

---

[6] Potocky-Tripodi, M. (2004). The role of social capital in immigrant and refugee economic adaptation. *Journal of Social Service Research, 31,* 59–91.

[7] O'Hare, T., & Sherrer, M. V. (2005). Assessment of youthful problem drinkers: Validating the drinking context scale (DCS-9) with freshmen first offenders. *Research on Social Work Practice, 15,* 110–117.

✓ Guideline 8:   Prepare note cards with short notable quotations that might be used very sparingly in your review.

Direct quotations should be used very sparingly in literature reviews. This is because the use of too many quotations can interrupt the flow of the narrative. In addition, the writer of a review is usually able to summarize and paraphrase points more succinctly than the original author, who is obligated to provide more details on the research than is the reviewer. Nevertheless, there are instances in which an especially apt statement might be worthy of being quoted in a literature review. For instance, in Example 4.8.1, the writers are reviewing literature on leadership in families, yet, near the beginning of their review they draw an analogy with leadership in business organizations. The quotation succinctly summarizes a major point that the authors are making. Note that this is the only quotation they used in their review.

Example 4.8.1[8]

As stated by Bennis and Nanus (1985), "A business short on capital can borrow money, and one with a poor location can move. But a business short on leadership has little chance for survival" (p. 20).

Another appropriate use of quotations is when citing legal matters, where the exact wording is important and even a small change in wording might change its legal meaning. Example 4.8.2 contains such a quotation, which appeared as the first sentence in a review.

Example 4.8.2[9]

On November 18, 2003, the Massachusetts Supreme Judicial Court (SJC) declared that it could find no "constitutionally adequate reason for denying civil marriage to same-sex couples," and ordered the state to begin issuing marriage licenses to same-sex couples.

Note that the quotations in Examples 4.8.1 and 4.8.2 are quite short. It is almost always inappropriate to include long quotations (i.e., longer than a few sentences) in a literature review. After all, a review should be an original synthesis, not a repeat of already published materials.

✓ Guideline 9:   Look for methodological strengths.

It is unlikely that you will find a single research article with definitive results about any aspect of the human condition. Inevitably, some studies will be stronger than others, and these strengths should be noted in your review. Ask yourself how strong the

---

[8] Galbraith, K. A., & Schvaneveldt, J. D. (2005). Family leadership styles and family well-being. *Family and Consumer Sciences Research Journal, 33*, 220–239.

[9] Lannutti, P. J. (2005). For better or worse: Exploring the meanings of same-sex marriage within the lesbian, gay, bisexual, and transgendered community. *Journal of Social and Personal Relationships, 22*, 5–18.

evidence is, and keep in mind that in your role as the reviewer, you have the right and the responsibility to make these subjective evaluations.

The strength of a research article may come from the research methodology used. Do the research methods of one study improve on the data-gathering techniques of earlier studies? Does the article's strength derive from the size and generalizability of its subject pool? Does a set of studies demonstrate that the same conclusion can be reached by using a variety of methods? These and other similar questions will guide you in determining the strengths of particular studies. Identifying methodological strengths is considered in more detail in Chapters 5 and 6.

✔ Guideline 10: Look for methodological weaknesses.

Remember that you should note any major weaknesses you encounter when reviewing research literature. The same process you used in identifying strengths should be used when identifying weaknesses. For instance, you should determine whether the author's research method has provided new insights into the research topic. Particularly, if an innovative methodology is used, does it seem appropriate, or does it raise the possibility of alternative explanations? Has an appropriate sample been used? Are the findings consistent with those of similar studies? Is enough evidence presented in the article for a reasonable person to judge whether the researcher's conclusions are valid?

Here again, it may be preferable to critique groups of studies together, especially if their flaws are similar. Generally, it is *inappropriate* to note each and every flaw in every study you review. Instead, note major weaknesses of individual studies, and keep your eye out for patterns of weaknesses across groups of studies. For instance, if all the research reports on a subtopic you are reviewing are based on very small samples, you might note this fact on a separate card that relates to the collection of articles on that subtopic.

Authors of research articles often discuss the weaknesses in their own studies. While this may be discussed at any point in a research article, it is conventional to discuss these in the Discussion section near the end of a research report. Usually, these are identified as "limitations" of the study. Example 4.10.1 shows such a statement. It is important to take notes in light of these self-disclosed methodological weaknesses.

Example 4.10.1[10]

The results and proposed implications [of the current research] for social work practice are based on a nonprobability sample with a small sample size from a single provider organization. Also, the severity of their illness was not taken into account.... Therefore, the results and implications for social work practice should be interpreted with these limitations in mind.

✔ Guideline 11: Distinguish between assertion and evidence.

A common mistake made in literature reviews is to report an author's assertions

---

[10] Lee, J. S. (2004). A profile of diabetic African American elderly receiving home health care: Implications for social work practice. *Journal of Social Work in Long-Term Care, 3*, 13–30.

as though they were findings. To avoid this mistake, make sure you have understood the author's evidence and its interpretation. A finding derives from the empirical evidence presented; an assertion is the author's opinion.

In Example 4.11.1, readers can easily distinguish between the assertions in the body of the paragraph and the evidence-based statements in the last sentence. Bold italics have been added for emphasis.

Example 4.11.1[11]

The risk factor for binge eating that has received the most attention is dieting (Lowe, 1994). Dieting *is thought to* increase the risk that an individual will over-eat to counteract the effects of caloric deprivation. Dieting *may* also promote binge eating because violating strict dietary rules can result in disinhibited eating (the abstinence–violation effect). Moreover, dieting entails a shift from a reliance on physiological cues to cognitive control over eating behaviors, which leaves the individual vulnerable to disinhibited eating when these cognitive processes are disrupted. In support of *these assertions*, dieting predicted binge eating onset in adolescent girls (Stice & Agras, 1998; Stice, Killen, Hayward, & Taylor, 1998), and acute caloric deprivation resulted in elevated binge eating in adult women (Agras & Telch, 1998; Telch & Agras, 1996). (p. 132).

✔ Guideline 12: Identify the major trends or patterns in the results of previous studies.

When you write your literature review, you will be responsible for pointing out major trends or patterns in the results reported in the research articles you review. This may take the form of a *generalization*, in which you generalize from the various articles, as was done in Example 4.12.1, which originally appeared in the last paragraph of a literature review article. Note that the references that support the generalization in the example were cited earlier in the review in which this excerpt appeared.

Example 4.12.1[12]

Of the nine interventions reviewed, the Arthritis Self-Help Course enjoys a well-established body of research supporting its efficacy and cost-effectiveness. (p. 60).

Of course, you may not be as fortunate as the reviewers who wrote Example 4.12.1. There may be considerable inconsistencies in results from one research article to another. When this is the case, you should try to make sense of them for your readers. For instance, you might state a generalization based on a *majority* of the articles, or you might state a generalization based only on those articles you think have the strongest research methodology. Either option is acceptable as long as you clearly describe to your

---

[11] Stice, E., Presnell, K., & Spangler, D. (2002). Risk factors for binge eating onset in adolescent girls: A 2-year prospective investigation. *Health Psychology, 21*, 131–138.
[12] Brady, T. J., Kruger, J., Helmick, C. G., Callahan, L. F., & Boutaugh, M. L. (2003). Intervention programs for arthritis and other rheumatic diseases. *Health Education & Behavior, 30*, 44–63.

reader the basis for your generalization. Once again, careful note taking during the analysis stage will help you in this process.

✔ Guideline 13: Identify gaps in the literature.

It is every graduate student's dream to discover a significant gap in the literature, especially one that can form the crux of the student's thesis or dissertation study. In fact, gaps often exist because research in these areas presents considerable obstacles for researchers. These gaps should be noted in a literature review, along with discussions of why they exist. If you identify a gap that you believe should be addressed, make note of it, and take it into consideration as you plan the organization of your review.

✔ Guideline 14: Identify relationships among studies.

As you read additional articles on your list, make note of any relationships that may exist among studies. For instance, a landmark research article may have spawned a new approach subsequently explored in additional studies conducted by others, or two articles may explore the same or a similar question but with different age groups or language groups. It is important to point out these relationships in your review. When you write, you probably will want to discuss related ones together.

✔ Guideline 15: Note how closely each article relates to your topic.

Try to keep your review focused on the topic you have chosen. It is inappropriate to include studies that bear no relationship to your area of study in your literature review. Therefore, your notes should include explicit references to the specific aspects of a study that relate to your topic.

If you determine that there is no literature with a direct bearing on one or more aspects of your research topic, it is permissible to review peripheral research, but this should be done cautiously. Pyrczak and Bruce (2005) cite the example of year-round school schedules, which were implemented in Los Angeles as a curricular innovation, as shown in Example 4.15.1.

Example 4.15.1[13]

When Los Angeles first started implementing year-round school schedules, for example, there was no published research on the topic. There was research, however, on traditional school-year programs in which children attended school in shifts, on the effects of the length of the school year on achievement, and on the effectiveness of summer school programs. Students who were writing theses and dissertations on the Los Angeles program had to cite such peripheral literature in order to demonstrate their ability to conduct a search of the literature and write a comprehensive, well-organized review of literature.

---

[13] Pyrczak, F., & Bruce, R. R. (2005). *Writing empirical research reports: A basic guide for students of the social and behavioral sciences* (5th ed.). Los Angeles, CA: Pyrczak Publishing.

Such examples are rare, and you are advised to consult your instructor before you reach the conclusion that no studies have dealt with your specific research topic.

✓ Guideline 16: Evaluate your reference list for currency and for coverage.

When you have finished reading the articles you have collected, you should re-evaluate your entire reference list once more to ensure that it is complete and up-to-date. A literature review should demonstrate that it represents the latest work done in the subject area. As a rule of thumb, use a five-year span from the present as a tentative limit of coverage, keeping in mind that you will extend further back when it is warranted. If your review is intended to present a historical overview of your topic, for example, you may have to reach well beyond the five-year span. However, remember that the reader of a literature review expects that you have reported on the most current research available. Thus, you should make explicit your reasons for including articles that are not current (e.g., Is it a landmark study? Does it present the only evidence available on a given topic? Does it help you to understand the evolution of a research technique?).

The question of how much literature is enough to include in a review is difficult to answer. In general, your first priority should be to establish that you have read the most current research available. Then, you should try to cover your topic as completely as necessary, not as completely as possible. Your instructor or faculty adviser can help you determine how much is enough.

Activities for Chapter 4

Directions: Refer to the printed list of sources you developed in Activity 5 at the end of Chapter 3.

1. Obtain copies of two articles from this list, and look over each of the articles.

   - Do the authors include a summary of the contents of the literature review at or near the beginning? If so, highlight or mark this summary for future reference.
   - Did the authors use subheadings?
   - Scan the paragraph(s) immediately preceding the heading "Method." Did the authors describe their hypotheses, research questions, or research purposes?
   - Without rereading any of the text of the article, write a brief statement describing what each article is about.

2. Based on your overview of all the articles on your list, make predictions of some of the likely categories and subcategories for your review. Reread the printed list of sources and try to group them by these categories and subcategories. Then, using these categories and subcategories, create an outline for describing the area of your topic.

3. Carefully review your outline and select the articles you will read first. Within each category, start with the earliest study and work toward the present. You now have your initial reading list.

Chapter 5

Analyzing Quantitative Research Literature

In the previous chapter, you were advised to make notes on important methodological strengths and weaknesses of the research articles you are reading prior to writing your literature review. This chapter will provide you with information on some points you may want to note regarding research methodology in quantitative studies. Those of you who have taken a course in research methods will recognize that this chapter contains only a very brief overview of some of the important issues.

✔ Guideline 1: Note whether the research is quantitative or qualitative.

Because quantitative researchers reduce information to statistics such as averages, percentages, and so on, their research articles are easy to spot. If an article has a results section devoted mainly to the presentation of statistical data, it is a safe bet that it is quantitative. The quantitative approach to research has dominated the social and behavioral sciences throughout the 1900s and into the 2000s, so for most topics, you are likely to locate many more articles reporting quantitative than qualitative research.

The literature on how to conduct quantitative research *emphasizes*:

1. Starting with one or more explicitly stated hypotheses that will remain unchanged throughout the study.[1] The validity of the hypotheses is evaluated only after the data have been analyzed (i.e., the hypotheses are not subject to change while the data are being collected).

2. Selecting an unbiased sample (such as a simple random sample obtained by drawing names out of a hat) from a particular population.

3. Using a relatively large sample of participants (typically, at least 30 for an experiment and sometimes as many as 1,500 for a national survey).

4. Measuring with instruments that can be scored objectively, such as multiple-choice achievement tests and forced-choice questionnaires, attitude scales or personality scales with choices that participants mark.

5. Presenting results using statistics and often making inferences to the population from which the sample was drawn (i.e., inferring that what the researchers found by studying a sample is similar to what they would have found if they had studied the whole population from which the sample was drawn).

---

[1] Quantitative researchers sometimes start with specific research questions or purposes instead of a hypothesis. As with hypotheses, the research questions or purposes remain unchanged throughout the study.

Qualitative research also has a long tradition in the social and behavioral sciences, but has gained a large following in many applied fields only in recent decades. It is sometimes easy to spot because the titles of the articles often contain the word "qualitative." In addition, qualitative researchers usually identify their research as qualitative in their introductions as well as in other parts of their reports.[2] You can also identify qualitative research because the results sections will be presented in terms of a narrative describing themes and trends—often accompanied by quotations from the participants.

The literature on how to conduct qualitative research *emphasizes*:

1. Starting with a general problem without imposing rigid, specific purposes and hypotheses to guide the study. As data are collected on the problem, hypotheses may emerge, but they are subject to change during the course of a study as additional data are collected.

2. Selecting a purposive sample—not a random one. For instance, a qualitative researcher may have access to some heroin addicts who attend a particular methadone clinic and may believe that these clients of the clinic might provide useful insights into the problems of recovering addicts. In other words, qualitative researchers use their *judgment* in selecting a sample instead of a mechanical, objective process such as drawing names out of a hat at random.

3. Using a relatively small sample—sometimes as small as one exemplary case such as a mathematics teacher who has received a national award for teaching (once again, a purposive sample—selecting someone who is judged as a potential source of important information).

4. Measuring with relatively unstructured instruments such as semistructured interviews with open-ended questions (i.e., without "choices" to be selected by participants), unstructured observations of behavior in natural contexts, and so on.

5. Measuring intensively (e.g., spending extended periods of time with the participants to gain in-depth insights into the phenomena of interest).

6. Presenting results mainly or exclusively in words, with an emphasis on understanding the particular purposive sample studied and usually de-emphasizing or ignoring generalizations to larger populations.

As you can see by comparing the two lists above, the distinction between quantitative and qualitative research will be important when you evaluate studies for their strengths and weaknesses. This chapter presents major guidelines for evaluating quantitative research, which you should consider when evaluating and synthesizing research in order to prepare a literature review. Guidelines for evaluating qualitative research are presented in the next chapter.

✔ Guideline 2: Note whether a study is experimental or nonexperimental.

An *experimental* study is one in which treatments are administered to participants

---

[2] Note that quantitative researchers rarely explicitly state that their research is quantitative.

for the purposes of the study and their effects are assessed. For instance, in an experiment, some hyperactive students might be given Ritalin™ while others are given behavior therapy (such as systematic application of reward systems) in order to assess the relative effectiveness of the two treatments in reducing the number of classroom discipline problems. (Note that almost all experiments are quantitative.) The purpose obviously would be to see how effective each treatment is and which treatment is more effective. More generally, the purpose is to identify cause-and-effect relationships.

A *nonexperimental* study is one in which participants' traits are measured without attempting to change them. For instance, hyperactive students might be interviewed to understand their perceptions of their own disruptive classroom behaviors without any attempt by the researcher to treat the students. Such a study might be quantitative (if the researcher uses highly structured interview questions with choices for students to select from and summarizes the results statistically) or qualitative (if a researcher uses semi-structured or unstructured interview questions[3] and uses words to summarize the results in terms of themes, models, or theories).[4]

Here is an important caveat: Do not fall into the habit of referring to all research studies as experiments. For instance, if you are reviewing nonexperimental studies, refer to them as "studies"—not "experiments." Use the term "experiment" only if treatments were administered to participants in order to observe the effects of the treatments.

✔ Guideline 3: In an experiment, note whether the participants were assigned at random to treatment conditions.

An experiment in which participants are assigned at random to treatments is known as a *true experiment*. Random assignment to treatments guarantees that there is no bias in the assignment (i.e., with random assignment, there is no bias that would systematically assign the more disruptive students to the behavior therapy treatment while assigning the rest to be treated with Ritalin™). Other things being equal, more weight should be given to true experiments than to experiments using other methods of assignment such as using the students in one school as the experimental group and the students in another school as the control group. Note that students are not normally assigned schools at random. Hence, there may be important preexisting differences between the students in the two schools, which may confound the interpretation of the results of such an experiment (e.g., socioeconomic status, language background, or self-selection, as occurs in "magnet" schools for the arts, the sciences, etc.).

✔ Guideline 4: Note attempts to examine cause-and-effect issues in nonexperimental studies.

The experimental method (with random assignment to treatment conditions) is widely regarded as the best quantitative method for investigating cause-and-effect issues. However, it is sometimes unfeasible or impossible to treat participants in certain ways.

---

[3] In addition, a qualitative researcher would be likely to conduct significantly longer interviews and possibly more than one interview.
[4] Obviously, then, nonexperimental research can be quantitative or qualitative while experimental research is almost always quantitative.

For instance, if a researcher was exploring a possible causal link between the divorce of parents and their children dropping out of high school, it would obviously be impossible to force some parents to get divorced while forcing others to remain married for the purposes of an experiment. For this research problem, the best that can be done is to obtain some students who have dropped out and some who have not dropped out but who are very similar in other important respects (such as socioeconomic status, the quality of the schools they attended, and so on) and then check to see if their parents' divorce rates differ in the hypothesized direction.[5] Suppose that the children of the divorced parents had somewhat higher drop-out rates than those of the children of nondivorced parents. Does this mean that divorce causes higher drop-out rates? Not necessarily. The conclusion is debatable because the researchers may have overlooked a number of other possible causal variables. Here is just one: Perhaps parents who tend to get divorced have poorer interpersonal skills and relate less well to their children. It may be this deficit in the children's upbringing (and not the divorce *per se*) that contributed to dropping out.[6]

The study we are considering is an example of a causal–comparative (or *ex post facto*) study. When using it, a researcher observes a current condition or outcome (such as dropping out) and searches the past for possible causal variables (such as divorce). Because causal–comparative studies are considered to be more prone to error than true experiments for examining causality, you should note when a conclusion is based on the causal–comparative method. In addition, you should consider whether there are other plausible causal interpretations the researcher may have overlooked.

✓ Guideline 5: Consider the test–retest reliability of the instrumentation.

Quantitative researchers refer to the measures they use (such as tests and questionnaires) as *instruments*. Thus, the term *instrumentation* refers to the process by which they measure key variables.

Reliability refers to consistency of results. Here is an example: Suppose we administered a college admissions test one week and then readministered it to the same examinees the following week. The test would be considered reliable if the same examinees who scored high the first week also tended to score high the second week.[7] By calculating a correlation coefficient, the reliability of a test can be quantified. Correlation coefficients can range from 0.00 to 1.00, with 1.00 indicating perfect reliability. Quantitative re-

---

[5] If the researcher had considerable resources and a long time frame, a prospective study could be conducted in which children are followed from the time they start school until they finish school, noting who drops out and who does not drop out as well as whose parents get divorced. This longitudinal method is also inferior to the experimental method for identifying cause-and-effect relationships because of possible confounding variables (i.e., many variables other than divorce may be responsible for the dropping-out behavior, and the researchers may fail to control for them all).

[6] If this limitation is still not clear, consider the example further. Suppose that based on the study in question, a dictatorial government made it illegal for parents to divorce in order to reduce the dropout rate. If the real cause of dropping out was parents' poor interpersonal skills, preventing divorce would not have the presumed effect because it was misidentified as a causal agent. Instead, the government should have mounted programs to assist parents to improve their interpersonal skills, especially in dealing with their children.

[7] Likewise, for high reliability, those examinees who scored low the first week also scored low the second week.

searchers generally regard a coefficient of 0.75 or higher to indicate adequate reliability. The type of reliability we are considering here is called *test–retest reliability*.[8]

When you analyze a quantitative study, examine the section on instrumentation to see if the researchers provide information on the reliability of the instruments they used in their research. Typically, this information is very briefly presented, as in Example 5.5.1.

Example 5.5.1
A brief statement in a research report on test–retest reliability:

The test–retest reliability of the instrument with a two-week interval between administrations was reported to be 0.81, which indicates adequate reliability (Doe, 2005).

While the statement in Example 5.5.1 is very brief, it assures you that the researcher whose research you are analyzing has considered the important issue of reliability. In addition, it provides you with a reference (i.e., Doe, 2005), which you could consult for more information on how reliability was determined.

✓ Guideline 6: Consider the internal consistency reliability of the instrumentation.

While test–retest reliability concerns the consistency of results over time (see Guideline 5), *internal consistency reliability* refers to consistency of results at one point in time. To understand this concept, consider a multiple-choice test with only two algebra test items. Suppose an examinee marked one item correctly and the other item incorrectly. This would indicate a *lack* of internal consistency because what we learned about the examinee's algebra knowledge varied from one item to the next (i.e., on one test item, the examinee earned one point, while on the other test item, the examinee earned zero points, which is the lowest possible score on a single item). Extending this concept to a test with a larger number of items and examinees, if those examinees who mark any one test item correctly *tend* to mark the other test items correctly (and if those examinees who mark any one test item *in*correctly *tend* to mark the other test items *in*correctly), the test would be said to have good internal consistency reliability. Put more generally, internal consistency refers to the idea that what is learned about an examinee's ability by examining responses to some of the items is similar to what is learned by examining responses to other items.[9]

Failure to have internal consistency indicates that some of the items are not operating as indicated. There may be many reasons for this. One obvious reason is that some items may be ambiguous, causing examinees with much knowledge to mark incorrect answers. Of course, this would be undesirable.

Internal consistency reliability is almost universally examined by computing a statistic known as Cronbach's alpha (whose symbol is α). Like a correlation coefficient, α

---

[8] Other methods for determining reliability are beyond the scope of this book.
[9] In other words, an instrument with high internal consistency may be viewed as consisting of a set of homogenous items (i.e., all items tend to tap similar skills, attitudes, and so on).

can range from 0.00 to 1.00, with values above 0.75 usually considered to indicate adequate internal consistency reliability for research purposes.[10] Example 5.6.1 shows how alpha might be reported in a research report.

Example 5.6.1[11]

A brief statement in a research report on two types of reliability:

The outcome of interest for this study was a self-reported measure of violent behavior.... The scale ranged from 0 to 70; higher scores indicate more violent behavior. In a pilot test, Cronbach's alpha (α) was .75, and the test–retest...correlation was .76 (Birnbaum et al., 2002).

While the statement in Example 5.6.1 is very brief, it assures you that the researchers have considered both test–retest and internal consistency reliability. In addition, it provides you with a reference (i.e., Birnbaum et al., 2002), which you could consult for more information on how reliability and internal consistency were determined.

✓ Guideline 7: Consider the validity of the instrumentation.

An instrument (such as a college admissions test) is said to be *valid* to the extent that it measures what it is supposed to measure. For instance, to the extent that a college admissions test correctly predicts who will and who will not succeed in college, the test is said to be valid. In practice, it is safe to assume that no instrument is perfectly valid. For instance, college admissions tests are at best only modestly valid.

In a *criterion-related validity* study, scores earned by examinees on an instrument (such as a college admissions test) are correlated with scores earned on some other measure (such as freshman GPAs earned in college). The extent of criterion-related validity is determined by calculating a correlation coefficient to describe the relationship. When this is done, the resulting correlation coefficient is called a *validity coefficient*.[12] Generally, coefficients above 0.30 indicate adequate validity for research purposes. Example 5.7.1 shows a brief statement regarding the *predictive criterion-related validity* of a college admissions test. It is called *predictive* because the admissions test was administered at one point in time, while the outcome (GPAs) was measured later, with the purpose being to determine how well the scores predict GPAs.

Example 5.7.1

A brief statement in a research report on predictive criterion-related validity:

Using a sample of 240 examinees who were admitted to a small liberal arts college, Doe (2005) correlated scores on the XYZ College Admissions test with freshmen grades. The test was found to have adequate criterion–related validity ($r = .49$).

---

[10] If you have studied statistics, you know that correlation coefficients can also have negative values. In practice, however, when estimating reliability and internal consistency, they are always positive in value.

[11] Blitstein, J. L., Murray, D. M., Lytle, L. A., Birnbaum, A. S, & Perry, C. L. (2005). Predictors of violent behavior in an early adolescent cohort: Similarities and differences across genders. *Health Education & Behavior, 32*, 175–194.

[12] A *validity coefficient* is a correlation coefficient whose symbol is *r*.

Example 5.7.2 shows a brief statement regarding *concurrent criterion–related validity*. The adjective "concurrent" refers to the fact that the two measures were administered at about the same time.

Example 5.7.2
A brief statement in a research report on concurrent criterion-related validity (predictive):

In a previous study, Doe (2005) correlated scores on the Smoking Cessation Questionnaire with data regarding smoking cessation gathered by trained and experienced interviewers. The questionnaire was administered to the participants on the same day that the participants were interviewed. Using the interview data as the criterion for judging the validity of the questionnaire, the questionnaire was found to have good criterion-related validity ($r = .68$). Thus, the Smoking Cessation Questionnaire is a reasonably valid substitute for the more expensive interview process for measuring smoking cessation behaviors.

Another major type of validity is *construct validity*. This term refers to any type of data-based study that sheds light on the validity of an instrument. Construct validity studies can take many forms, most of which are beyond the scope of this book. However, to illustrate how such a study might be conducted, consider Example 5.7.3.

Example 5.7.3
A brief statement in a research report on construct validity:

Scores on the new ABC Anxiety Scale were correlated with scores on the well-established Beck Depression Inventory, resulting in a correlation of .45. This result is consistent with major theories as well as previous studies (e.g., Doe, 2004) that indicate that individuals who are anxious have a moderate tendency to also be depressed. Thus, the correlation provides indirect evidence on the validity of the new anxiety scale.

The last major type of validity is *content validity*. Content validity is determined by having one or more experts evaluate the contents of an instrument. It is especially important to determine the content validity of achievement tests. For instance, experts can be asked to compare the instructional objectives with the material covered by an achievement test designed to measure attainment of those objectives in order to determine the extent to which they match. Content validity can also be determined for other types of instruments as illustrated in Example 5.7.4.

Example 5.7.4
A brief statement in a research report on content validity:

The Infant Development Checklist was used as the measure of the outcome in this experiment. In a previous study, Doe (2004) reported that it had adequate content validity, as judged by three professors whose specialty is developmental psychology.

✓ Guideline 8: Consider whether an instrument is valid for a particular research purpose.

An instrument that has been shown to be reasonably valid in previous research may not be especially valid for use in all other studies. For instance, an attitude scale that has been shown to be valid for use with adolescents may have some unknown amount of validity for use with younger children in another study. Thus, if the purpose of the study is to study attitudes of younger children, the validity of the instrument might be unknown. Put in more general terms, the validity of an instrument is *relative* to the purposes of a study. It may be more valid in a study with one purpose (e.g., determine attitudes of adolescents) than in another study with some different purpose (e.g., determine attitudes of young children).

✓ Guideline 9: Note differences in how a variable is measured across studies.

When you examine various published studies in which a variable of interest to you has been measured, you will often find that different researchers used different instruments to measure the variable. For instance, one researcher may have measured attitude toward school with a forced-choice questionnaire (e.g., items to which participants respond to choices from "Strongly Agree" to "Strongly Disagree"), while another researcher might have used an observational checklist for classroom behaviors that indicate positive or negative attitudes (e.g., children working cooperatively on classroom projects). If similarities are found in results across studies using different instruments, this lends support to the results. Obviously, differences in results among studies could be attributable to differences in the instrumentation.

Note that part of the measurement process is to determine the sources from which to collect data. For instance, to study violent juvenile delinquent behavior, one researcher might seek data from the participants' peers, while another might seek it from the participants themselves using essentially the same questions.[13] Differences in the sources with which the instrument is used could also account for differences in results.

In light of the above, you should look for patterns across studies that might be attributed to instrumentation. For instance, do all the studies that support a certain conclusion use one method or type of instrument while those that support a different conclusion use a different method? If your notes reveal this, you might consider making a statement such as the one in Example 5.9.1.

Example 5.9.1

A statement from a literature review that points out differences in measurement techniques (desirable):

While the two studies that used mailed questionnaires support the finding that inhalant use among adolescents is extremely rare (less than one-half of 1%), the three studies that used face-to-face interviews reported an incidence of more than 5%.

---

[13] For instance, peers might be asked, "Has your friend John told you about any fights he has had in the last week?" while the participant might be asked, "Have you had any fights in the last week?"

Note that Example 5.9.1 is much more informative than Example 5.9.2.

Example 5.9.2
A statement from a literature review that fails to point out differences in measurement techniques (undesirable):

The research on the incidence of adolescent inhalant use has yielded mixed results, with two studies reporting that it is extremely rare and three others reporting an incidence of more than 5%.

✔ Guideline 10: Note how the participants were sampled.

Most quantitative researchers study only samples from which they make inferences about the populations from which the samples were drawn. You should make notes on whether the samples studied seem likely to be representative of the populations to which one might wish to generalize. From a quantitative researcher's point of view, drawing a sample at random is best.

Unfortunately, most researchers cannot use random samples (at least not in their purest form). This is true for two reasons. First, many researchers work with limited funds and have limited cooperative contacts that might be required to obtain random samples. Because most researchers in the social and behavioral sciences are professors, it is not surprising that they often use students at the colleges or universities at which they teach as samples. Of course, what is true of college students might not generalize to other groups of individuals.

Second, even if a random sample of names is drawn, almost invariably, some of those individuals selected refuse to participate. This is especially problematic in mailed surveys in which response rates are often notoriously low. It would not be surprising, for instance, to receive only a 25% response rate in a national survey that was mailed to, for example, a random sample of members of a professional association (e.g., an association of public school teachers).

Studies without random sampling and with low response rates should be interpreted with considerable caution. Such studies usually should be regarded as *suggestive* because they do not offer firm evidence.

✔ Guideline 11: Make notes on the demographics of the participants.

Making notes on the demographics[14] of the participants can also help you identify patterns in the literature. For instance, have the researchers who studied the transition from welfare to work using urban samples obtained different results from researchers who have studied rural samples? Could the differences in the urban–rural status of the participants (a demographic characteristic) help explain the differences in the findings? Note that you cannot answer such a question with certainty, but you could raise the possibility in your literature review. Other demographic characteristics often reported in research reports are gender, race/ethnicity, age, and socioeconomic status.

---

[14] "Demographics" are background characteristics of the participants.

Research reports in which demographics are not reported in detail are generally less useful than ones in which demographics are reported in detail.

✓ Guideline 12: Note how large a difference is—not just whether it is statistically significant.

When a researcher says a difference is statistically significant, he or she is reporting that a statistical test has indicated that the difference is greater than might be created by chance alone. It does *not* mean that the difference is necessarily large. It would take several chapters of a statistics textbook to explain the reasons why this is true. However, the following analogy may help you understand this point: Suppose there is a very tight race for the United States Senate, and Candidate A wins over Candidate B by 10 votes. This is indeed a very small difference, but it is quite significant (i.e., by counting all the votes systematically and carefully, we have identified a very small nonchance, "real" difference).

Given that even a small difference is often statistically significant, you will want to make note of the sizes of the differences you find in the literature.[15] Suppose you read several studies that showed that computer-assisted instruction in English composition led to very slight, but statistically significant, increases in students' achievement. In fairness to your reader, you should point out the size of the differences, as illustrated in Example 5.12.1. You will be prepared to write such statements if you make appropriate notes as you read and analyze the literature.

Example 5.12.1

In a series of true experiments at various colleges throughout the United States, the experimental groups receiving computer-assisted instruction in English composition consistently made very small but statistically significant gains than the control groups in mathematics achievement. On average, the gains were only about one percentage point on multiple-choice tests. Despite their statistical significance, these very small gains make the use of the experimental treatment on a widespread basis problematic because of the greatly increased cost of using it instead of the conventional (control) treatment.

✓ Guideline 13: It is safe to presume that all quantitative studies are flawed.

All quantitative studies are subject to errors of various kinds, so no one study should be taken as providing the definitive answer(s) to a given research problem. In fact, that is why you are combing through the evidence reported in original reports of research—to weigh the various pieces of evidence, all of which are subject to error—in or-

---

[15] Increasingly, quantitative researchers are reporting a relatively new statistic called "effect size," which measures the size of a difference between groups of participants relative to the differences among individual participants. While a discussion of this statistic is beyond the scope of this book, should you encounter this statistic while reviewing literature, use this rough guideline: Effect sizes of less than about .25 indicate a small difference, and effect sizes above .50 indicate a large difference.

der to arrive at some reasonable conclusions based on a body of literature. This brings us to an important caveat: Never use the word "prove" when discussing the results of empirical research. Empirical studies do not offer proof. Instead, they offer *degrees of evidence*, with some studies offering stronger evidence than others. While analyzing research articles, make notes on how convincing the evidence is in each article. Other things being equal, you should emphasize in your literature review the research articles that present the strongest evidence.

This guideline leads to another important principle. Namely, you will not be expected to dissect and discuss every flaw of every study you cite because flaws abound in studies. Instead, you should make notes on major flaws, especially in studies that you plan to emphasize in your review. In addition, you should critique the methodology of studies in groups, whenever possible. For instance, you might point out that all studies in a group you are reviewing have common weaknesses. Good note-taking while you are reading the articles will help you identify such commonalities.

Concluding Comment

This chapter briefly covers only some major methodological issues you might consider when you make notes on reports of quantitative research in preparation for writing a review of literature. As you read the articles you have selected for your review, you will find additional information on these as well as other issues because researchers often critique their own research as well as that of others in their journal articles. Reading these critiques carefully will help you comprehend more fully the research articles you will be reviewing.

Activities for Chapter 5

Directions: Locate an original report of quantitative research, preferably on a topic you are reviewing, and answer the following questions. For learning purposes, your instructor may choose to assign an article for all students in your class to read.

1. What characteristics of the report you located led you to believe that it is an example of quantitative research?

2. Is the study experimental *or* nonexperimental? On what basis did you decide?

3. If the study is experimental, were the participants assigned at random to treatment conditions? If not, how were they assigned?

4. If it is nonexperimental, was the researcher attempting to examine cause-and-effect issues? If yes, did he or she use the causal–comparative method? Explain.

5. What types of measures (i.e., instruments) were used? Did the researcher provide enough information about them to allow you to make judgments on their adequacy for use in the research? If yes, do you believe they were adequate in light of the information provided? If no, what types of additional information about the measures should have been reported?

6. How did the researcher obtain a sample of participants? Was it at random from a population? If the study is a mailed survey, what was the response rate?

7. Has the researcher described the demographics of the participants in sufficient detail? Explain.

8. If the researcher reported statistically significant differences, did he or she discuss whether they were large differences? In your opinion, are the differences large enough to be of practical importance? Explain.

9. Did the researcher critique his or her own research by describing its limitations? Explain.

10. Briefly describe any major flaws in the research that you did not cover in your answers to Questions 1 through 9.

Chapter 6

Analyzing Qualitative
Research Literature

The major differences between qualitative and quantitative research are described under Guideline 1 in Chapter 5. This chapter was written with the assumption that you have already carefully considered the material under that guideline. While Chapter 5 emphasizes the analysis of quantitative research prior to writing a literature review, this chapter explores criteria for analyzing qualitative research.

✔ Guideline 1: Note whether the research was conducted by an individual or by a research team.

While both published quantitative and qualitative research are very frequently conducted by teams of researchers, the use of a team is more important in qualitative research than in quantitative research. For instance, if a quantitative researcher administers an objective attitude scale, scores it, and analyzes the data using a statistical software package, it is reasonable to expect that anyone else who uses care in scoring and entering the data would obtain the same results as the original researcher obtained. However, if a qualitative researcher conducts open-ended, semistructured interviews, the resulting raw data typically consist of many pages of transcripts of what the participants said in the interviews. It is possible that different researchers might analyze and interpret such data differently, calling into question the validity of the analysis of the data. However, if a team of researchers analyzes a set of qualitative data and arrives at a consensus on its meaning, consumers of research can have more confidence in the results of the research than if it were conducted by an individual.

It is not necessary for research to be conducted by a team. In fact, there may not be other qualified researchers available to work with a researcher, or the requirements for a thesis or a dissertation might be that the researcher work as an individual. When this is the case, it is especially important for consumers of qualitative research to check to see that the individual who conducted the qualitative research used at least one of the techniques described under Guidelines 3 and 4 in this chapter.

✔ Guideline 2: When there is a research team, note whether analysis of the data was initially conducted independently.

Researchers who analyze a set of qualitative data should first analyze it independently (i.e., without consulting each other) in order to prevent one or more researchers from unduly influencing the others in interpreting the data. After the initial analysis, researchers then resolve any discrepancies, usually by discussing them until a consensus is reached. This process is described in Example 6.2.1.

Example 6.2.1[1]
Description of independent analysis followed by reaching a consensus:

Qualitative data were analyzed by a research team.... We first independently scrutinized the raw data to become familiar with all responses generated by participants. Second, we each combined responses that appeared similar in content. Finally, we met to reach consensus on a list of items that represented the entire data set.

Other things being equal, qualitative research in which a team of researchers first analyze the data independently and then discuss their analyses to reach a consensus is stronger than research in which this is not done.

✓ Guideline 3: Note whether outside expert(s) were consulted.

Consultation with one or more outside experts increases the confidence consumers of research can have in the research results obtained in a qualitative study. Consultation is especially important if an individual (and not a team) has conducted the research (see Guideline 1).

Qualitative researchers usually refer to obtaining input on the adequacy of the results of the data analysis from outside experts as a *peer review* process. When the expert reviews the entire process of conducting the research as well as reviews the results of the data analysis, the expert is usually referred to as an *auditor*, as was done in Example 6.3.1.

Example 6.3.1[2]
Description of independent analysis followed by reaching a consensus:

The auditor was an African American female doctoral student with expertise in counseling African immigrants and international college students. The audit process entailed checking to ensure that raw data were appropriately sorted into domains and abstracted into accurate and complete core summaries. The auditor made several written suggestions for changes, and the researchers who originally constructed the domains and core ideas evaluated the auditor's comments and made changes by consensus judgment.

✓ Guideline 4: Note whether the participants were consulted on the interpretation of the data.

The literature on how to conduct qualitative research emphasizes conducting research in such a way that the results reflect the realities *as perceived by the participants*. In other words, the goal of qualitative research is to understand how participants perceive their own reality—not to establish a so-called "objective reality." Thus, it is appropriate

---

[1] Schuck, K., & Liddle, B. J. (2004). The female manager's experience: A concept map and assessment tool. *Consulting Psychology Journal: Practice*, 75–87.
[2] Modified from Friedman, M. L., Friedlander, M. L., & Blustein, D. L. (2005). Toward an understanding of Jewish identity: A phenomenological study. *Journal of Counseling Psychology, 52*, 77–83.

for qualitative researchers to write up a tentative report of results and ask the participants (or a sample of them) to review the report and provide feedback on how well it reflects their perceptions. Qualitative researchers call this process *member checking*. This term has its origins in the idea that the participants in qualitative research are in fact *members* of the research team who are *checking* the results for accuracy. Example 6.4.1 illustrates how this might be described in a research report.

Example 6.4.1[3]
Description of the use of member checking:

After the initial analysis, three of the participants (one male and two female) were asked to review the tentative draft of results and to consider how accurate it was. Overall, the participants agreed that the draft accurately reflected the ideas expressed by all the participants in the focus group session. Based on this review, however, the wording of the label for one of the key concepts was modified.

While member checking is not essential for qualitative research to be judged adequate, it is especially helpful to an individual who is conducting research alone (as opposed to a research team, who can reflect with each other on the accuracy of results).

✓ Guideline 5:   Note whether the researchers used a purposive sample or a sample of convenience.

As you know from the material under Guideline 1 in Chapter 5, qualitative researchers strive to use *purposive samples*. These are samples of individuals who are selected on purpose based on the careful judgment of the researchers regarding what types of individuals would be especially good sources of data for a particular research topic. For instance, a qualitative researcher who is evaluating a clinical program might select for interviews several individuals who are just beginning the program and several who have been attending the program for more than a certain length of time. Selection criteria might also include gender (for instance, selecting some men and some women), age, and attendance (for instance, selecting only those who have attended regularly).

In contrast, a *sample of convenience* is one in which the participants are selected solely or primarily on the basis that they are readily available (i.e., convenient to work with). For instance, a researcher might be personal friends with several individuals who participate in a clinical program and use them as participants solely because they are available and cooperative. Note that both qualitative and quantitative researchers regard samples of convenience as undesirable, although sometimes such a sample is the only type available to a researcher with limited contacts and resources. Nevertheless, research employing samples of convenience yields results that should be interpreted very cautiously.

---

[3] Modified from Friedman, M. L., Friedlander, M. L., & Blustein, D. L. (2005). Toward an understanding of Jewish identity: A phenomenological study. *Journal of Counseling Psychology, 52*, 77–83.

✓ Guideline 6:   Note whether the demographics of the participants are described.

As you know from Guideline 11 in Chapter 5, it is a good idea to make notes on the demographics of participants in preparation for analyzing research for inclusion in your literature review. By providing demographics relevant to the research topic, consumers of research can "see" the participants and make judgments on the adequacy of the sample. For instance, the researchers who wrote the description of demographics in Example 6.6.1 were studying how domestic violence affects women's employment. As you can see, the demographics they reported are relevant to the topic of their research.

Example 6.6.1[4]

Description of demographics in a qualitative study:

Participants' mean age was 38 years, with a range between 22 and 54 years. Twenty-two percent of women had some high school education, 37.5% had completed high school or earned a General Equivalency Degree (GED), 6% had an associate's degree, and 34% had some college, including completing a bachelor's degree or higher. Sixty-nine percent of participants identified as white, 22% identified as black, 3% identified as Native American, and 6% identified as other. Seventy-one percent of respondents had children under age 18, ranging in ages from 1 year to 18 years.

All of the participants had been employed within the past 2 years; 87.5% were either currently employed or employed within the last year, and 12.5% had been employed sometime within the past 24 months. Respondents were employed in jobs within the service-producing sector (93.5%) and trades industry (12.5%). Specifically, women were employed in positions including grocery cashier, waitress, motel clerk, nurse's aide, factory worker, machine operator, tobacco stripper, video store manager, restaurant manager, receptionist, house painter, health club manager, and taxi driver. The average wage in U.S. dollars for women ranged between $5.15 hourly (minimum wage in the United States) and $10 hourly.

All of the women reported experiencing psychological abuse in their life, and 78% reported experiencing psychological abuse by an intimate partner in the past year. Psychological or emotional violence frequently co-occurs with both physical and sexual violence and includes verbal attacks such as ridicule, verbal harassment, and name-calling; isolation; and verbal threats of harm (Dutton et al., 1997; Follingstad, Rutledge, Berg, Hause, & Polek, 1990). All of the women reported being stalked in their lifetime, with 67.7% reporting being stalked by an intimate partner in the past year. All of the women experienced physical aggression (being pushed, shoved, kicked, or bitten) in their lifetime, with 75% reporting physical aggression in the past year. About 88% of the women reported severe violence by an intimate partner (being beaten up, threatened with a weapon, or actually had a weapon used on them), and 59.4% reported severe violence by an intimate partner in the past year. Three quarters of the sample reported sexual assault by an intimate partner in their lifetime, and one-third reported sexual assault in the past year.

✓ Guideline 7:   Consider whether the method of qualitative analysis is described in sufficient detail.

To qualify as "research," the method used to analyze the data must be carefully planned and systematic. In contrast, casual observation followed by a purely subjective discussion of it does not qualify as research.

---

[4] Swanberg, J. E., & Logan, T. K. (2005). Domestic violence and employment: A qualitative study. *Journal of Occupational Health Psychology, 10*, 3–17.

To help consumers of research determine whether a given qualitative report qualifies as "qualitative research," qualitative researchers should describe in some detail how they analyzed the data. Note that it is insufficient for a researcher to say only that "the grounded theory approach was used" or that "the analysis was based on a phenomenological approach." In Example 6.7.1, the researchers begin by naming "consensual qualitative research" (CQR) as the method of analysis and provide references where more information on the approach can be obtained. They follow this by summarizing the steps in CQR that they applied in the analysis.

Example 6.7.1[5]
Description of the use of Consensual Qualitative Research Methodology:

Analyses consisted of using consensual qualitative research (CQR) methodology (Bogdan & Biklen, 1992; Henwood & Pidgeon, 1992; Hill, Thompson, & Williams, 1997; Stiles, 1993). CQR is a highly reliable and cost-effective method of analyzing qualitative data, making use of multiple researchers, the process of reaching consensus, and a systematic way of examining representativeness of results across cases. Once the responses to the open-ended questions are transcribed, CQR involves three steps: developing and coding domains, constructing core ideas, and developing categories to describe consistencies across cases (cross-analysis).

Development and Coding Into Domains

Two independent research psychologists developed a list of *domains* or *topic areas* based on the content of the discussions and the focus group questions used to organize information into similar topics. Once each reviewer had independently identified their domains, the two reviewers compared their separate lists of domains until consensus was reached. The final seven domains were (1) sex with men, (2) sex with women, (3) the importance of family including having children, (4) gender roles and social expectations, (5) sex or "partying" with drugs and alcohol, (6) church and religion, and (7) living with HIV. Each reviewer, along with all the investigators, independently read through the transcripts and assigned sentences or paragraphs to a domain. Attempts were made to avoid double coding the data by careful review of domains. Reviewers compared their coding, differences were discussed, and consensus was obtained.

Constructing Core Ideas

The two independent reviewers along with the investigators reread all the raw data and attempted to summarize the data into core ideas. This process, called *boiling down* or *abstracting*, summarizes the content and accurately reflects the participants' statements in fewer words while avoiding inferences. Once the team members developed the core ideas independently, the reviewers and the investigators met again as a team to discuss their ideas until consensus was achieved.

Cross-Analyses

While in the first and second steps of CQR the investigators examined the statements of individuals, the purpose of cross-analyses was to determine whether there were similarities among the cases in the sample. The team in this step attempted to look across cases to determine whether there were similarities among the cases. The independent reviewers and the investigators identified all of the core ideas for each domain across cases and determined how these core ideas clustered into *categories*. Individual team members reviewed the core ideas within a single domain and assigned them to relevant categories. The team compared categories again and determined which ones were significant on the basis of the self-report of participants. Consensus by the independent reviewers and the investigators was obtained. After consensus, the team reviewed the cross-analysis, ensuring that each core idea fit and the category label adequately described the core ideas listed.

---

[5] Williams, J. K., Wyatt, G. E., Resell, J., Peterson, J., & Asuan-O'Brien, A. (2004). Psychosocial issues among gay- and non-gay-identifying HIV-seropositive African American and Latino MSM. *Cultural Diversity and Ethnic Minority Psychology*, *10*, 268–286.

✔ Guideline 8:   Note whether quantities are provided when qualitative researchers discuss quantitative matters.

Just because research is qualitative does not mean that no quantities should be reported. For instance, it is appropriate to use statistics when describing demographics of participants in qualitative research, as in Example 6.6.1, in which the mean age as well as a large number of percentages are provided.

When describing the results, it is usually undesirable to make statements such as "a few of the participants raised the issue of…." or "many of the participants perceived the issue as…."

One approach to quantifying qualitative results is to use what qualitative researchers call literal *enumeration*, which merely means reporting specific numbers of participants for each statement of results. However, reporting many numbers can clutter up a report of qualitative research results. An alternative is to establish quantitative categories for otherwise vague terms such as "many." This is illustrated in Example 6.8.1. Such a statement near the beginning of the results section helps to clarify how the terms were defined and used by the researchers.

Example 6.8.1[6]
Definitions of otherwise vague terms that refer to quantities:

Enumeration data were used in the results section that follows. Specifically, the word "many" indicates that more than 50% of the participants gave a particular type of response, the term "some" indicates that between 25% and 50% did so, while the term "a few" indicates that less than 25% did so.

Other things being equal, qualitative reports that provide guidance on quantities are more useful to consumers of research than those that do not.

Concluding Comment

This chapter briefly covers only some major methodological issues you might consider when you make notes on reports of qualitative research in preparation for writing a review of literature. As you read the articles you have selected for your review, make notes on any other methodological issues and decisions made by the researchers that might affect the validity of the research results.

---

[6] This example is drawn from Orcher, L. T. (2005). *Conducting research: Social and behavioral science methods*, p. 72. Glendale, CA: Pyrczak Publishing.

Activities for Chapter 6

Directions: Locate an original report of qualitative research, preferably on a topic you are reviewing, and answer the following questions. For learning purposes, your instructor may choose to assign an article for all students in your class to read.

1. What characteristics of the report you located led you to believe that it is an example of qualitative research?

2. Was the study conducted by an individual *or* by a research team?

3. Was the initial analysis of the results conducted *independently* by more than one researcher?

4. Were outside experts consulted for peer review? For an audit? If yes, does this increase your confidence in the validity of the results?

5. Did the participants participate in *member checking*? If yes, does this increase your confidence in the validity of the results?

6. Is it clear whether a purposive *or* a convenience sample was used? Explain.

7. Has the researcher described the demographics of the participants in sufficient detail? Explain.

8. Did the researcher name a specific method of qualitative data analysis (e.g., consensual qualitative research)? Is it described in sufficient detail? Explain.

9. Did the researcher provide sufficiently specific qualitative information in the results section? Explain.

10. Briefly describe any major flaws in the research that you did not cover in your answers to Questions 1 through 9.

Notes:

Chapter 7

Building Tables to Summarize Literature

The guidelines in the previous chapters have helped you select a topic, identify literature, and conduct a preliminary analysis. Building tables that summarize literature is an effective way to help you get an overview of the literature you have considered. In addition, you may want to include in your literature review one or more of the tables you build, which will also help provide an overview for the readers of your review.

✔ Guideline 1: Consider building a table of definitions.

Each of the variables you are considering should be defined early in your review. Building a table of definitions helps you and your readers under two circumstances. First, if there are a number of definitions of closely related variables, a table of definitions, such as the one in Example 7.1.1, makes it easy to scan the definitions in order to identify similarities and differences.

Example 7.1.1[1]

Table 7.1.1
Definitions of Psychological Empowerment Relevant to Tobacco Control Initiatives

Domain	Attributes	Definitions
Intrapersonal	Domain-specific efficacy	Beliefs in one's capabilities to organize and execute the courses of action required to produce specific changes related to tobacco control.
	Perceived sociopolitical control	Beliefs about one's capabilities and efficacy in social and political systems.
	Participatory competence	Perceived ability to participate in and contribute to the operations of the group or organization, through talking at meetings, working as a team member, etc.
Interactional	Knowledge of resources	Awareness of whether resources exist to support the group and how to acquire them.
	Assertiveness	Ability to express your feelings, opinions, beliefs, and needs directly, openly, and honestly while not violating the personal rights of others.
	Advocacy	Pursuit of influencing outcomes, including public policy and resource allocation decisions within political, economic, and social systems and institutions that directly affect people's lives.

Second, a table of definitions can be helpful if there are diverse definitions of a given variable. Consider arranging them chronologically by year to see if there are historical trends in how the variable has been defined across time. Example 7.1.2 illustrates the organization of such a table.

---

[1] Holden, D. J., Evans, W. D., Hinnant, L. W., & Messeri, P. (2005). Modeling psychological empowerment among youth involved in local tobacco control efforts. *Health Education & Behavior, 32,* 264–278. Reprinted with permission.

Example 7.1.2

Table 7.1.2
Definitions of Child Abuse Over Time (1945 to 2005)

Author	Definition	Notes
Doe (1945)	Defined as....	First published definition. Does not include psychological abuse.
Smith (1952)	Defined as....	
Jones (1966)	Defined as....	First one to mention sexual abuse.
Lock (1978)	Defined as....	
Black & Clark (1989)	Defined as....	
Solis (2000)	Defined as....	Legal definition in Texas.
Ty (2003)	Defined as....	Most widely cited definition in recent literature.
Bart (2005)	Defined as....	

✓ Guideline 2: Consider building a table of research methods.

Because different research methods can cause differences in the outcomes of studies, it is helpful to build a table summarizing the methods employed, such as the one in Table 7.2.1. In addition to the methods described in Table 7.2.1, for experiments (see Guidelines 2 and 3 in Chapter 5), it is desirable to include a row indicating the type of experimental design that was used (e.g., randomized control group design) in each study.

Example 7.2.1[2]

Table 7.2.1
Primary Study Characteristics (Methods)

	Pope (1994)	Preyde (2000)	Cherkin (2001)
Sample size	$n = 164$	$n = 98$	$n = 267$
Recruitment of participants	Those attending clinic	University e-mail & advertisements in newspaper	Mailed letters to HMO
Presenting condition	Nonspecific low back pain	Subacute low back pain	Persistent low back pain
Type of massage	Massage	Comprehensive massage	Therapeutic massage
Duration of study	Not indicated	1 year	6 months
Outcome measure	Visual Analog Scale	Roland Disability Questionnaire	Symptom Bothersomeness Scale

✓ Guideline 3: Consider including a summary of research results in the methods table.

Results can be summarized in a table showing the research methods (see Guideline 2) by adding an additional row or column to the table.

Instead of having authors' names at the top of the columns, as in Example 7.2.1, they can be placed at the beginning of the rows, as in Example 7.3.1. In this example, the results of the studies are briefly summarized.

---

[2] Loosely based on Dryden, T., Baskwil, A., & Preyde, M. (2004). Massage therapy for the orthopaedic patient: A review. *Orthopaedic Nursing, 23*, 327–332.

Example 7.3.1[3]

Table 7.3.1
Longitudinal Studies Linking Religion and Adolescent Sexual Behavior

Publication date, authors	Location, year, SES, sample N	Age or grade, gender, ethnicity	Religiosity measures	Sexual behavior measures	Impact of religion on sex behavior
(1975) Jessor & Jessor	Small city in Rocky Mountain region, 1969 to 1971, middle class, $N = 424$	High school, M and F, white	Religiosity; church attendance	Ever had sexual intercourse at Time 1	High school females who initiated sexual intercourse between Time 1 and Time 2 were less religious and attended church less frequently.
(1983) Jessor, Costa, Jessor, & Donovan	Rocky Mountains, 1969 to 1972 and 1979, $N = 346$ virgins	Grades 7, 8, and 9 in 1969, M and F, white	Church attendance; religiosity[a]	Age at first coitus	Religiosity and more frequent attendance predicted later initiation of first coitus.
(1991) Beck, Cole, & Hammond[b]	United States; 1979, 1983; $N = 2,072$	14 to 17 years old M and F, white virgins in 1979	Religious affiliation of adolescents and parents (Catholic, Baptist, mainline Protestant, institutional sect, Fundamentalist)	Coital experience (yes or no)	White adolescent females and males with institutionalized sect affiliation (e.g., Pentecostal, Mormon, Jehovah's Witness) were less likely than were mainline Protestants (e.g., Episcopalian, Lutheran, Methodist) to engage in first coitus between 1979 and 1983. Even when controlling for attendance, females with Baptist affiliation and males with Fundamentalist affiliation were less likely than were mainline Protestants to experience first coitus.
(1996) Crockett, Bingham, Chopack, & Vicary	Single rural school district in eastern United States, 1985, lower SES, $N = 289$	7th to 9th grades, M and F, white	Attendance	Age at first coitus	Females (but not males) who attended more frequently were more likely to be older (more than age 17) at first coitus.
(1996) Mott, Fondell, Hu, Kowaleski-Jones, & Menaghan[c]	United States; 1988, 1990, and 1992; $N = 451$	At least 14 years old in 1992, M and F, white (black and Hispanic over-sampled)	Attendance; do friends attend same church?	Early initiation of first coitus (using age 14 as criterion for *early*)	Frequent attendees who also had peers attending the same church were less likely to be engaging in sexual intercourse at age 14.
(1996) Pleck, Sonenstein, Ku, & Burbridge[d]	United States; 1988 (Wave I, $N = 1,880$) 1990 to 1991 (Wave II, $N = 1,676$)	15 to 19 years old in 1988; males; 37% black, 21% Hispanic, 3% other	Importance of religion, frequency of church attendance	Number of coital acts in past 12 months that did not include use of a condom	Males who attended church more frequently in mid-adolescence showed a decline (relative to predicted levels) in the frequency of unprotected sex in late adolescence.
(1997) Miller, Norton, Curtis, Hill, Schvaneveldt, & Young[e]	United States; 1976, 1981, and 1987; $N = 759$	7 to 11 years old in 1976, M and F, white and black	Attendance (parent report); attitudes toward attending	Age at first coitus (reported retrospectively in Wave III)	Families who reported positive attitudes toward attending religious services were more likely to delay sexual debut.
(1999) Bearman & Bruckner[f]	United States, 1994 to 1996, $N = 5,070$	7th to 12th grades, females only, white, black, Asian, Hispanic	Religious affiliation	First sexual intercourse (yes or no); age of first coitus; pregnancy risk (yes or no)	Beyond the effects of age on sexual debut, conservative Protestants and Catholics were less likely than were mainstream Protestants to experience first intercourse (sexual debut) between Time 1 and Time 2.
(1999) Whitbek, Yoder, Hoyt, & Conger	Midwestern state, 1989 to 1993, rural, $N = 457$	8th to 10th grades, M and F, white	Composite: attendance, importance (mother and adolescent)	Sexual intercourse (yes or no)	Mother's religiosity decreased likelihood of adolescent's sexual debut in 9th and 10th grades. Adolescent religiosity had strong negative effects on sexual debut.
(2001) Bearman & Bruckner	United States; 1994 to 1995 (Wave I), 1996 (Wave II); $N = 14,787$	7th to 12th grades; M and F, white, Hispanic, Asian, black	Composite of attendance, perceived importance, and frequency of praying	Age at first coitus; contraceptive use at first coitus (yes or no); virginity pledger (yes or no)	Higher religiosity decreased the risk of sexual debut for white, Asian, and Hispanic adolescents of both genders. For black adolescents, no relation between religiosity and risk of sexual debut was found. Religiosity delayed sexual debut in middle and late, but not early, adolescence. (Analyses conducted with nonblack respondents only.) Religiosity and contraceptive use at first coitus were unrelated.

Note: M = male; F = female.
a. The religiosity measure is not described for this article.
b. Data are from the National Longitudinal Survey of Youth (NLSY).
c. Data are from the National Longitudinal Survey of Youth (NLSY).
d. Data are from the National Survey of Adolescent Males (NSAM).
e. Data are from all three waves of the National Survey of Children (NSC)
f. Data are from Waves I and II of the National Longitudinal Study of Adolescent Health (Add Health).
g. Data are from Waves I and II of the National Longitudinal Study of Adolescent Health (Add Health).

---

[3] Rostosky, S. S., Wilcox, B. L., Wright, M. L. C., & Randall, B. A. (2004). The impact of religiosity on adolescent sexual behavior: A review of the evidence. *Journal of Adolescent Research, 19,* 677–697. Reprinted with permission.

Note that the summaries of results of the various studies in Example 7.3.1 are in words (not statistics). Often, this is the best way to present the summaries of results. It is acceptable to present statistics, however, if they are straightforward and are comparable from study to study. For instance, if there are five studies that estimate the prevalence of inhalant use by high school students, and they all present results in terms of percentages, including the percentages would be appropriate in the summaries of results. On the other hand, if the statistics reported on a topic are diverse from study to study, it would be less desirable to present them because they are not directly comparable from one study to another (e.g., one study presents percentages, one presents means and medians, another presents a frequency distribution, and so on). This is true because a reader should be able to scan columns and rows to note differences among studies. Scanning and comparing mixed statistics in a column can be confusing.

✓ Guideline 4: When there is much literature on a topic, establish criteria for determining which ones to summarize in a table.

Summary tables that will be inserted into a literature review do not necessarily need to include all studies on the topic of the review. However, if only some are included you should describe the criteria for inclusion. Examples 7.4.1 and 7.4.2 show sample statements that inform readers of such criteria.

Example 7.4.1
Description of criterion (i.e., only true experiments) for inclusion in a table:

Table 1 summarizes characteristics of the participants, the treatments applied, and the outcome measures. This table includes only *true experiments* (i.e., experiments in which participants were assigned at random to experimental and control groups).

Example 7.4.2
Description of criterion (i.e., only recent surveys) for inclusion in a table:

Table 2 summarizes the research methods and results of the five most recent surveys on the topic. Because the literature indicates that opinions on the issue vary over time, the most recent surveys provide the best indication of current public opinion on this issue.

✓ Guideline 5: When there is much literature on a topic, consider building two or more tables to summarize it.

Even after establishing criteria for inclusion of studies in a table (see Guideline 4), there may be too many studies to include in a single table. When this is the case, consider how the literature might be divided into groups so a different table may be built for each group of studies. For instance, one table might summarize the theories relevant to the topic, another might summarize the quantitative studies on a topic, and a third table might summarize the qualitative studies.

✓ Guideline 6: Present tables in a literature review only for complex material.

During the early stages of synthesizing literature, there is no limit to how many tables you may create to help you get an overview of the literature. However, you should include in your literature review only tables that deal with complex matters that might be difficult for your readers to follow in the text (i.e., difficult to follow in the narrative of the literature review).

A literature review should *not* be a collection of tables. Instead, it should primarily be a narrative in which you summarize, synthesize, and interpret the literature on a topic, with only a small number of tables inserted to assist readers in comprehending complex material.

✔ Guideline 7: Discuss each table included in a literature review.

All tables in a literature review should be introduced and discussed in the narrative of the literature review. Example 7.7.1 illustrates how this might be done.

Example 7.7.1
Discussion of a table:

Table 1 summarizes the five studies in which the effectiveness of cognitive/behavioral therapy was examined using the Beck Depression Inventory as the outcome measure. Overall, the sample sizes were quite small, ranging from $n = 4$ to $n = 16$. Despite this limitation, the results show promise for use of cognitive/behavioral therapy because all the treated groups (i.e., experimental groups) showed statistically significant decreases in depression in comparison with the control groups.

While you should discuss each table, it is not necessary to describe every element in it. For instance, Example 7.7.1 discusses a table that summarizes five studies, yet the sample sizes used in only two of the studies ($n = 4$ and $n = 16$) are mentioned in the narrative.

✔ Guideline 8: Give each table a number and descriptive title.

All tables should have a number (e.g., Table 1, Table 2, and so on) as well as a descriptive title (i.e., a caption). Note that all tables in this chapter have table numbers and titles.

✔ Guideline 9: Master table-building using your word processor.

Modern word processing programs have features that facilitate building tables with columns and rows. For instance, in Microsoft Word®, clicking on "Table"[4] near the top of the screen will give you the option to "Insert" table. After clicking on "Insert," click on "Table" in the drop-down list. Doing this will produce a dialog box in which you can indicate the number of columns and rows you need. Doing this for a table with five columns and four rows will produce a raw table such as this one:

---

[4] An underlined letter such as the a in Table indicates a keyboard shortcut for touch typists who are more efficient when they do not use the mouse. For instance, holding down the "Alt" key on the keyboard while typing the letter "a" will produce the drop-down list that will permit building a table without using the mouse.

To refine the table, you need to bring up the "Tables and Borders" toolbar. To do this, click on "View," then click on "Toolbars" from the drop-down list, and then click on "Tables and Borders." The toolbar will appear on your screen. Scrolling the cursor across the toolbar (with a slight pause on each icon) will produce pop-up boxes that indicate the function of each icon. For instance, you will find one that says "Merge Cells." This can be used to merge the cells in the first row of the table to provide room for the table number and title. Specifically, to do this, highlight the first row of the table by dragging the cursor across it. (It will become black.) Then, click on the "Merge Cells" icon, and the table will look like this:

The table number is placed here. No italics (e.g., "Table 1"). The title is placed here (italicize title; cap the first letter of each word; no period).[5]			

While it is beyond the scope of this book to provide comprehensive directions on using a word processor to build tables, in programs such as Word®, with only a little experimentation while paying attention to the pop-up boxes in the "Tables and Borders" toolbar, it is rather easy to learn how to modify tables.

✔ **Guideline 10: Insert "Continued" when tables split across pages.**

While it is desirable to fit each table on a single page, it is not always possible. When a table splits across pages, put "(*continued*)" at the bottom of the table so that readers know to turn the page to continue reading the table. At the top of the second part of the table on the next page repeat the table number followed by "(*continued*)."

Activities for Chapter 7

Directions: It is assumed that you have already read many of the articles that you will be evaluating and synthesizing in your literature review. Answer the following questions to the extent that you can based on your preliminary reading of the literature.

1. Do you plan to build a table of definitions? Explain.

2. Do you plan to build a table of research methods? Will it also include a row or column that summarizes the results of the studies?

3. Will you apply criteria to select among studies to include in a table? Explain.

---

[5] This table format is consistent with guidelines outlined in the *Publication Manual of the American Psychological Association.*

4. Do you anticipate inserting more than one table in your literature review? Explain.

5. Have you considered how you will discuss the literature that you plan to summarize in one or more tables?

6. Have you explored table building using your word processor? How easy is it to use? Have you experienced any difficulties in using it? If so, have you consulted with others (e.g., other students) to resolve your difficulties? Explain.

Notes:

Chapter 8

Synthesizing Literature Prior to Writing a Review

At this point, you should have read and analyzed a collection of research articles and prepared detailed notes, possibly including summary tables (see Chapter 7). You should now begin to synthesize these notes and tabled material into a new whole, the sum of which will become your literature review. In other words, you are now ready to begin the process of *writing* a literature review. This chapter will help you develop an important product: a detailed writing outline.

✔ Guideline 1: Consider your purpose and voice before beginning to write.

Begin by asking yourself what your purpose is in writing a literature review. Are you trying to convince your professor that you have expended sufficient effort in preparing a term paper for your class? Are you trying to demonstrate your command of a field of study in a thesis or dissertation? Or, is your purpose to establish a context for a study you hope to have published in a journal? Each of these scenarios will result in a different type of final product, in part because of the differences in the writer's purpose, but also because of differences in readers' expectations. Review the descriptions of these three types of literature reviews in Chapter 2.

After you establish your purpose and have considered your audience, decide on an appropriate *voice* (or style of writing) for your manuscript. A writer's voice when preparing a literature review should be formal because that is what the academic context dictates. The traditional *voice* in scientific writing dictates that the writer de-emphasize himself or herself in order to focus the readers' attention on the content. In Example 8.1.1, the writer's *self* is too much in evidence; it distracts the reader from the content of the statement. Example 8.1.2 is superior because it focuses on the content.

Example 8.1.1[1]

Improper "voice" for academic writing:

In this review, I will show that the literature on treating juvenile murderers is sparse and suffers from the same problems as the general literature on juvenile homicide (Benedek, Cornell, & Staresina, 1989; Myers, 1992) and violent juvenile delinquents (Tate, Reppucci, & Mulvery, 1995). Unfortunately, I have found that most of the treatment results are based on clinical case reports of a few cases referred to the author for evaluation and/or treatment (e.g., see Agee, 1979…).

---

[1] This is a hypothetical example based on Example 8.1.2 on the next page.

Example 8.1.2[2]

Suitable "voice" for academic writing:

The literature on treating juvenile murderers is sparse and suffers from the same problems as the general literature on juvenile homicide (Benedek, Cornell, & Staresina, 1989; Myers, 1992) and violent juvenile delinquents (Tate, Reppucci, & Mulvery, 1995). Most of the treatment results are based on clinical case reports of a few cases referred to the author for evaluation and/or treatment (e.g., see Agee, 1979…).

Notice that academic writers tend to avoid using the first person. Instead, they let the material, including statistics and theories, speak for themselves. This is not to say that the first person should never be used. However, it is traditional to use it exceedingly sparingly.

✔ Guideline 2: Consider how to reassemble your notes.

Now that you have established the purpose for writing your review, identified your audience, and established your voice, you should reevaluate your notes to determine how the pieces you have described will be reassembled. At the outset, you should recognize that it is almost always unacceptable in writing a literature review to present only a series of annotations of research studies. That would be, in essence, like describing trees when you really should be describing a forest. In the case of a literature review, you are creating a unique new forest, which you will build by using the trees you found in the literature you have read. In order to build this new whole, you should consider how the pieces relate to one another while preparing a topic outline, which is described in more detail under the next guideline.

✔ Guideline 3: Create a topic outline that traces your argument.

Like any other kind of essay, the review should *first* establish for the reader the line of argumentation you will follow (this is called the *thesis* in composition classes). This can be stated in the form of an assertion, a contention, or a proposition; *then*, you should develop a traceable narrative that demonstrates that the line of argumentation is worthwhile and justified. This means that you should have formed judgments about the topic based on the analysis and synthesis of the literature you are reviewing.

The topic outline should be designed as a road map of the argument, which is illustrated in Example 8.3.1. Notice that it starts with an assertion (that there is a severe shortage of donor organs, which will be substantiated with statistics, and that the review will be delimited to the psychological components of the decision to donate). This introduction is followed by a systematic review of the relevant areas of the research literature (points II and III in the outline), followed by a discussion of methodological issues in the relevant research (point IV). It ends with a summary, implications, and a discussion of

---

[2] Heide, K. M., & Solomon, E. P. (2003). Treating today's juvenile homicide offenders. *Youth Violence and Juvenile Justice, 1,* 5–31.

suggestions for future research and conclusions that relate back to the introduction (point I).

Note that the authors of Example 8.3.1 have chosen to discuss weaknesses in research methodology in a separate section (point IV in the outline). Using a separate section for such a discussion is especially appropriate when all or many of the studies suffer from the same weaknesses. If different studies have different weaknesses, it is usually best to refer to the weaknesses when each study is cited (as opposed to discussing them in a separate section of the literature review).

Because the following outline will be referred to at various points throughout the rest of this chapter, please take a moment to examine it carefully. Place a flag on this page or bookmark it for easy reference to the outline when you are referred to it later.

Example 8.3.1[3]

Sample topic outline:

Topic: Psychological Aspects of Organ Donation: Individual and Next-of-Kin Donation Decisions

I. Introduction
    A. Establish importance of the topic (cite statistics on scarcity of organs).
    B. Delimit the review to psychological components of decisions.
    C. Describe organization of the paper, indicating that the remaining topics in the outline will be discussed.
II. Individual decisions regarding posthumous organ donation
    A. Beliefs about organ donation.
    B. Attitudes toward donating.
    C. Stated willingness to donate.
    D. Summary of research on individual decisions.
III. Next-of-kin consent decisions
    A. Beliefs about donating others' organs.
    B. Attitudes toward next-of-kin donations.
    C. Summary of research on next-of-kin consent decisions.
IV. Methodological issues and directions for future research
    A. Improvement in attitude measures and measurement strategy.
    B. Greater differentiation by type of donation.
    C. Stronger theoretical emphasis.
    D. Greater interdisciplinary focus.
V. Summary, Implications, and Discussion
    A. Summary of points I–IV.
    B. Need well-developed theoretical models of attitudes and decision making.
    C. Current survey data limited in scope and application points to need for more sophisticated research in the future.
    D. Need more use of sophisticated data analysis techniques.
    E. Conclusions: Psychology can draw from various subdisciplines for an understanding of donation decisions so intervention strategies can be identified. Desperately need to increase the available supply of donor organs.

---

[3] The outline is based on the work of Radicki, C. M., & Jaccard, J. (1997). Psychological aspects of organ donation: A critical review and synthesis of individual and next-of-kin donation decisions. *Health Psychology, 16*, 183–195.

✔ Guideline 4:   Reorganize your notes according to the path of your argument.

The topic outline described in the previous guideline describes the path of the authors' argument. The next step is to reorganize the notes according to the outline. Begin by coding the notes with references to the appropriate places in the outline. For example, on the actual note cards write a "I" beside notations that cite statistics on the scarcity of donated organs, a "II" beside notations that deal with individual decisions about organ donations, a "III" beside notations that deal with next-of-kin decisions, and a "IV" beside notations that pertain to methodological issues. Then, return to the topic outline and indicate the specific references to particular studies. For example, if Doe and Smith (2005) cite statistics on the scarcity of donated organs, write their names on the outline to the right of point I.

✔ Guideline 5:   Within each topic heading, note differences among studies.

The next step is to note on your topic outline the differences in content among studies. Based on any differences, you may want to consider whether it is possible to group the articles into subtopics. For instance, for "Beliefs about organ donation" (point II.A. in Example 8.3.1), the literature can be grouped into the five subcategories shown in Example 8.5.1.

Example 8.5.1

Additional subtopics for point II.A. in Example 8.3.1:

1. Religious beliefs
2. Cultural beliefs
3. Knowledge (i.e., beliefs based on "facts" people have gathered from a variety of sources)
4. Altruistic beliefs
5. Normative beliefs (i.e., beliefs based on perceptions of what is acceptable within a particular social group)

These would become subtopics under point II.A. ("Beliefs about organ donation") in the topic outline. In other words, your outline will become more detailed as you identify additional subtopics.

The other type of difference you will want to consider is the consistency of results from study to study. For instance, the reviewers on whose work Example 8.3.1 is based found three articles suggesting that there are cultural obstacles that reduce the number of organ donations among Hispanics, while one other article indicated a willingness to donate and a high level of awareness about transplantation issues among this group. When you discuss such discrepancies, assist your reader by providing relevant information about the research, with an eye to identifying possible explanations for the differences. Were the first three articles older and the last one more current? Did the first three use a different methodology for collecting the data (e.g., did those with the negative results examine hospital records while the one with a positive result used self-report question-naires)? Noting differences such as these may give you important issues to discuss when writing your literature review.

✔ Guideline 6: Within each topic heading, look for obvious gaps or areas needing more research.

In the full review based on the topic outline in Example 8.3.1, the reviewers noted that whereas much cross-cultural research has been conducted on African Americans, Asian Americans, and Hispanics, only a few studies have focused on Native Americans. Thus, any conclusions may not apply to the latter group. In addition, this points to an area that might be recommended for consideration in planning future research.

✔ Guideline 7: Plan to briefly describe relevant theories.

The importance of theoretical literature is discussed in Chapter 1. You should plan to briefly describe each theory. Example 8.7.1 illustrates a brief description of social comparison theory. Note that the authors start with a summary of the original theory and then proceed to discuss how the theory has been modified over time. This organization helps readers more fully understand the theory.

Example 8.7.1[4]

Brief definition of a relevant theory:

Festinger's (1954) social comparison theory asserts that (1) individuals have a drive to evaluate their opinions and abilities; (2) in the absence of objective, nonsocial criteria, individuals engage in social comparison (i.e., they compare their opinions and abilities to other individuals); and (3) whenever possible, social comparisons are made with similar others.

Since its original formulation, social comparison theory has undergone a number of revisions. First, it is now acknowledged that unsought comparisons may occur, and that the referent point used in the comparison process may be an individual dissimilar to oneself (Martin & Kennedy, 1993). Second, social comparison also may occur on dimensions such as physical appearance....

✔ Guideline 8: Plan to discuss how individual studies relate to and advance theory.

You should consider how individual studies, which are often narrow, help to define, illustrate, or advance theoretical notions. Often, researchers will point out how their studies relate to theory, which will help you in your considerations of this matter. Specify that one or more theories will be discussed in your literature review by including it in the topic outline, which was done in point V.B. in Example 8.3.1, which indicates that the reviewer will discuss the need for well-defined theoretical models.

---

[4] Morrison, T. G., Kalin, R., & Morrison, M. A. (2004). Body-image evaluation and body-image investment among adolescents: A test of sociocultural and social comparison theories. *Adolescence, 39*, 571–592.

If there are competing theories in your area, plan to discuss the extent to which the literature you have reviewed supports each of them, keeping in mind that an inconsistency between the results of a study and a prediction based on theory may result from *either* imperfections in the theoretical model *or* imperfections in the research methodology used in the study.

✔ Guideline 9: Plan to summarize periodically and, again, near the end of the review.

It is helpful to summarize the inferences, generalizations, and/or conclusions you have drawn from your review of the literature in stages. For instance, the outline in Example 8.3.1 calls for summaries at two intermediate points in the literature review (i.e., points II.D. and III.C.). Long, complex topics within a literature review often deserve their own separate summaries. These summaries help readers to understand the direction the author is taking and invite readers to pause, think about, and internalize difficult material.

You have probably already noticed that the last main topic (Topic V.) in Example 8.3.1 calls for a summary of all the material that preceded it. It is usually appropriate to start the last section of a long review with a summary of the main points already covered. This shows readers what the writer views as the major points and sets the stage for a discussion of the writer's conclusions and any implications he or she has drawn. In a very short literature review, a summary may not be needed.

✔ Guideline 10: Plan to present conclusions and implications.

Note that a *conclusion* is a statement about the state of the knowledge on a topic. Example 8.10.1 illustrates a conclusion. Note that it does not say that there is "proof." Reviewers should hedge and talk about degrees of evidence (e.g., "it seems safe to conclude that...," "one conclusion might be that...," "there is strong evidence that...," or "the evidence overwhelmingly supports the conclusion that...").

Example 8.10.1

In light of the research on cultural differences in attitudes toward organ donation, *it seems safe to conclude that* (emphasis added) cultural groups differ substantially in their attitudes toward organ donation and that effective intervention strategies need to take account of these differences. Specifically,....

If the weight of the evidence on a topic does not clearly favor one conclusion over the other, be prepared to say so. Example 8.10.2 illustrates this technique.

Example 8.10.2

Although the majority of the studies indicate Method A is superior, several methodologically strong studies point to the superiority of Method B. In the absence of additional evidence, *it is difficult to conclude that* (emphasis added)....

An *implication* is usually a statement of what individuals or organizations should do in light of existing research. In other words, a reviewer usually should make suggestions as to what actions seem promising based on the review of the research. Thus, it is usually desirable to include the heading "Implications" near the end of a topic outline. Example 8.10.3 is an implication because it suggests that a particular intervention might be effectively used with a particular group.

Example 8.10.3

The body of evidence reviewed in this paper suggests that when working with Asian Americans, Intervention A seems most promising for increasing the number of organ donations made by this group.

At first, some novice writers believe that they should describe only "facts" from the published research and not venture to offer their own conclusions and related implications. Keep in mind, however, that an individual who thoroughly and carefully reviewed the literature on a topic has, in fact, become an expert on it. To whom else should we look for advice on the state of a knowledge base (conclusions) and what we should do to be more effective (implications) than an expert who has up-to-date knowledge of the research on a topic? Thus, it is appropriate for you to express your conclusions regarding the state of knowledge on a topic and the implications that follow from them.

✔ Guideline 11: Plan to suggest specific directions for future research near the end of the review.

Note that in the outline in Example 8.3.1, the reviewers plan to discuss future research in point V.C. As you plan what to say, keep in mind that it is inadequate to simply suggest that "more research is needed in the future." Instead, make specific suggestions. For instance, if all (or almost all) the researchers have used self-report questionnaires, you might call for future research using other means of data collection such as direct observation of physical behavior and an examination of records kept by agencies that coordinate donations. If there are understudied groups such as Native Americans, you might call for more research on them. If almost all the studies are quantitative, you might call for additional qualitative studies. The list of possibilities is almost endless. Your job is to suggest those that you think are most promising for advancing knowledge in the area you are reviewing.

✔ Guideline 12: Flesh out your outline with details from your analysis.

The final step before you will begin to write your first draft is to review the topic outline and flesh it out with specific details from your analysis of the research literature. Make every effort, as you expand the outline, to include enough details to be able to write clearly about the studies you are including. Make sure to note the strengths and weaknesses of studies as well as the gaps, relationships, and major trends or patterns that emerge in the literature. At the end of this step, your outline should be several pages in length, and you will be ready to write your first draft.

Example 8.12.1 illustrates how a small portion of the topic outline in Example 8.3.1 (specifically, point II.A.1. in Example 8.12.1) would look if it were fleshed out with additional details.

Example 8.12.1

Part of a fleshed-out outline:

II. Individual decisions regarding posthumous organ donation
    A. Beliefs about organ donation (Research can be categorized into 5 major groupings)
        1. Religious beliefs
           a. Define the term "religious beliefs"
           b. Religions that support organ donation
               (1) Buddhism, Hindu (Ulshafer, 1988; Woo, 2002)
               (2) Catholicism (Ulshafer, 1988)
               (3) Judaism (Bulka, 1990; Cohen, 1988; Pearl, 1990; Weiss, 1988)
               (4) Protestantism (Walters, 1988)
               (5) Islam (Gatrad, 1994; Rispler-Chaim, 1989; Sachedina, 2003)
           c. Religions that do not support it
               (1) Jehovah's Witnesses (Corlett, 2003; Pearl, 2004)
               (2) Orthodox Judaism (Corlett, 2003; Pearl, 2004)
           d. Other sources that have commented on religion as a barrier (Basu et al., 1989; Gallup Organization, 1993; Moore et al., 2004)

Notice that several of the references in Example 8.12.1 appear in more than one place. For instance, Corlett's 2003 report will be referred to under a discussion of both Jehovah's Witnesses and Orthodox Judaism. This is appropriate because a reviewer should *not* be writing a series of summaries in which Corlett's study is summarized in one place and then dropped from the discussion. Instead, it should be cited as many times as needed, depending on how many specific points on which it bears in the outline.

Activities for Chapter 8

Directions: For each of the model literature reviews that your instructor assigns, answer the following questions. The model reviews are near the end of this book.

1. Did the author use an appropriate academic "voice"? Did the author write in the first person? Explain.

2. Does the author's "argument" move logically from one topic to another? Explain.

3. Has the author pointed out areas needing more research? Explain.

4. Has the author discussed how the individual studies help to define, illustrate, and/or advance theory? Explain.

5. If the review is a long one, does it include one or more summary(ies)? Explain.

6. Has the author clearly discussed conclusions and implications?

7. Has the author suggested specific directions for future research?

Notes:

Chapter 9

Guidelines for Writing a First Draft

Up to this point, you have searched for literature on the topic of your review, made careful notes of specific details of the literature, and analyzed these details to identify patterns, relationships among studies, gaps in the body of literature, as well as strengths and weaknesses in particular research studies. Then, in Chapter 8, you reorganized your notes and developed a detailed writing outline as you prepared yourself to begin to write your literature review.

In other words, you have already completed the most difficult steps in the writing process: the analysis and synthesis of the literature and the charting of the course of your argument. These preliminary steps constitute the intellectual process of preparing a literature review. The remaining steps—drafting, editing, and redrafting—will now require you to translate the results of your intellectual labor into a narrative account of what you have found.

The guidelines in this chapter will help you to produce a first draft of your literature review. The guidelines in Chapter 10 will help you to develop a coherent essay and avoid producing a series of annotations, and Chapter 11 presents additional guidelines that relate to style, mechanics, and language usage.

✔ Guideline 1: Begin by identifying the broad problem area, but avoid global statements.

Usually, the introduction of a literature review should begin with the identification of the broad problem area under review. The rule of thumb is, "Go from the general to the specific." However, there are limits on how general to be in the beginning. Consider Example 9.1.1. As the beginning of a literature review on a topic in higher education, it is much too broad. It fails to identify any particular area or topic. You should avoid starting your review with such global statements.

Example 9.1.1

Beginning of a literature review in education that is too broad:

Higher education is important to both the economy of the United States and to the rest of the world. Without a college education, students will be unprepared for the many advances that will take place in this millennium.

Contrast Example 9.1.1 with Example 9.1.2, which is also on a topic in education but clearly relates to the specific topic that will be reviewed: reduction of alcohol consumption by undergraduates.

Example 9.1.2[1]

Beginning of a literature review on education that is sufficiently specific:

[The] high rate of alcohol-related crimes, accidents, and other problem behaviors on college campuses has led school administrators to implement a range of initiatives designed to reduce undergraduate drinking (Abbey, 1991; Scott, Schafer, & Greenfield, 1999…).

✔ Guideline 2:   Early in the review, indicate why the topic being reviewed is important.

As early as the first paragraph in a literature review, it is desirable to indicate why the topic is important. The authors of Example 9.2.1 have done this by pointing out that their topic deals with a life-or-death issue.

Example 9.2.1[2]

Beginning of a literature review indicating the importance of the topic:

Considering that more than 48,762 people have died while waiting for an organ transplant in the United States from 1993 through 2002, the need to increase the number of available organs is not difficult to defend (Department of Health and Human Services [DHHS]…2004). Furthermore, although the number of individuals on the organ waiting list in 1993 was 33,014, the number of men, women, and children awaiting a life-saving transplant procedure was 80,000 at the start of 2003 (DHHS et al., 2004). Moreover.…

Of course, not all issues are of as much universal importance as the one in Example 9.2.1. Nevertheless, the topic of the review should be of importance to some group(s), and this should be pointed out, as in Example 9.2.2, which establishes the importance of understanding how educators' attitudes on dyslexia affect students.

Example 9.2.2[3]

Beginning of the second paragraph of a literature review in which the importance of the topic, for students with dyslexia, is pointed out:

Students with learning disabilities such as dyslexia (reading disability) report that the attitudes of educators profoundly affect the way they perceive themselves as well as their success in school and life (Helendoorn & Ruijssenaars, 2000…).

---

[1] Novak, K. B., & Crawford, L. A. (2001). Perceived drinking norms, attention to social comparison information, and alcohol use among college students. *Journal of Alcohol and Drug Education, 46*, 18–32.

[2] Siegel, J. T., Alvaro, E. M., & Jones, S. P. (2005). Organ donor registration preferences among Hispanic populations: Which modes of registration have the greatest promise? *Health Education & Behavior, 32*, 242–252.

[3] Wadlington, E. M., & Wadlington, P. L. (2005). What educators really believe about dyslexia. *Reading Improvement, 42*, 16–33.

✔ Guideline 3:   Distinguish between research findings and other sources of information.

If you describe points of view that are based on anecdotal evidence or personal opinions rather than on research, indicate the nature of the source. For instance, the three statements in Example 9.3.1 contain key words (e.g., "speculated"), which indicate that the material is based on personal points of view (not research).

Example 9.3.1

Beginnings of statements that indicate that the material that follows is based on personal points of view (not research):

"Doe (2004) speculated that...."

"It has been suggested that.... (Smith, 2004)."

"Black (2004) related a personal experience, which indicated that...."

Contrast the statements in Example 9.3.1 with those in Example 9.3.2, which is for introducing research-based findings in a literature review.

Example 9.3.2

Beginnings of statements that indicate that the material that follows is based on research:

"In a statewide survey, Jones (2004) found that...."

"Hill's (2004) research in urban classrooms suggests that...."

"Recent findings indicate that.... (Barnes, 2003; Hanks, 2004)."

If there is little research on a topic, you may find it necessary to review primarily literature that expresses only opinions (without a research base). When this is the case, consider making a general statement to indicate this situation before discussing the literature in more detail in your review. This technique is indicated in Example 9.3.3.

Example 9.3.3[4]

Statement indicating a lack of research:

...the *ERIC* database contains...more than 500 *ERIC* documents, journal articles, and monographs devoted to the topic of block scheduling. However, only ten of those documents focus on block scheduling in the context of the school media center, and none report findings based on designed research studies...

Of the reports that do exist, most are anecdotal in nature. Lincoln (1999), Ready (1999), and Richmond (1999) all give their personal experiences with the impact of block scheduling on their library media centers. Each one discusses....

---

[4] Huffman, S., Thurman, G., & Thomas, L. K. (2005). An investigation of block scheduling and school library media centers. *Reading Improvement, 42,* 3–15.

✔ Guideline 4: Indicate why certain studies are important.

If you believe a particular study is important, state clearly why you think so. For instance, the authors of Example 9.4.1 identify a study as "one of the largest studies in the field," thereby indicating its importance.

Example 9.4.1[5]

States why a study is important (in this case, "one of the largest studies"):

Big Brothers/Big Sisters may be the best-known volunteer mentoring program in the United States, matching at-risk youth with adult mentors. In one of the largest studies in the field (Tierney & Grossman, 1995), 995 youth who asked to be matched with a Big Brother/Big Sister during 1992–1993 were randomly assigned to one of two groups: a mentoring group or a control group (the latter youth were put on the 18-month waiting list). Both groups were interviewed....

A study may also be important because it represents a pivotal point in the development of an area of research, such as a research article that indicates a reversal of a prominent researcher's position or one that launched a new methodology. These and other characteristics of a study may justify its status as an important study. When a study is especially important, make sure your review makes this clear to the reader.

✔ Guideline 5: If you are commenting on the timeliness of a topic, be specific in describing the time frame.

Avoid beginning your review with unspecific references to the timeliness of a topic, as in, "In recent years, there has been an increased interest in...." This beginning would leave many questions unanswered for the reader, such as: What years are being referenced? How did the writer determine that the "interest" is increasing? Who has become more interested, the writer or others in the field? Is it possible that the writer became interested in the topic recently while others have been losing interest?

Likewise, an increase in a problem or an increase in the size of a population of interest should be specific in terms of numbers or percentages and the specific years being referred to. For instance, it is not very informative to state only that "The number of people of Hispanic origin probably will increase in the future." The authors of Example 9.5.1 avoided this problem by being specific in citing percentages and the time frame (italics and bold added for emphasis).

Example 9.5.1[6]

Names a specific timeline:

According to the U.S. Census Bureau (2001), there are an estimated 32.8 million people of Hispanic origin living in the United States. Projections indicate this

---

[5] Keating, L. M., Tomishima, M. A., Foster, S., & Alessandri, M. (2002). The effects of a mentoring program on at-risk youth. *Adolescence, 37*, 717–734.
[6] Sharma, P., & Kerl, S. B. (2002). Suggestions for psychologists working with Mexican American individuals and families in health care settings. *Rehabilitation Psychology, 47*, 230–239.

number *will increase from about 10% of the U.S. population in 1990 to 14% or 15% by the year 2020*, making this group one of the four largest ethnic groups in this country (Garcia & Marotta, 1997). Baruth and Manning (1999) wrote that Mexican Americans accounted for 61% of the total Hispanic population. Approximately half of the....

✔ Guideline 6: If citing a classic or landmark study, identify it as such.

Make sure that you identify the classic or landmark studies in your review. Such studies are often pivotal points in the historical development of the published literature. In addition, they are often responsible for framing a particular question or a research tradition, and they also may be the original source of key concepts or terminology used in the subsequent literature. Whatever their contribution, you should identify their status as classics or landmarks in the literature. Consider Example 9.6.1, in which a landmark (first of its kind) study is cited.

Example 9.6.1[7]

Identifies a landmark study:

The *first content analysis* (emphasis added) of gender biases in magazine advertisements was published by Courtney and Lockeretz (1971). Those authors found that magazine advertisements reflected four general stereotypes: (1) "A woman's place is in the home," (2) "Women do not make important decisions or do important things," (3) "Women are dependent and need men's protection," and (4) "Men regard women primarily as sex objects; they are not interested in women as people."

✔ Guideline 7: If a landmark study was replicated, mention that and indicate the results of the replication.

As noted in the previous guideline, landmark studies typically stimulate additional research. In fact, many are replicated a number of times, using different groups of participants or by adjusting other research design variables. If you are citing a landmark study and it has been replicated, you should mention that fact and indicate whether the replications were successful. This is illustrated in Example 9.7.1, which is an elaboration on Example 9.6.1.

Example 9.7.1

Points at replications:

Since the time of this study, a number of *other content analyses have replicated these results* (emphasis added) (Belkaoui & Belkaoui, 1976; Busby & Leichty, 1993; Culley & Bennett, 1976; England, Kuhn, & Gardner, 1983; Lysonski, 1983; Sexton & Haberman, 1974; Venkatesan & Losco, 1975; Wagner & Banos, 1973).

---

[7] Neptune, D., & Plous, S. (1997). Racial and gender biases in magazine advertising. *Psychology of Women Quarterly*, *21*, 627–644.

During the past 40 years, only one of the stereotypes found by Courtney and Lockeretz (1971) has shown evidence of amelioration: the image of women as homebound. As women have entered the workforce in growing numbers, advertisements have increasingly shown them in work settings outside the home (Busby & Leichty, 1993; Sullivan & O'Connor, 1988).

✔ Guideline 8: Discuss other literature reviews on your topic.

If you find an earlier published review on your topic, it is important to discuss it in your review. Before doing so, consider the following questions:

How is the other review different from yours?
   Is yours substantially more current?
   Did you delimit the topic in a different way?
   Did you conduct a more comprehensive review?
   Did the earlier reviewer reach the same major conclusions that you reached?
   Did you reach the same major conclusions as the earlier reviewers?

How worthy is the other review of your readers' attention?
   What will they gain, if anything, by reading it?
   Will they encounter a different and potentially helpful perspective on the problem area?
   What are its major strengths and weaknesses?

✔ Guideline 9: Refer the reader to other reviews on issues that you will not be discussing in detail.

If you find it necessary to refer to a *related issue* that cannot be covered in depth in your review, it is appropriate to refer the reader to other reviews, as in Example 9.9.1. Needless to say, your review should completely cover the specific topic you have chosen. It is not acceptable to describe just a portion of the literature on your topic (as you defined it) and then refer the reader to another source for the remainder. However, the technique illustrated in Example 9.9.1 can be useful for pointing out literature that may be of interest to the reader but will not be reviewed in detail in the review you are writing (italics and bold added for emphasis).

Example 9.9.1[8]

Refers readers to other sources for details:

Throughout the 20th century, interest in the psychological impact of trauma has peaked during and after wartime, with the first major study of combat-related psychological sequelae (then called *physioneurosis*) published in 1941 by A. Kardiner (***see Kolb, 1993, for a more detailed accounting***). Dealing with survivors of World War II prisoner-of-war camps brought some insight....

---

[8] Ozer, E. J., Best, S. R., Lipsey, T. L., & Weiss, D. S. (2003). Predictors of posttraumatic stress disorder and symptoms in adults: A meta-analysis. *Psychological Bulletin, 129,* 52–73.

✔ Guideline 10: Justify comments such as "no studies were found."

If you find a gap in the literature that deserves mention in your literature review, explain how you arrived at the conclusion that there is a gap. At the very least, explain how you conducted the literature search, which databases you searched, and the dates and other parameters you used. You do not need to be overly specific, but the reader will expect you to justify your statement about the gap.

To avoid misleading your reader, it is a good idea early in your review to make statements such as the one shown in Example 9.10.1. This will protect you from criticism if you point out a gap when one does not actually exist. In other words, you are telling your reader that there is a gap based on the use of *a particular search strategy*.

Example 9.10.1[9]

Describes the strategy for searching literature:

We used five methods to locate relevant studies. First, we reviewed reference lists from previously published reviews of self-concept development (Demo, 1992; Harter, 1982, 1998; Wylie, 1979) and from two recent meta-analyses of gender differences in self-esteem (Kling, Hyde, Showers, & Buswell, 1999; Major, Barr, Zubek, & Babey, 1999). Second, we searched the *PsycINFO* and *ERIC* databases for articles published between 1887 (the earliest entry in the *PsycINFO* database) and June 2002, using the keyword "self-esteem" paired with each of the following keywords: "age differences," "change," "consistency," "continuity," "development," "literature review," "longitudinal," "meta-analysis," and "stability." Third, we paired the keyword "self-esteem" with every journal title that contained a previously identified article (from the keyword search). Fourth, we searched *PsycINFO* using the names of common self-esteem scales as the keyword (e.g., Rosenberg Self-Esteem Scale, Self-Esteem Inventory, Piers-Harris Self-Concept Scale). These keyword searches resulted in 9,410 citations (7,150 were from peer-reviewed journals). Fifth, we searched for relevant articles by reviewing the reference lists of the articles identified in the *PsycINFO* and *ERIC* searches that met the inclusion criteria.

✔ Guideline 11: Avoid long lists of nonspecific references.

In academic writing, references are used in the text of a written document for at least two purposes. First, they are used to give proper credit to an author of an idea or, in the case of a direct quotation, of a specific set of words. A failure to do so would constitute plagiarism. Second, references are used to demonstrate the breadth of coverage given in a manuscript. In an introductory paragraph, for example, it may be desirable to include references to several key studies that will be discussed in more detail in the body of the review. However, it is inadvisable to use long lists of references that do not specifically relate to the point being expressed. For instance, in Example 9.11.1, the long list of nonspecific references in the first sentence is probably inappropriate. Are these all empirical

---

[9] Trzesniewski, K. H., Donnellan, M. B., & Robins, R. W. (2003). Stability of self-esteem across the life span. *Journal of Personality and Social Psychology, 84*, 205–220.

studies? Do they report their authors' speculations on the issue? Are some of the references more important than others? It would have been better for the authors to refer the reader to a few key studies, which themselves would contain references to additional examples of research in that particular area, as illustrated in Example 9.11.2.

Example 9.11.1

First sentence in a literature review (too many nonspecific references):

Numerous writers have indicated that children in single-parent households are at greater risk for academic underachievement than children from two-parent households (Adams, 1999; Block, 2002; Doe, 2004; Edgar, 2000; Hampton, 1995; Jones, 2003; Klinger, 1991; Long, 1992; Livingston, 1993; Macy, 1985; Norton, 1988; Pearl, 1994; Smith, 1996; Travers, 1997; Vincent, 1994; West, 1992; Westerly, 1995; Yardley, 2004).

Example 9.11.2

An improved version of Example 9.11.1:

Numerous writers have suggested that children in single-parent households are at greater risk for academic underachievement than children from two-parent households (e.g., see Adams, 1999, and Block, 2002). Three recent studies have provided strong empirical support for this contention (Doe, 2004; Edgar, 2000; Jones, 2003). Of these, the study by Jones is the strongest, employing a national sample with rigorous controls for....

Notice the use of "e.g., see...," which indicates that only some of the possible references are cited for the point that the writers "have suggested." You may also use the Latin abbreviation *cf.* (which means "compare").

✓ Guideline 12:   If the results of previous studies are inconsistent or widely varying, cite them separately.

It is not uncommon for studies on the same topic to produce inconsistent or widely varying results. If so, it is important to cite the studies separately in order for the reader to interpret your review correctly. The following two examples illustrate the potential problem. Example 9.12.1 is misleading because it fails to note that the previous studies are grouped according to the two extremes of the percentage range given. Example 9.12.2 illustrates a better way to cite inconsistent findings.

Example 9.12.1

Inconsistent results cited as a single finding (undesirable):

In previous studies (Doe, 2004; Jones, 2005), parental support for requiring students to wear school uniforms in public schools varied considerably, ranging from only 19% to 52%.

Example 9.12.2

Improved version of Example 9.12.1:

In previous studies, parental support for requiring students to wear school uniforms have varied considerably. Support from rural parents varied from only 19% to 28% (Doe, 2004) while support from suburban parents varied from 35% to 52% (Jones, 2005).

✔ Guideline 13:   Cite all relevant references in the review section of a thesis, dissertation, or journal article.

When writing a thesis, a dissertation, or an article for publication in which the literature review precedes a report of original research, you should usually first cite all the relevant references in the literature review of your document. Avoid introducing new references to literature in later sections such as the results or discussion sections. Make sure you have checked your entire document to ensure that the literature review section or chapter is comprehensive. You may refer back to a previous discussion of a pertinent study when discussing your conclusions, but the study should have been referenced first in the literature review at the beginning of the thesis, dissertation, or article.

✔ Guideline 14:   Emphasize the need for your study in the literature review section or chapter.

When writing a thesis, a dissertation, or an article for publication in which the literature review precedes a report of original research, you should use the review to help justify your study. You can do this in a variety of ways, such as pointing out that your study (1) closes a gap in the literature, (2) tests an important aspect of a current theory, (3) replicates an important study, (4) retests a hypothesis using new or improved methodological procedures, (5) is designed to resolve conflicts in the literature, and so on.

Example 9.14.1 was included in the literature review portion of a research report designed to explore the relationship between self-reported marijuana use and opinions on drug testing and treatment programs. In their review of the literature, the authors point out gaps in the literature and indicate how their study fills them. This is a strong justification for the study.

Example 9.14.1[10]

Justifies a study:

The present study fills these three gaps. First, this study focuses on reactions to organizational drug treatment programs. Specifically, we considered issues such as job safety sensitivity, drug use, and type of treatment program. Second, we focused specifically on the relationship of....

---

[10] Paronto, M. E., Truxillo, D. M., Talya, N. B., & Leo, M. C. (2002). Drug testing, drug treatment, and marijuana use: A fairness perspective. *Journal of Applied Psychology, 87*, 1159–1166.

Activities for Chapter 9

Directions: For each of the model literature reviews that your instructor assigns, answer the following questions. The model reviews are presented near the end of this book.

1. Did the author begin by identifying the broad problem area while avoiding global statements? Explain.

2. Did the author indicate why the topic being reviewed is important? Explain.

3. Did the author distinguish between research findings and other sources of information by using appropriate wording? Explain.

4. Did the author indicate why certain studies are important? Explain.

5. If the author commented on the timeliness of the topic, was he or she specific in describing the time frame? Explain.

6. Was a landmark study cited? If yes, was it identified as a landmark? Was there any indication that it was replicated?

7. Are other literature reviews on the same topic discussed?

8. Are there references to other reviews on related issues that are not discussed in detail in the model literature review?

9. If the author said "no studies were found" on some aspect of the topic, was this statement justified (as indicated in this chapter)?

10. Did the author provide long lists of nonspecific references?

11. If results of previous studies are inconsistent or widely varying, were they cited separately?

Chapter 10

Guidelines for Developing a Coherent Essay

This chapter is designed to help you refine your first draft by guiding you in developing a coherent essay. Remember that a literature review should not be written as a series of connected summaries (or annotations) of the literature you have read. Instead, it should have a clearly stated argument, and it should be developed in such a way that all of its elements work together to communicate a well-reasoned account of that argument.

✔ Guideline 1: If your review is long, provide an overview near the beginning of the review.

When writing a long literature review, it is important to provide readers with an explicit road map of the author's argument. This is usually done in the introductory section of the review, which should include an overview of what will be covered in the rest of the document. Example 10.1.1 illustrates this.

Example 10.1.1[1]

An effective "road map" at the beginning of a review:

Given the adverse outcomes they expose themselves to by delaying and failing to act, why do humans so frequently engage in decision avoidance? Herein I consider a variety of choice behaviors as reflections of an individual's underlying decision avoidance, a pattern of behavior in which individuals seek to avoid the responsibility of making a decision by delaying or choosing options they perceive to be nondecisions. This review reveals that in all such cases, there is a mixture of a few good, rational reasons for avoidance and a more complex and rationally questionable role played by emotions such as regret and fear. These issues form the basis of this article: (1) the delineation of boundary conditions under which persons hesitate, defer, or choose options that require no action on their part or no change to the status quo and (2) the explanation for that behavior.

✔ Guideline 2: Near the beginning of a review, state explicitly what will and will not be covered.

Some topics are so broad that it will not be possible for you to cover the research completely in your review, especially if you are writing a term paper, which may have page-length restrictions imposed by your instructor, or an article for publication, in which

---

[1] Anderson, C. J. (2003). The psychology of doing nothing: Forms of decision avoidance result from reason and emotion. *Psychological Bulletin, 129*, 139–167.

reviews traditionally are relatively short. In such cases, you should state explicitly, near the beginning of your review, what will and will not be covered (i.e., the delimitations of your review). The excerpt in Example 10.2.1 illustrates application of this guideline. Note that the reviewers first provide a definition and indicate that their review includes *deceiving* and *lying* (as being interchangeable). They then state that the review will be limited to two criteria.

Example 10.2.1[2]

A statement of the delimitations of a review:

We define deception as a deliberate attempt to mislead others. Falsehoods communicated by people who are mistaken or self-deceived are not lies, but literal truths designed to mislead are lies. Although some scholars draw a distinction between *deceiving* and *lying* (e.g., Bok, 1978), we use the terms interchangeably. As Zuckerman et al. (1981) did in their review, we limit our analysis to behaviors that can be discerned by human perceivers without the aid of any special equipment. We also limit our review to studies of adults, as the dynamics of deceiving may be markedly different in children (e.g., Feldman, Devin-Sheehan, & Allen, 1978; Lewis, Stanger, & Sullivan, 1989; Shennum & Bugental, 1982).

✔ Guideline 3:   Specify your point of view early in the review.

As has been emphasized previously, your literature review should be written in the form of an essay that has a particular point of view in looking at the reviewed research. This point of view serves as the thesis statement of your essay (the assertion or proposition that is supported in the remainder of the essay).

The expression of your point of view does not need to be elaborate or detailed (although it can be). In Example 10.3.1, the reviewers briefly indicate their point of view (that SES, cognitive–emotional factors, and health may be dynamically linked). This informs readers very early in the review that this overarching point of view guides the interpretation and synthesis of the literature.

Of course, you should settle on a point of view only *after* you have read and considered the body of literature as a whole. In other words, this guideline indicates when you should *express* your point of view (early in the review), not when you should develop a point of view.

Example 10.3.1[3]

Early summary of the path of an argument:

The associations between SES and cognitive–emotional factors have not been presented in any recent, enumerative reviews (but see the review of SES and psychiatric disorders by Kohn, Dohrenwend, & Mirotznik, 1998), and we therefore analyze this research in more detail. Following our review and critical analysis, we present a framework for understanding the pathways that may dynamically

---

[2] DePaulo, B. M. et al. (2003). Cues to deception. *Psychological Bulletin, 129*, 74–118.

[3] Gallo, L. C., & Matthews, K. A. (2003). Understanding the association between socioeconomic status and physical health: Do negative emotions play a role? *Psychological Bulletin, 129*, 10–51.

link SES, cognitive–emotional factors, and health. Finally, we conclude with recommendations for future research to better address the proposed mediation hypothesis.

✓ Guideline 4: Aim for a clear and cohesive essay; avoid annotations.

It has been emphasized several times thus far that an effective literature review should be written in the form of an essay. Perhaps the single most reported problem for novice academic writers is their difficulty in abandoning the use of annotations in the body of a literature review.

Annotations are brief summaries of the contents of articles. Stringing together several annotations in the body of a review may describe what research is available on a topic, but it fails to organize the material for the reader. An effective review of literature is organized to make a point. The writer needs to describe how the individual studies relate to one another. What are the relative strengths and weaknesses? Where are the gaps, and why do they exist? All these details and more need to support the author's main purpose for writing the review. The detailed outline developed in Chapter 8 describes the path of the argument, but it is up to the writer to translate this into a prose account that integrates the important details of the research literature into an essay that communicates a point of view.

Example 10.4.1 shows how a number of studies can be cited together as part of a single paragraph. The paragraph starts with a topic sentence and ends with an elaboration on the topic sentence based on the citations from the literature within the paragraph. Note that one of the points made by the reviewers is supported by three references. Clearly, then, the organization of the paragraph is topical—not around the reports of individual authors.

Example 10.4.1[4]

A single paragraph with multiple sources:

At the family level, the nature of relationships between parents and children could play a role in asthma hospitalizations. Children with asthma have been found to have higher rates of clinically significant family stress as compared with healthy children (Bussing, Burket, & Kelleher, 1996). Children whose families are more cohesive are more likely to have controlled rather than uncontrolled asthma (Meijer, Griffioen, van Nierop, & Oppenheimer, 1995). Additionally, parenting difficulties early in a child's life, particularly during times of high stress, have been found to predict the onset of asthma in childhood (Klinnert, Mrazek, & Mrazek, 1994; Klinnert et al., 2001; Mrazek et al., 1999). Thus, strain in the family, in terms of both conflicts among family members and impact of illness on family relationships, could be associated with more frequent hospitalizations among children with asthma.

---

[4] Chen, E., Bloomberg, G. R., Fisher, E. B., & Strunk, R. C. (2003). Predictors of repeat hospitalizations in children with asthma: The role of psychosocial and socioenvironmental factors. *Health Psychology, 22,* 12–18.

✔ Guideline 5: Use subheadings, especially in long reviews.

Because long reviews, especially those written for theses and dissertations, often deal with articles from more than one discipline area, it is advisable to use subheadings. If you decide to use subheadings, place them strategically to help advance your argument and allow the reader to follow your discussion more easily. The topic outline you prepared in Chapter 8 can help you to determine where they should be placed, though you may need to recast some of the topic headings as labels rather than statements.

✔ Guideline 6: Use transitions to help trace your argument.

Strategic transitional phrases can help readers follow your argument. For instance, you can use transitions to provide readers with textual clues that mark the progression of a discussion, such as when you begin paragraphs with "First," "Second," and "Third" to mark the development of three related points. Of course, any standard writing manual will contain lists of transitional expressions that are commonly used in formal writing.

These transitions should not be overused, however. Especially in a short review, it may not be necessary to use such phrases to label the development of three related points when each is described in three adjacent paragraphs. Another problem often found in short reviews is the overuse of what Bem (1995) calls "meta-comments," which are comments about the review *itself* (as opposed to comments about the literature being reviewed).[5] For instance, in Example 10.6.1, the writer restates the organization of the review (i.e., this is an example of a meta-comment) partway through the document. While there is nothing inherently wrong with making meta-comments, you should avoid frequent restatements that rehash what you have already stated.

Example 10.6.1

Example of overuse of meta-comments:

Recall that this paper deals with how question asking in children has been used to explain a variety of learning styles. Also recall that we have reviewed the research on the use of question asking in the classroom and have reached some tentative conclusions regarding its conclusions. Now, we will consider two basic types of questions that young children frequently ask, noting that....

✔ Guideline 7: If your topic reaches across disciplines, consider reviewing studies from each discipline separately.

Some topics naturally transcend discipline boundaries. For instance, if you were writing about diabetes management among teenage girls, you would find relevant sources in several discipline areas, including health care, nutrition, and psychology. The health care literature, for example, may deal with variations in insulin therapies (such as variations in types of insulin used or the use of pumps vs. syringes to deliver the insulin). The nutrition journals, on the other hand, may include studies on alternative methods for

---

[5] Bem, D. J. (1995). Writing a review article for *Psychological Bulletin. Psychological Bulletin, 118,* 172–177.

managing food intake in the search for more effective methods to control episodes of insulin shock. Finally, the psychological literature may offer insights into the nature of the stressors common to adolescent girls, especially with respect to how these stressors may interfere with the girls' decision-making processes concerning self-monitoring, nutrition choices, and value orientations. While these examples are hypothetical, it is easy to see how such a review might benefit from being divided into three sections, with the findings from each discipline area reviewed separately.

✔ Guideline 8: Write a conclusion for the end of the review.

The end of your literature review should provide closure for the reader, that is, the path of the argument should end with a conclusion of some kind. How you end a literature review, however, will depend on your reasons for writing it. If the review was written to stand alone, as in the case of a term paper or a review article for publication, the conclusion needs to make clear how the material in the body of the review has supported the assertion or proposition presented in the introduction. On the other hand, a review in a thesis, dissertation, or journal article presenting original research usually leads to the research questions that will be addressed.

If your review is long and complex, you should briefly summarize the main threads of your argument, and then present your conclusion. Otherwise, you may cause your reader to pause in order to try to reconstruct the case you have made. Shorter reviews usually do not require a summary, but this judgment will depend on the complexity of the argument you have presented. You may need feedback from your faculty adviser or a friend to help you determine how much you will need to restate at the end. Example 10.8.1 presents a brief summary and conclusion section that appeared at the end of a long literature review. In most cases, for very long reviews, a more detailed summary would be desirable.

Example 10.8.1[6]

A summary and conclusion section at the end of a long review:

Evidence from a wide range of psychological disciplines converges to suggest that physical and social pain operate via common mechanisms. Both were necessary to promote the survival of social animals, functioning to guide animals away from threats and toward others [who are helpful]. Both motivate quick, defensive behavior and are extremely emotionally aversive. Both types of pain share common psychological correlates and physiological pathways. Finally, both appear to prime generalized threat-response mechanisms.

In general, we believe this review contributes to the emerging notion that people's social and physical worlds are deeply entangled. We have focused specifically on how individuals' feelings for other people may stem in part from the same pain that keeps them physically safe. We also believe that social pain theory helps emphasize the vital role of connection with others in human behavior. Those of us living in individualistic societies are inundated with messages trum-

---

[6] MacDonald, G., & Leary, M. R. (2005). Why does social exclusion hurt? The relationship between social and physical pain. *Psychological Bulletin, 131*, 202–223.

peting autonomy and individuality. Yet, a picture is emerging that people are so vitally important to each other that social needs are ingrained in our very biology. We hold social pain to be one such example of our deep, physical need for each other.

✓ Guideline 9: Check the flow of your argument for coherence.

One of the most difficult skills to learn in academic writing is to evaluate one's own writing for coherence. Coherence refers to how well a manuscript holds together as a unified document. It is important for you to ask yourself how well the various elements of your review connect with one another. This requires that you carefully evaluate the effectiveness of the rhetorical elements of your document that tell the reader about its structure and about the relationships among its elements. Subheadings often go a long way in identifying a manuscript's structure. Transitional expressions and other kinds of rhetorical markers also help to identify relationships among sections, as in "the next example," "in a related study," "a counter-example," and "the most recent (or relevant) study." Obviously, there are many more such examples. Remember, these kinds of rhetorical devices are useful navigational tools for your reader, especially if the details of the review are complex.

Activities for Chapter 10

Directions: For each of the model literature reviews that your instructor assigns, answer the following questions. The model reviews are presented near the end of this book.

1. If the review is long, did the author provide an overview of the review near its beginning? Explain.

2. Did the author explicitly state what would and would not be covered in the review? Explain.

3. Is the review a clear and cohesive essay? Explain.

4. Did the author avoid annotations? Explain.

5. If the review is long, did the author use subheadings? Explain.

6. Did the author use transitions to help trace his or her argument? Explain.

7. If the topic reaches across disciplines, did the author review studies from each discipline separately?

8. Did the author write a conclusion for the end of the review?

9. Is the flow of the "argument" coherent?

Notes:

Chapter 11

Guidelines on Style, Mechanics, and Language Usage

The previous two chapters dealt with general issues involved in writing a literature review. This chapter presents guidelines that focus on more specific issues related to style, mechanics, and language usage. These issues are important in producing a draft that is free of mechanical errors.

✔ Guideline 1: Compare your draft with your topic outline.

The topic outline you prepared after reading Chapter 8 traced the path of the argument for the literature review. Now that your first draft is completed, compare what you have written with the topic outline to make sure you have properly fleshed out the path of the argument.

✔ Guideline 2: Check the structure of your review for parallelism.

The reader of a literature review, especially a long, complex review, needs to be able to follow the structure of the manuscript while internalizing the details of the analysis and synthesis. A topic outline will typically involve parallel structural elements. For instance, a discussion of weaknesses will be balanced by a discussion of strengths, arguments for a position will be balanced by arguments against, and so on. These expectations on the part of the reader stem from long-standing rhetorical traditions in academic writing. Therefore, you need to check your manuscript to make sure that your descriptions are balanced properly. This may require that you explain a particular lack of parallelism, perhaps by stating explicitly that no studies were found that contradict a specific point (see Guideline 10 in Chapter 9 if this applies to your review).

✔ Guideline 3: Avoid overusing direct quotations, especially long ones.

One of the most stubborn problems for novice academic writers in the social and behavioral sciences is the overuse of quotations. This is understandable, given the heavy emphasis placed in college writing classes on the correct use of the conventions for citing others' words. In fact, there is nothing inherently wrong with using direct quotations. However, problems arise when they are used inappropriately or indiscriminately.

A direct quotation presented out of context may not convey the full meaning of the original author's intent. When a reader struggles to understand the function of a quotation in a review, the communication of the message of the review is interrupted. Explaining the full context of a quotation can further confuse the reader with details that are not essential for the purpose of the review in hand. By contrast, paraphrasing the main ideas of an author is usually more efficient and makes it easier to avoid extraneous details. In addition, paraphrasing eliminates the potential for disruptions in the flow of a review due to the different writing styles of various authors.

Finally, it is seldom acceptable to begin a literature review with a quotation. Some students find it hard to resist doing this. Remember that it is usually very difficult for the reader to experience the intended impact of the quotation when it is presented before the author of the literature review has established the proper context.

✔ Guideline 4: Check your style manual for correct use of citations.

Make sure to check the style manual used in your field for the appropriate conventions for citing references in the text. For example, the *Publication Manual of the American Psychological Association* specifies the following guidelines for citations.

a. You may formally cite a reference in your narrative in one of several ways. At the conclusion of a statement that represents someone else's thoughts, you cite the author's last name and the year of publication, separated by a comma, set off in parentheses, as in this example: (Doe, 2005). If you use the author's name in the narrative, simply give the year of publication in parentheses immediately following the name, as in "Doe (2005) noted that...."

b. When you cite multiple authors' names in parentheses, use the ampersand (&) instead of the word "and." If the citation is in the narrative, use the word "and."

c. Use semicolons to separate multiple citations in parentheses, as in this example: (Black, 2004; Brown, 2005; Green, 2005).

d. When you cite a secondary source, be sure you have made it clear, as in this example: (Doe, as cited in Smith, 2004). Note that only Smith (2004) would be placed in the reference list.

✔ Guideline 5: Avoid using synonyms for recurring words.

The focus of a review of empirical research should be on presenting, interpreting, and synthesizing other writers' ideas and research findings as clearly and precisely as possible. This may require you to repeat words that describe routine aspects of several studies. Students who are new to academic writing sometimes approach the task as though it were a creative writing exercise. *It is not!* Literature reviews should include information about many studies (and other types of literature), all of which readers should be able to internalize quickly. Therefore, it is important to adhere to the use of conventional terms, even if they should recur. Clarity is best achieved when the writer consistently uses conventional terms throughout, especially when referring to details about a study's methodology or some other technical aspect of the research.

In general, it is best not to vary the use of labels. For example, if a study deals with two groups of participants, and the researcher has labeled them Groups 1 and 2, you should usually avoid substituting more creative phrases (e.g., "the Phoenix cohort" or "the original group of youngsters"). On the other hand, if alternative labels help clarify a study's design (e.g., when Group 1 is the control group and Group 2 the experimental group), use the substitute expressions instead, but remain consistent throughout your discussion. Example 11.5.1 illustrates how the use of synonyms and "creative" sentence construction can confuse readers. At various points, the first group is referred to as the "Phoenix cohort," as "Group I," and as the "experimental group," which is bound to cause confusion. Example 11.5.2 is an improved version in which the writer consistently uses the terms "experimental group" and "control group" to identify the two groups.

Example 11.5.1

Inconsistent use of identifying terms:

The Phoenix cohort, which was taught to correctly identify the various toy animals by name, was brought back to be studied by the researchers twice, once after six months and again at the end of the year. The other group of youngsters was asked to answer the set of questions only once, after six months, but they had been taught to label the animals by color rather than by name. The performance of Group I was superior to the performance of Group II. The superior performance of the experimental group was attributed to....

Example 11.5.2

Improved version of Example 11.5.1:

The experimental group was taught to identify toy animals by color and was retested twice at six-month intervals. The control group, which was taught to identify the toys by name, was retested only once after six months. The performance of the experimental group was superior to the performance of the control group. The superior performance of the experimental group was attributed to....

✔ Guideline 6:   Spell out all acronyms when you first use them, and avoid using too many.

So many acronyms have become part of our everyday lexicon that it is easy to overlook them during the editing process. Some examples are school acronyms, such as UCLA and USC; professional acronyms, such as APA and MLA; and acronyms from our everyday lives, such as FBI, FDA, and GPA. As obvious as this guideline may seem, it is quite common to find these and other examples of acronyms that are never spelled out. Make sure to check your document carefully for acronyms and spell them out the first time you use them.

Sometimes, it is useful to refer to something by its acronym, especially if its full title is long and you need to refer to it several times. For example, the Graduate Writing Assessment Requirement for students in the California State University system is commonly referred to as the GWAR. In general, you should avoid using too many acronyms, especially ones that are not commonly recognized, like GWAR. In a complex literature review, using a few acronyms may be helpful, but using too many of them may be confusing.

✔ Guideline 7:   Avoid the use of contractions; they are inappropriate in formal academic writing.

Contractions are a natural part of language use. They are one example of the natural process of linguistic simplification that accounts for how all languages change, slowly but surely, across time. Many instructors, even some English composition instructors, tolerate the use of contractions on the assumption that their use reflects the changing standards of acceptability in modern-day American English. In spite of such attitudes, however, it is almost always *inappropriate* to use contractions in formal academic writing.

✔ Guideline 8: When used, coined terms should be set off in quotations.

It is sometimes useful to coin a term to describe something in one or two words that would otherwise require a sentence or more. Coined terms frequently become part of common usage, as in the noun "lunch," which is now commonly used as a verb (Did you *lunch* with Jane yesterday?). However, coined terms should be used sparingly in formal academic writing. If you decide to coin a term, set it off with quotation marks to indicate that its meaning cannot be found in a standard dictionary.

✔ Guideline 9: Avoid slang expressions, colloquialisms, and idioms.

Remember that academic writing is *formal* writing. Therefore, slang, colloquialisms, and idioms are not appropriate in a literature review. While many slang terms such as "cool" (meaning "good") and "ain't" are becoming part of our conversational language repertoires, they should be avoided altogether in formal writing. Colloquialisms, such as "thing" and "stuff," should be replaced by appropriate noncolloquial terms (e.g., "item," "feature," and "characteristic"). Similarly, idioms, such as "to rise to the pinnacle" and "to survive the test," should be replaced by more formal expressions, such as "to become prominent" or "to be successful."

✔ Guideline 10: Use Latin abbreviations in parenthetic material; elsewhere, use English translations.

The Latin abbreviations shown below with their English translations are commonly used in formal academic writing. With the exception of et al., these abbreviations are limited to parenthetic material. For instance, the Latin abbreviation in parentheses at the end of this sentence is proper: (i.e., this is a correct example). If this was not in parentheses, you should use the English translation: that is, this is also a correct example. Additionally, note the punctuation that is required for each of these abbreviations. Note especially that there is no period mark after "et" in et al.

cf.	compare	e.g.,	for example	et al.	and others
etc.	and so forth	i.e.,	that is	vs.	versus, against

✔ Guideline 11: Check your draft for common writing conventions.

There are a number of additional writing conventions that all academic disciplines require. Check your draft to ensure you have applied all the following items before you give it to your instructor to read.

a. Make sure you have used complete sentences.

b. It is sometimes acceptable to write a literature review in the first person. However, you should avoid excessive use of the first person.

c. It is inappropriate to use sexist language in academic writing. For instance, it is incorrect to always use masculine or feminine pronouns (he, him, his vs. she, her, hers) to refer to a person when you are not sure of the person's gender (as in, "the teacher left her classroom...," when the teacher's gender is not known). Often, sexist language can be avoided by using the plural form ("the teachers left their classrooms..."). If you must use singular forms, alternate between masculine and feminine forms or use "he or she."

d. You should strive for clarity in your writing. Thus, you should avoid indirect sentence constructions, such as "In Smith's study, it was found...." An improved version would be, "Smith found that ...."

e. In general, numbers from zero through nine are spelled out, but numbers 10 and above are written as numbers. Two exceptions to this rule are numbers assigned to a table or figure and measurements expressed in decimals or in metrical units.

f. Always capitalize nouns followed by numerals or letters when they denote a specific place in a numbered series. For instance, this is Item f under Guideline 11 in Chapter 11. (Note that "I," "G," and "C" are capped.)

g. Always spell out a number when it is the first word or phrase in a sentence, as in, "Seventy-five participants were interviewed...." Sometimes a sentence can be rewritten so that the number is not at the beginning. For example: "Researchers interviewed 75 participants...."

✔ Guideline 12: Write a concise and descriptive title for the review.

The title of a literature review should identify the field of study you have investigated as well as tell the reader your point of view. However, it should also be concise and describe what you have written. In general, the title should not draw attention to itself; rather, it should help the reader to adopt a proper frame of reference with which to read your paper. The following suggestions will help you to avoid some common problems with titles.

a. **Identify the field, but do not describe it fully.** Especially with long and complex reviews, it is not advisable for you to try to describe every aspect of your argument. If you do, the result will be an excessively long and detailed title. Your title should provide your reader an easy entry into your paper. It should not force the reader to pause in order to decipher it.

b. **Consider specifying your bias, orientation, or delimitations.** If your review is written with an identifiable bias, orientation, or delimitation, it may be desirable to specify it in the title. For instance, if you are critical of some aspect of the literature, consider using a phrase such as "A Critique of..." or "A Critical Evaluation of..." as part of your title. Subtitles often can be used effectively for this purpose. For example, "The Politics of Abortion: A Review of the Qualitative Research" has a subtitle that indicates that the review is delimited to qualitative research.

   c. **Avoid "cute" titles.** Avoid the use of puns, alliteration, or other literary devices that detract from the content of the title. While a title such as "Phonics vs. 'Hole' Language" may seem clever if your review is critical of the whole language approach to reading instruction, it will probably distract readers. A more descriptive title, such as "Reading as a Natural or Unnatural Outgrowth of Spoken Language," will give the reader of your review a better start in comprehending your paper.

   d. **Keep it short.** Titles should be short and to the point. Professional conference organizers will often limit titles of submissions to about nine words in order to facilitate the printing of hundreds of titles in their program books. While such printing constraints are not at play with a term paper or a chapter heading, it is still advisable to try to keep your review title as simple and short as possible. A good rule of thumb is to aim for a title of about 10 words, plus or minus three.

✔ Guideline 13: Strive for a user-friendly draft.

You should view your first draft as a work in progress. As such, it should be formatted in a way that invites comments from your readers. Thus, it should be legible and laid out in a way that allows the reader to react to your ideas easily. The following list contains some suggestions for ensuring that your draft is user-friendly. Ask your faculty adviser to review this list, and add additional items as appropriate.

   a. **Spell-check, proofread, and edit your manuscript.** New word processing programs have spell-check functions. Use the spell-check feature before asking anyone to read your paper. However, there is no substitute for editing your own manuscript carefully, especially because the spell-check function can overlook some of your mistakes (e.g., "see" and "sea" are both correctly spelled, but the spell-check function will not highlight them as errors if you mistakenly type the wrong one). Remember that your goal should be to have an error-free document that communicates the content easily and does not distract the reader with careless mechanical errors.

   b. **Number all pages.** Professors sometimes write general comments in the form of a memo in addition to their notes in the margins. Unnumbered pages make such comments more difficult to write because professors cannot refer to page numbers in their memos.

   c. **Double-space the draft.** Single-spaced documents make it difficult for the reader to write specific comments or suggest alternative phrasing.

   d. **Use wide margins.** Narrow margins may save paper, but they restrict the amount of space available for your instructor's comments.

   e. **Use a stapler or a strong binder clip to secure the draft.** Your draft is one of many papers your instructor will read. Securing the document with a stapler or a strong clip will make it easier to keep your paper together. If you use a folder or a binder to hold your draft, make sure that it opens flat. Plastic folders that do not open flat make it difficult for your professor (or editor) to write comments in the margins.

f. **Identify yourself as the author, and include a telephone number or e-mail address.** Because your draft is one of many papers your instructor will read, it is important to identify yourself as the author. Always include a cover page with your name and a telephone number or e-mail address in case your professor wants to contact you. If you are writing the literature review as a term paper, be sure to indicate the course number and title as well as the date.

g. **Make sure the draft is printed clearly.** In general, you should avoid using printers with ribbons unless you make sure the print is dark enough for it to be read comfortably. Similarly, if you submit a photocopy of your draft, make sure the copy is dark enough. Always keep a hard copy for your records! Student papers sometimes get misplaced, and hard drives on computers sometimes crash.

h. **Avoid "cute" touches.** In general, you should avoid using color text for highlighted words (use italics instead), mixing different size fonts (use a uniform font size throughout except for the title), or using clip art or any other special touches that may distract the reader by calling attention to the physical appearance of your paper instead of its content.

✓ Guideline 14: Use great care to avoid plagiarism.

If you are uncertain about what constitutes plagiarism, consult your university's student code of conduct. It is usually part of your university's main catalog and is reprinted in several other sources readily available to students. For example, the University of Washington's Psychology Writing Center makes a handout on Plagiarism and Student Writing available on its Web site at http://depts.washington.edu/psywc/. On the main page, click the "Handouts" link, which will take you to a list of handouts in PDF format. Under the "About Plagiarism" heading, you will find a statement on academic responsibility prepared by the university's Committee on Academic Conduct (1994),[1] which discusses six types of plagiarism.

(1) Using another writer's words without proper citation;

(2) using another writer's ideas without proper citation;

(3) citing a source but reproducing the exact words of a printed source without quotation marks;

(4) borrowing the structure of another author's phrases or sentences without crediting the author from whom it came;

(5) borrowing all or part of another student's paper or using someone else's outline to write your own paper; and

(6) using a paper-writing service or having a friend write the paper for you. (p. 23)

It is easy to quarrel about whether borrowing even one or two words would constitute plagiarism or whether an "idea" is really owned by an author. However, plagiarism is easily avoided simply by making sure that you cite your sources properly. If you have

---

[1] Committee on Academic Conduct. (1994). *Bachelor's degree handbook.* University of Washington.

any doubt about this issue with respect to your own writing, ask your instructor. This is a very serious matter.

✔ Guideline 15: Get help if you need it.

It should be obvious from the content of this chapter that the expectations for correctness and accuracy in academic writing are quite high. If you feel that you are unable to meet these demands at your current level of writing proficiency, you may need to get help. International students are often advised to hire proofreaders to help them meet their instructors' expectations. Most universities offer writing classes, either through the English department or in other disciplines. Some offer workshops for students struggling with the demands of thesis or dissertation requirements, and many universities have Writing Centers that provide a variety of services for students. If you feel you need help, talk with your instructor about the services available at your university. You should not expect your instructor to edit your work for style and mechanics.

Activities for Chapter 11

1. Examine the titles of the model literature reviews near the end of this book.

    • How well does each title serve to identify the field of the review?

    • Do the titles of the articles specify the authors' points of view in the review?

2. Now consider your own first draft of your literature review.

    • Compare your first draft with the topic outline you prepared. Do they match? If not, where did your draft vary from the outline? Does this variation affect the path of the "argument" of your review?

    • Find two or three places in your review where your discussion jumps to the next major category of your topic outline. How will the reader know that you have changed to a new category (i.e., did you use subheadings or transitions to signal the switch)?

Chapter 12

Incorporating Feedback
and Refining the First Draft

At this point in the writing process, you have completed the major portion of your critical review of the literature. However, your work is not yet done. You should now undertake the important final steps in the writing process—redrafting your review.

New writers often experience frustration at this stage because they are now expected to take an impartial view of a piece of writing in which they have had a very personal role. In the earlier stages, as the writer, you were the one who was analyzing, evaluating, and synthesizing other writers' work. Now, your draft is the subject of your own and your readers' analysis and evaluation. This is not an easy task, but it is a critical *and* necessary next step in writing an *effective* literature review.

The first step in accomplishing this role reversal is to put the manuscript aside for a period of time, thereby creating some distance from the manuscript and from your role as the writer. Second, remind yourself that the writing process is an ongoing negotiation between a writer and the intended audience. This is why the role reversal is so important. You should now approach your draft from the perspective of someone who is trying to read and understand the argument that is being communicated.

The redrafting process typically involves evaluating and incorporating feedback. That feedback may come from an instructor and your peers, or it may come from your own attempts to refine and revise your own draft. If you are writing a literature review as a term paper, solicit feedback from your professor at key points during the writing process, either by discussing your ideas during an office visit or, if your professor is willing, by submitting a first draft for comments. If it is for a thesis or dissertation, your earliest feedback will be from your faculty adviser, although you should also consider asking fellow students and colleagues for comments. If the review is for an article intended for publication, you should seek feedback from instructors, fellow students, and colleagues.

As the writer, you should determine which comments you will incorporate and which you will discard, but the feedback you receive from these various sources will give you valuable information on how to improve the communication of your ideas to your audience. The following guidelines are designed to help you through this process.

✔ Guideline 1: The reader is always right.

This guideline is deliberately overstated to draw your attention to it because it is the most important one in the redrafting process. If an educated reader does not understand one of your points, the communication process has not worked. Therefore, you should almost always seriously consider changing the draft to make it clearer for the reader. It will usually be counterproductive to defend the draft manuscript. Instead, you should try to determine why the reader did not understand it. Did you err in your analysis? Did you provide insufficient background information? Would the addition of more explicit transitions between sections make it clearer? These questions, and others like these, should guide your discussions with your readers whom you chose to provide you with feedback.

✔ Guideline 2: Expect your instructor to comment on the content.

It is important for you to obtain your instructor's feedback on the *content* of your manuscript early in the redrafting process. If your first draft contained many stylistic and mechanical errors, such as misspellings or misplaced headings, your instructor may feel compelled to focus on these matters and defer the comments on the content until the manuscript is easier to read.

✔ Guideline 3: Concentrate first on comments about your ideas.

As the previous two guidelines suggest, your first priority at this stage should be to make sure that your ideas have come across as you intended. Of course, you should note comments about stylistic matters and eventually attend to them, but your first order of business should be to ensure that you have communicated the argument you have developed. Thus, you need to carefully evaluate the feedback you receive from all your sources—your fellow students as well as your instructor—because at this stage you need to concentrate your efforts on making sure that your paper communicates your ideas effectively and correctly. (Some important matters concerning style, language use, and grammar are covered in the next chapter.)

✔ Guideline 4: Reconcile contradictory feedback by seeking clarification.

You may encounter differences of opinion among those who review your draft document. For instance, it is not unusual for members of a thesis or dissertation committee to give you contradictory feedback. One member may ask that you provide additional details about a study while another member may want you to de-emphasize it. If you encounter such differences of opinion, it is your responsibility to seek further clarification from both sources and negotiate a resolution of the controversy. First, make sure that the different opinions were not due to one person's failure to comprehend your argument. Second, discuss the matter with both individuals and arrive at a compromise.

✔ Guideline 5: Reconcile comments about style with your style manual.

Make sure that you have carefully reviewed the particular style manual that is required for your writing task. If your earliest experience with academic writing was in an English department course, you may have been trained to use the style manual of the Modern Language Association.[1] Many university libraries advise that theses and disserta-

---

[1] Gibaldi, J. (1998). *MLA style manual and guide to scholarly publishing* (2nd ed.). New York: Modern Language Association of America.

tions follow the University of Chicago style manual.[2] However, the most widely used manual in the social and behavioral sciences is the style manual of the American Psychological Association.[3] If you are preparing a paper for publication, check the specific periodical or publisher for guidelines on style before submitting the paper. Finally, many academic departments and schools will have their own policies with respect to style. Regardless of which style manual pertains to your writing task, remember that you are expected to adhere to it meticulously. As you consider incorporating any feedback you receive, make sure that it conforms to the required style manual.

✓ Guideline 6: Allow plenty of time for the feedback and redrafting process.

Students often experience frustration when they are faced with major structural or content revisions and have an imminent deadline. You can expect to have to prepare at least one major redraft of your literature review, so you should allow yourself plenty of time for it. Professional writers often go through three or more drafts before they consider a document to be a final draft. While you may not have quite so many drafts, you should allow enough time to comfortably go through at least several revisions of your document.

Activities for Chapter 12

1. Ask two friends to read the draft of your literature review and comment on the content. Compare their comments.

   - On which points did your friends agree?

   - On which points did they disagree? Which of the two opinions will you follow? Why?

   - Consider the places in your review that your friends found hard to follow. Rewrite these passages, keeping in mind that you want your friends to understand your points.

2. Write five questions designed to guide your instructor or your friends in giving you feedback on the content of your review.

   - Reread your review draft, and respond to your own questions by pretending you are your instructor.

   - Revise your draft according to your own feedback.

   - Reconsider the five questions you wrote for your instructor or your friends. Which questions would you leave on your list? What questions would you add?

---

[2] University of Chicago Press. (2003). *The Chicago manual of style* (15th ed.). Chicago: University of Chicago Press.
[3] American Psychological Association. (2001). *Publication manual of the American Psychological Association* (5th ed.). Washington, DC: American Psychological Association.

Notes:

Chapter 13

Comprehensive Self-Editing Checklist for Refining the Final Draft

The final draft should be as accurate and error-free as possible, both in terms of its content as well as its mechanics and style. After you have carefully considered the feedback you received from your peers and academic advisers and after you have revised the manuscript in light of their input, you should carefully edit your manuscript a final time. The purpose for this final review is accuracy.

The items in the following checklist are grouped according to some of the major criteria instructors use in evaluating student writing. Most of these criteria are absolutely critical when writing a thesis or dissertation. However, your instructor may relax some of them in the case of term papers written during a single semester.

You will find that most of the items on the checklist were presented in the earlier chapters as guidelines, but many additional ones have been added in an attempt to cover common problems that are sometimes overlooked by student writers. You should show this checklist to your instructors and ask that they add or eliminate items according to their own preferences.

Keep in mind that the checklist is designed to help you to refine the manuscript. Ultimately, the extent of perfection you achieve will depend on how meticulously you edit your own work.

Adherence to the Writing Process for Editing and Redrafting

_____ 1. Have you asked your instructors to review this checklist and to add or delete items according to their preferences?

_____ 2. After finishing your last draft, did you set your manuscript aside for several days before you began to revise it (i.e., did you create an appropriate *distance* from your manuscript before changing roles from "writer" to "reader")?

_____ 3. Did you ask another person to review your manuscript?

_____ 4. Have you addressed all the questions raised by your reviewers?

_____ 5. Did you reconcile all differences of opinion among your reviewers?

Importance or Significance of the Topic

_____ 6. Is your topic important, either from a theoretical or a practical perspective?

_____ 7. Does it present a fresh perspective or identify a gap in the literature (i.e., does it address a question not previously addressed)?

_____ 8. Is your topic's significance or importance demonstrated and justified?

_____ 9. Is this an appropriate topic for your field of study?

_____ 10. Is the topic timely in terms of what is being reported in the research literature?

_____ 11. Does the title of your manuscript adequately describe the subject of your review?

Organization and Other Global Considerations

_____ 12. Does your review include an introduction and a discussion and conclusions section?

_____ 13. Did you include a reference list?

_____ 14. Does the length and organization of your review follow the criteria set forth by (1) your instructor, if you are writing a term paper; (2) your committee chair, if you are writing a thesis or dissertation; or (3) the publication guidelines of the journal you have targeted, if you are writing for publication?

Effectiveness of the Introduction

_____ 15. Does your introduction describe the scope of the literature you have reviewed and why the topic is important?

_____ 16. Did you describe in your introduction the general structure of your paper?

_____ 17. Does your introduction identify the line of argumentation you have followed in your manuscript?

_____ 18. Does the introduction state what will and will not be covered, if this is appropriate?

_____ 19. Does the introduction specify your thesis statement or point of view, if this is relevant?

Currency and Relevance of the Literature Cited

_____ 20. Did you review the most current articles on the topic?

_____ 21. Are the studies you reviewed current?

_____ 22. If you have included older articles, did you have a good reason for including them?

_____ 23. Have you explained why you have described some findings as being strong?

_____ 24. Have you explained why you have described other findings as being weak?

_____ 25. Did you identify the major patterns or trends in the literature?

_____ 26. Have you identified in your manuscript the classic or landmark studies you cited?

_____ 27. Did you specify the relationship of these classic studies to subsequent studies they may have influenced?

Thoroughness and Accuracy of the Literature Reviewed

_____ 28. Is the coverage of your review adequate?

_____ 29. Have you noted and explained the gaps in the literature?

_____ 30. Have you described any pertinent controversies in the field?

_____ 31. If you answered yes to item 30, did you make clear which studies fall on either side of the controversy?

_____ 32. Have you checked the draft for parallelism?

_____ 33. Have you noted and explained the relationships among studies, such as which ones came first? Which ones share similarities? Which ones have differences?

_____ 34. Did you indicate the source of key terms or concepts?

_____ 35. Are there gaps in the body of your manuscript?

Coherence and Flow of the Path of the Argument

_____ 36. Does each study you reviewed correspond with a specific part of your topic outline?

_____ 37. Have you deleted citations to studies you decided not to include in your review because they do not relate to the path of your argument?

_____ 38. Is the path of your argument made clear throughout the manuscript?

_____ 39. Does each part of your review flow logically from the preceding part?

_____ 40. If you have used "meta-comments" (see Chapter 10, Guideline 6), are they essential?

_____ 41. If you have used subheadings, do they help advance your argument?

_____ 42. If you have not used subheadings, would adding them help advance your argument?

_____ 43. Is your manuscript coherent, or would additional transitional devices help to clarify how it holds together?

Effectiveness of the Conclusion

_____ 44. Does your conclusion provide closure for the reader?

_____ 45. Does your conclusion make reference to the line of argumentation you specified in the introduction?

Accuracy of Citations and the Reference List

_____ 46. Have you checked your style manual's guidelines for citing references in the narrative (e.g., when to use parentheses, how to cite multiple authors, and how to cite a secondary source)?

_____ 47. Have you checked each citation in the manuscript to make sure that it appears on your reference list?

_____ 48. Have you checked all entries on the reference list to make sure that each one is cited in your manuscript?

_____ 49. Have you eliminated all entries from your reference list that are not cited in the manuscript?

_____ 50. Have you checked for accuracy and consistency between the dates in your manuscript and the dates in your reference list?

_____ 51. Have you checked for accuracy between the spelling of the authors' names in your manuscript and in your reference list?

_____ 52. Are most of the dates of the studies included in the reference list within the recent past?

Mechanics and Overall Accuracy of the Manuscript

_____ 53. Did you read and edit your manuscript carefully?

_____ 54. Did you perform a final spell-check of the entire manuscript?

_____ 55. Are your margins set appropriately?

_____ 56. Did you number all the pages?

_____ 57. Is your manuscript double-spaced?

_____ 58. Did you include your full name (and, for theses and dissertations, your telephone number or e-mail address)?

Appropriateness of Style and Language Usage

_____ 59. Have you carefully reviewed the appropriate style manual for your field?

_____ 60. Have you checked your manuscript for consistency with your style manual?

_____ 61. Are your headings formatted in accordance with the guidelines specified in the appropriate style manual?

_____ 62. If you used Latin abbreviations (i.e., e.g., etc.), are they in parentheses, and have you checked for the required punctuation?

_____ 63. If you have used long quotations, are they absolutely necessary?

_____ 64. Does each quotation contribute significantly to the review?

_____ 65. Can any of these quotations be paraphrased?

_____ 66. Did you avoid the use of synonyms for important key terms and concepts?

_____ 67. If you have coined a new term, is it set off in quotations?

_____ 68. Have you avoided slang terms, colloquialisms, and idioms?

_____ 69. Have you avoided using contractions?

_____ 70. Have you included any annotations that are not linked to the path of the argument of your review?

_____ 71. Have you avoided using a series of annotations?

_____ 72. Have you spelled out all acronyms on first mention?

_____ 73. If you have used the first person, is it appropriate?

_____ 74. Have you avoided using sexist language?

_____ 75. If you used numbers in the narrative of your review, did you check to see if you spelled out the numbers zero through nine?

_____ 76. If you used a noun followed by a number to denote a specific place in a sequence, did you capitalize the noun (as in Item 76 of this checklist)?

_____ 77. If you used a number to begin a sentence, did you spell it out?

Grammatical Accuracy

_____ 78. Did you check your manuscript for grammatical correctness?

_____ 79. Is every sentence of your manuscript a complete sentence?

_____ 80. Have you avoided using indirect sentence constructions (as in, "In Galvan's study, it was found….")?

_____ 81. Have you been consistent in your use of tenses (e.g., if you use the present tense in describing one study's findings, do you use this same tense throughout, unless you are commenting on the historical relationship among studies)?

_____ 82. Have you checked for the proper use of commas and other punctuation marks?

_____ 83. Have you attempted to avoid using complicated sentence structures?

_____ 84. If you have any long sentences (e.g., several lines), have you attempted to break them down into two or more sentences?

_____ 85. If you have any long paragraphs (e.g., a page or longer), have you attempted to break them down into two or more paragraphs?

Additional Editing Steps for Non-Native English Speakers and Students with Serious Writing Difficulties

_____ 86. If your proficiency in English is not at a high level, have you asked a proof-reader for assistance?

_____ 87. Have you checked the entire manuscript for the proper article (e.g., a, an, the) usage?

_____ 88. Have you checked the manuscript for proper use of prepositions?

_____ 89. Have you checked each sentence for proper subject–verb agreement?

_____ 90. Have you checked the manuscript for the proper use of idiomatic expressions?

Guidelines Suggested by Your Instructor

_____ 91. _____

_____ 92. _____

_____ 93. _____

_____ 94. _____

_____ 95. _____

Notes:

Model Literature Reviews for Discussion and Evaluation

Notes:

MODEL LITERATURE REVIEW A

Maintaining Change Following Eating Disorder Treatment[1]

One of your eating disorder clients is nearing her date of discharge, and she tells you that she is worried about being able to maintain the changes that she worked so hard to make during her admission. She tells you that her family and friends also worry that she may relapse. You suggest that she keep a log of her thoughts and feelings in a journal, use the coping skills she has developed in the program, follow her meal plan, maintain appointments with her therapist, and join a support group in the community. However, deep down you share the uncertainty about her ability to choose non-eating disorder coping strategies when her distress level runs high. You consider keeping her in the program longer, but even if this were feasible, you are aware that this may simply delay the inevitable. Is there anything that you can do to help her with this inherently destabilizing transition? Is there anything that you can say to help her maintain the changes she has made? Is there anything that you can recommend to outpatient practitioners who will provide her with follow-up care?

There is a growing body of research investigating ways to enhance readiness to change eating disorder behaviors (Cockell, Geller, & Linden, 2002, 2003; Geller, Williams, & Srikameswaran, 2001; Treasure & Schmidt, 2001; Vitousek, Watson, & Wilson, 1998), but relatively little attention has been given to an equally important topic—how to promote the maintenance of change once it has been achieved. Learning more about this critical phase of change is important, as relapse rates in eating disorders are reported to range from 33% to 63% (Field et al., 1997; Herzog et al., 1999; Keel & Mitchell, 1997; Olmstead, Kaplan, & Rockert, 1994), and repeated admissions to treatment programs are common (Woodside, Kohn, & Kerr, 1998).

High relapse and readmission rates are understandable when the challenges of treating eating disorders are acknowledged. First, eating disorders have a tremendous impact on physical, psychological, and social systems, all of which need to be considered when working with clients. Accordingly, many physicians welcome collaboration with psychologists and other mental health professionals because they recognize that medical interventions alone do not address the powerful psychological underpinnings of the disorder. Likewise, nonmedical professionals often seek permission to consult with a client's general practitioner, because they recognize that some of the presenting symptoms (e.g., fatigue, sleep disturbance, cognitive impairment, obsessive thinking) can be explained best by malnutrition and that the malnutrition needs to be closely monitored and addressed. The coordination of medical and nonmedical treatment is not always available, however, and as a result, clients receive less than optimal interventions, which may account for poor prognosis.

Second, most individuals with eating disorders present with multiple problems. For instance, many clients report comorbid depressive, anxiety, and/or substance abuse disorders, and some report self-harm and/or suicidal ideation. These individuals may also have rigid interpersonal styles (e.g., passive, dependent, borderline) and defense strategies (e.g., magnification, minimization, displacement of emotions onto the body) that support their eating disorders. At a deeper level, core beliefs (e.g., I am not good enough; something is wrong with me; I never fit in) and difficult life experiences that have contributed to the development of these beliefs need to be addressed. Given these issues, it is not surprising that recovery from an eating disorder takes a great deal of time and commitment (Strober, Freeman, & Morrell, 1997). The unfortunate reality, however, is that intensive treatment programs tend to be time limited, and even when longer periods of treatment are available, clients often have trouble completing the treatment.

Third, individuals with eating disorders tend to be ambivalent about treatment and recovery. This is not surprising given that the eating disorder often represents an individual's best attempt to cope. Many negative consequences may be identified, but the functional value of the eating disorder tends to outweigh the cost. Each person's reasons for engaging in eating disorder behaviors vary, but there seems to be a general theme of avoidance coping. Typical areas of avoidance include thoughts and feelings related to difficult early life experiences, as well as current intra- and interpersonal conflict and distress (Cockell et al., 2003). Thus, recovery requires not only developing new ways of thinking and behaving in relation to eating, shape, and weight, but addressing core issues with new coping strategies. When one takes these various

---

[1] Literature review excerpt from: Cockell, S. J., Zaitsoff, S. L., & Geller, J. (2004). Maintaining change following eating disorder treatment. *Professional Psychology: Research and Practice*, 35, 527–534. Copyright © 2004 by the American Psychological Association. All rights reserved. Reprinted with permission.

95 factors into consideration, it is not surprising that the process of recovery is often slow and bumpy.

What Supports Recovery?

Although recovery from an eating disorder is an enormous challenge, many individuals do attain partial or full recovery. For instance, in one of the more comprehensive assessments of treatment outcome, Strober
100 et al. (1997) found that 76% of individuals were free of the physical and cognitive-behavioral signs of their eating disorder at completion of follow-up, some 10 to 15 years after initial assessment for specialized treatment. It is important to note, however, that the process
105 toward both partial and full recovery is protracted. Although eating disorder symptoms are reduced by the end of treatment, the probabilities of partial or full recovery are only 10% and 0%, respectively, 2 years following hospitalization, and they are 21% and 1%,
110 respectively, at the end of 3 years. At the end of 4 years, recovery rates rise and continue to accelerate fairly steadily until 6 years follow-up, at which point they decelerate. Rates then rise again after 8 years and finally reach a plateau after 10 years (Strober et al.,
115 1997).

While it is well-understood that the course of recovery from an eating disorder is slow, what remains unclear is an understanding of what factors support a favorable outcome. A small number of published
120 qualitative studies have assessed factors that assist clients in their recovery process (Beresin, Gordon, & Herzog, 1989; Hsu, Crisp, & Callender, 1992; Pettersen & Rosenvinge, 2002; Rorty, Yager, & Rossotto, 1993). Participants in these studies had a past diagno-
125 sis of anorexia nervosa or bulimia nervosa, and assessments were conducted between 1 and 20 years posttreatment. With the exception of one study (Hsu et al., 1992), semistructured interviews were audiotaped and transcribed, and responses were coded according
130 to a categorical system developed by author consensus. Two general findings emerged from these studies. First, social support from professionals, family, and friends was identified as helpful in maintaining recovery behaviors. Having the opportunity to identify and
135 express feelings and to receive empathic, nonjudgmental responses was said to promote movement toward health. Connecting with individuals who had recovered was reported to be particularly helpful, as this contact generated feelings of acceptance and provided
140 hope for the future (Beresin et al., 1989; Pettersen & Rosenvinge, 2002; Rorty et al., 1993). Second, experiences that increased positive emotions and self-esteem were identified as helpful in maintaining change. Clients noted that these positive experiences nurtured an
145 identity separate from the eating disorder, which in turn supported recovery behaviors (Beresin et al.,

1989; Hsu et al., 1992; Pettersen & Rosenvinge, 2002; Rorty et al., 1993).

150 In the most thorough study to date, 30 women (17 recovered, 13 partially recovered) who had received treatment for bulimia nervosa participated in qualitative interviews (Peters & Fallon, 1994). Their responses were coded according to content, sorted by computer, and analyzed for themes and response pat-
155 terns. Levels of recovery ranged along three continua from denial, alienation, and passivity at one end to reality, connection, and personal power, respectively, at the other. The continuum from denial to reality reflected the cognitive and emotional shifts that occur in
160 response to eating and appearance issues. This included challenging distorted beliefs about nutrition and evaluating shape and weight more accurately. The continuum from alienation to connection reflected an improvement in communication and relationships.
165 This included talking openly about the eating disorder, being assertive in social situations, and taking on new interpersonal roles. The continuum from passivity to personal power reflected an increasing sense of capability to change and control one's future. These find-
170 ings intuitively fit well with those identified in other relevant studies. For instance, the ability to connect with others is likely related to the establishment of social supports, and personal power is likely related to positive emotions, self-esteem enhancement, and iden-
175 tity development. Moreover, these findings add to the literature by suggesting how these factors promote recovery. This focus on the process of change and maintenance merits further investigation and discussion, particularly in the context of generating clinical
180 practice guidelines for professionals working with clients who are in the later stages of change (see the transtheoretical model of change; Prochaska, DiClemente, & Norcross, 1992).

What Hinders Recovery?

We found two published qualitative studies of
185 factors that interfered with recovery. In a study of 40 women who had recovered from bulimia nervosa, a lack of understanding from partners, friends, or family and societal insensitivity to eating disorders were identified as barriers to recovery (Rorty et al., 1993). Simi-
190 larly, a study of 13 women who had recovered from anorexia nervosa also identified lack of social support as an impediment to recovery (Beresin et al., 1989). This second study revealed a number of other factors that interfered with recovery, including the following:
195 (a) spending too much time in therapy focusing on parent shortcomings and related angry feelings, as opposed to understanding parent limitations and working toward forgiveness; (b) being told covertly or explicitly how to appear, feel, or think; (c) comparing
200 oneself to other "skeletons" and competing for the role

of most impaired; and (d) learning bad habits (e.g., water loading before being weighed, purging techniques) from fellow patients. Given the lack of research in this area, replication studies are needed to assess the extent to which these findings generalize to other samples and can be incorporated into professional practice recommendations.

In summary, although few research studies have examined the maintenance of change in eating disorders, a few findings are noteworthy. Three factors are consistently mentioned as helpful in promoting lasting change: (a) social factors, including adopting an assertive style and establishing effective social supports; (b) cognitive factors, including challenging core beliefs about eating, shape, and weight; and (c) affective factors, including enhancing positive emotions, especially a sense of empowerment and hope for the future. The only factor consistently identified as impeding recovery is lack of effective social support. The extent to which these findings apply to clients who have recently completed treatment is not known. However, the answer to this question has great clinical value because the period immediately following discharge has been identified as challenging (Fichter & Quadflieg, 1996; Herzog et al., 1999; Olmstead et al., 1994; Woodside et al., 1998) and a time when individuals are most prone to slips and relapse (Strober et al., 1997). The purpose of this study was to identify factors that help or hinder the maintenance of change and the ongoing promotion of recovery during the critical 6 months immediately following eating disorder treatment. The use of qualitative methodology was selected so that a highly detailed account of clients' phenomenological experiences could be obtained and examined.

References

Beresin, E. V., Gordon, C., & Herzog, D. B. (1989). The process of recovering from anorexia nervosa. *Journal of the American Academy of Psychoanalysis, 17,* 103–130.

Cockell, S. J., Geller, J., & Linden, W. (2002). The development of a decisional balance scale for anorexia nervosa. *European Eating Disorders Review, 10,* 359–375.

Cockell, S. J., Geller, J., & Linden, W. (2003). Decisional balance in anorexia nervosa: Capitalizing on the ambivalence. *European Eating Disorders Review, 11,* 75–89.

Fichter, M. M., & Quadflieg, N. (1996). Course and two-year outcome in anorexic and bulimic adolescents. *Journal of Youth and Adolescence, 25,* 545–562.

Field, A. E., Herzog, D. B., Keller, M. B., West, J., Nussbaum, K., & Colditz, G. A. (1997). Distinguishing recovery from remission in a cohort of bulimic women: How should asymptomatic periods be described? *Journal of Clinical Epidemiology, 50,* 1339–1345.

Geller, J., Williams, K., & Srikameswaran, S. (2001). Clinician stance in the treatment of chronic eating disorders. *European Eating Disorders Review, 9,* 365–373.

Herzog, D. B., Dorer, D. J., Keel, P. K., Selwyn, S. E., Ekeblad, E. R., Flores, A. T. et al. (1999). Recovery and relapse in anorexia and bulimia nervosa: A 7.5 year follow-up study. *Journal of the American Academy of Child and Adolescent Psychiatry, 38,* 829–837.

Hsu, L., Crisp, A. H., & Callender, J. S. (1992). Recovery in anorexia nervosa: The patient's perspective. *International Journal of Eating Disorders, 11,* 341–350.

Keel, P. K., & Mitchell, J. E. (1997). Outcome in bulimia nervosa. *American Journal of Psychiatry, 154,* 313–321.

Olmstead, M. P., Kaplan, A. S., & Rockert, W. (1994). Rate and prediction of relapse in bulimia nervosa. *American Journal of Psychiatry, 151,* 738–743.

Peters, L., & Fallon, P. (1994). The journey of recovery: Dimensions of change. In P. Fallon, M. Katzman, & S. Wooley (Eds.), *Feminist perspectives on eating disorders* (pp. 339–354). New York: Guilford Press.

Pettersen, G., & Rosenvinge, J. H. (2002). Improvement and recovery from eating disorders: A patient perspective. *Eating Disorders: The Journal of Treatment and Prevention, 10,* 61–71.

Prochaska, J. O., DiClemente, C. C., & Norcross, J. C. (1992). In search of how people change. *American Psychologist, 47,* 1102–1114.

Rorty, M., Yager, J., & Rossotto, E. (1993). Why and how do women recover from bulimia nervosa? The subjective appraisals of forty women recovered for a year or more. *International Journal of Eating Disorders, 14,* 249–260.

Strober, M., Freeman, R., & Morrell, W. (1997). The long-term course of severe anorexia nervosa in adolescence: Survival analysis of recovery, relapse, and outcome predictors over 10–15 years in a prospective study. *International Journal of Eating Disorders, 22,* 339–360.

Treasure, J., & Schmidt, U. (2001). Ready, willing and able to change: Motivational aspects of the assessment and treatment of eating disorders. *European Eating Disorders Review, 9,* 4–18.

Vitousek, K. B., Watson, S., & Wilson, G. T. (1998). Enhancing motivation for change in treatment-resistant eating disorders. *Clinical Psychology Review, 18,* 391–420.

Woodside, D. B., Kohn, M., & Kerr, A. (1998). Patterns of relapse and recovery following intensive treatment for eating disorders: A qualitative description. *Eating Disorders: The Journal of Treatment and Prevention, 6,* 231–239.

About the authors: *Sarah J. Cockell* received her PhD in clinical psychology in 2001 from the University of British Columbia. She is currently the coordinator of the Quest Program at the St. Paul's Hospital Eating Disorders Program in Vancouver, as well as working in private practice. Her current research interests are ambivalence about change, relapse prevention, eating disorders, and quality of life. *Shannon L. Zaitsoff* received her MA in child clinical psychology from the University of Windsor in Ontario. She is currently working on her PhD. Her current area of research is readiness and motivation for change in adolescents with eating disorders. *Josie Geller* received her PhD in clinical psychology from the University of British Columbia in 1996. She is currently the director of research at the St. Paul's Hospital Eating Disorders Program and an associate professor in the Department of Psychiatry at the University of British Columbia. Her current research interests are motivational interviewing, clinician stance, eating disorders, and HIV.

Acknowledgment: This research was supported by a grant from the British Columbia Health Research Foundation.

Address correspondence to: Sarah J. Cockell, c/o Eating Disorders Program, St. Paul's Hospital, 1081 Burrard Street, Vancouver, British Columbia, Canada, V6Z 1Y6. E-mail: scockell@providencehealth.bc.ca

MODEL LITERATURE REVIEW B

Office versus Home-Based Family Therapy for Runaway, Alcohol-Abusing Adolescents: Examination of Factors Associated with Treatment Attendance[1]

Even when substance-abusing individuals contact a treatment system, early drop-out is a significant problem. Lawendowski (1998) suggested that adolescents tend to be more ambivalent and resistant to change. Indeed, Szapocznik, Perez-Vidal, Brickman, Foote, Santisteban, Hervis, and Kurtines (1988), in a study of treatment engagement, found that 62% of youth between the ages of 12 and 21 years refused to attend treatment sessions. Several studies have examined the relationship between age and dropout rates directly and some found evidence that, along the age continuum of substance abusers, youth is linked to higher treatment dropout rates (Ball, Lange, Meyers, & Friedman, 1988; Feigelman, 1987).

The general consensus is that runaway youth are difficult to engage and maintain in therapy (Morrissette, 1992; Smart & Ogborne, 1994) and are "difficult to work with" (Kufeldt & Nimmo, 1987). Given that treatment attendance is often a complicating factor for successful treatment outcome (Institute of Medicine, 1990), and that few studies have examined predictors of treatment attendance among runaway youth and their families, further research in this area is needed to help guide treatment providers. This paper examines factors associated with treatment attendance among alcohol-abusing runaway youth and their families utilizing a home-based versus office-based family therapy intervention.

Runaway youth are beset with many problems, including physical and sexual abuse, high levels of alcohol and drug use, depression, teen pregnancy, and frequent prostitution (Johnson, Aschkenasy, Herbers, & Gillenwater, 1996; Zimet, Sobo, Zimmerman, Jackson, Mortimer, Yanda, & Lazebnik, 1995). The alcohol abuse rate of runaway and homeless youths is estimated to range from 70% to 85% (Rotheram-Borus, Selfridge, Koopman, Haignere, Meyer-Bahlburg, & Ehrhardt, 1989; Shaffer & Caton, 1984; Yates, MacKenzie, Pennbridge, & Cohen, 1988), and the level of alcohol involvement in runaways is at least double that of school youths (Forst & Crim, 1994). Limited evidence suggests that rates of alcohol abuse are similar to rates reported among homeless adults (Robertson, 1989). Runaway and homeless youth use alcohol at a younger age and experience greater impaired social functioning owing to alcohol use compared to nonhomeless adolescents (Kipke, Montgomery, & MacKenzie, 1993). Even given their severe alcohol abuse and related problem behaviors, one study determined that only 15% of this population of youth had ever received treatment for alcohol problems (Robertson, 1989).

Research suggests that family disturbance is highly correlated to the act of running away; hence, family therapy is identified as an important treatment to evaluate with this population. Engaging parents in counseling is almost always advisable given their involvement in precipitating the running-away behavior (Rohr & James, 1994), an obvious role in reunification with their child. In fact, Teare, Furst, Peterson, and Authier (1992) found that in their sample of shelter youths, those not reunified with their family had higher levels of hopelessness, suicide ideation, and reported more family problems than those reunified. Youths' perceptions of family dysfunction were significantly associated with reunification and those not reunified were at greater risk of suicide, had more overall dissatisfaction with life, and more generalized negative expectations about the future.

Post and McCoard (1994) found that during a crisis, runaway youths and families may be more amenable than usual to counseling, and the need for intervention is intense, with the timing (when they have sought help at a shelter) critical. These researchers also noted that runaways who go to shelters, unlike many, are asking for help. Their reported greatest needs concerned living arrangements, family relationships, and communication with their parents.

Reviews of formal clinical trials of family-based treatments consistently found that more drug-abusing adolescents enter, engage in, and remain in family therapy longer than in other modalities (Liddle & Dakof, 1995; Waldron, 1997). However, few studies have directly compared family therapy models, making conclusions about the superiority of one approach over another difficult. Moreover, researchers have noted

---

limited variation in theoretical orientation across models (Stanton & Shadish, 1997). For example, the vast majority of family-based interventions (i.e., traditional approaches) for substance abuse problems focus on family interaction patterns and parenting behaviors as major targets of change. The two approaches examined in this paper include the office-based Functional Family Therapy (FFT) and Ecologically Based Family Therapy (EBFT), which is conducted in the home.

Functional Family Therapy (FFT; Barton & Alexander, 1981; Alexander & Parsons, 1982) has a family systems conceptual base. Similar to other systems models, problems with alcohol and drugs are viewed as behaviors which occur in the context of and have meaning for family relationships. FFT has received considerable research attention during the past 30 years. It was initially developed and empirically supported for crisis intervention with juvenile offenders, including runaway adolescents and their families (Alexander, 1971). Alexander and his colleagues conducted several treatment outcome studies examining the effectiveness of FFT with runaway and status delinquents in reducing out-of-home placement, improving parent–child process, and reducing negativity using a 12-week format (Alexander, 1971; Alexander & Parsons, 1973; Barton, Alexander, Waldron, Turner, & Warburton, 1985). In these studies, FFT made significantly more improvements in adolescent and family functioning compared to individual therapy, a client-centered family therapy approach and a control group with minimal attention from probation officers.

EBFT is a multisystemic, home-based treatment based on the recognition that substance use and other related problem behaviors derive commonly from many sources of influence and occur in the context of multiple systems. It is based largely on family systems (Haley, 1976; Minuchin, 1974) conceptualizations of behavior, and behavior change. EBFT posits that behavior problems can be maintained by problematic transactions within any given system or between some combination of pertinent systems, including the intrapersonal system of the individual adolescent, the interpersonal systems of the family and peers, and the extra-personal systems of the shelter, juvenile justice system, school, and the community.

In-home therapy has been successful with families assessed as disorganized, chaotic, and with few resources (Henggeler, Borduin, Melton, Mann, Smith, Hall, Cone, & Fucci, 1991). Henggeler et al. (1991) noted that home-based interventions are particularly successful in facilitating treatment engagement of multiproblem youth. That is, working with the family in their home and in their neighborhood allows the assessment of multiple ecological influences impacting the adolescent and family. In-home sessions also allow the intervention to be perceived as a natural process and enhances treatment engagement and acceptability (Henggeler et al., 1991; Joanning, Thomas, Quinn, & Millen, 1992; Kazdin, Stolar, & Marciano, 1995). A high percentage of missed or canceled office-based appointments occurs because a family does not have reliable transportation or because the meeting time conflicts with a parent's work schedule (Henggeler & Borduin, 1995). These authors note that a therapist's time is often used most efficiently when sessions are conducted in the family's home, as it is much easier for unmotivated families to ignore an appointment at a clinic than to ignore the therapist who knocks at their door at the scheduled time.

It is expected that treatment engagement and overall attendance will be significantly higher for families assigned to the home-based intervention, as it removes many barriers for chaotic and disadvantaged families that otherwise would preclude their attendance in the session, as noted by Henggeler et al. (1991). Thus, based upon the theoretical model of home-based therapy, we expected that lower income, more family chaos, and more adolescent problem behaviors (externalizing behaviors and substance use) would predict higher treatment attendance for the home-based compared to the office-based intervention.

References

Alexander, J. F. (1971). *Evaluation summary: Family groups treatment program.* Report to Juvenile Court, District 1, State of Utah, Salt Lake City.

Alexander, J. F., & Parsons, B. V. (1973). Short-term behavioral intervention with delinquent families: Impact on family process and recidivism. *Journal of Abnormal Psychology, 81,* 219–225.

Alexander, J. F., & Parsons, B. V. (1982). *Functional family therapy: Principles and procedures.* Carmel, CA: Brooks/Cole.

Ball, J. C., Lange, W. R., Meyers, C. P., & Friedman, S. R. (1988). Reducing the risk of AIDS through methadone maintenance treatment. *Journal of Health and Social Behavior, 29,* 214–226.

Barton, C., & Alexander, J. F. (1981). Functional family therapy. In A. S. Gurman & D. P. Kniskern (Eds.), *Handbook of family therapy* (pp. 403–443). New York: Brunner/Mazel.

Barton, C., Alexander, J. F., Waldron, H., Turner, C. W., & Warburton, J. (1985). Generalizing treatment effects of Functional Family Therapy: Three replications. *American Journal of Family Therapy, 17,* 335–347.

Feigelman, W. (1987). Day-care treatment for multiple drug abusing adolescents: Social factors linked with completing treatment. *Journal of Psychoactive Drugs, 19,* 335–344.

Forst, M. L., & Crim, D. (1994). A substance use profile of delinquent and homeless youths. *Journal of Drug Education, 24,* 219–231.

Haley, J. (1976). *Problem-solving therapy.* San Francisco: Jossey-Bass.

Henggeler, S. W., & Borduin, C. M. (1995). Multisystemic treatment of serious juvenile offenders and their families. In I. M. Scwartz and P. AuClaire (Eds.), *Home-based services for troubled children.* Lincoln: University of Nebraska Press.

Henggeler, S. W., Borduin, C. M., Melton, G. B., Mann, B. J., Smith L. A., Hall, J. A., Cone, L., & Fucci, B. R. (1991). Effects of multisystemic therapy on drug use and abuse in serious juvenile offenders: A progress report from two outcome studies. *Family Dynamics of Addiction Quarterly, 1,* 40–51.

Institute of Medicine (1990). *Treating drug problems (Vol. 1.).* Washington, DC: National Academy Press.

Joanning, H., Thomas, F., Quinn, W., & Millen, R. (1992). Treating adolescent drug abuse: A comparison of family systems therapy, group therapy, and family drug education. *Journal of Marital and Family Therapy, 18,* 345–356.

Johnson, T. P., Aschkenasy, J. R., Herbers, M. R., & Gillenwater, S. A. (1996). Self-reported risk factors for AIDS among homeless youth. *AIDS Education and Prevention, 8,* 308–322.

Kazdin, A. E., Stolar, M. J., Marciano, P. L. (1995). Risk factors for dropping out of treatment among white and black families. *Journal of Family Psy-*

chology: JFP: Journal of the Division of Family Psychology of the American Psychological Association (Division 43), *9*, 402–416.

Kipke, M., Montgomery, S., & MacKenzie, R. (1993) Substance use among youth seen at a community-based health clinic. *Journal of Adolescent Health*, *14*, 289–294.

Kufeldt, K., & Nimmo, M. (1987). Youth on the street: Abuse and neglect in the eighties. *Child Abuse and Neglect*, *11*, 531–543.

Lawendowski, L. A. (1998). A motivational intervention for adolescent smokers. *Preventive Medicine*, *27*, A39.

Liddle, H. A., & Dakof, G. A. (1995). Family-based treatment for adolescent drug use: State of the science. *NIDA Research Monograph*, *156*, 218–254.

Minuchin, S. (1974). *Families and family therapy*. Cambridge: Harvard University Press.

Morrissette, P. (1992). Engagement strategies with reluctant homeless young people. *Psychotherapy*, *29*, 447–451.

Post, P., & McCoard, D. (1994). Needs and self-concept of runaway adolescents. *The School Counselor*, *41*, 212–219.

Robertson, M. (1989). *Homeless youth in Hollywood: Patterns of alcohol use*. A report of the National Institute on Alcohol Abuse and Alcoholism. Berkeley, CA: Alcohol Research Group, School of Public Health, University of Southern California.

Rohr, M. E., & James, R. (1994). Runaways: Some suggestions for prevention, coordinating services, and expediting the reentry process. *The School Counselor*, *42*, 40–47.

Rotheram-Borus, M. J., Selfridge, C., Koopman, C., Haignere, C., Meyer-Bahlburg, H. F. L., & Ehrhardt, A. (1989). The relationship of knowledge and attitudes towards AIDS to safe sex practices among runaway and gay adolescents. In *Abstracts: V International Conference on AIDS*. Ottawa, Ontario, Canada: International Development Research Centre, p. 728. *Runaway and homeless youth and programs that serve them*. Washington, DC

Shaffer, D., & Caton, C. L. M. (1984). *Runaway and homeless youth in New York City*. A report to the Ittleson Foundation, New York City.

Smart, R. G., & Ogborne, A. C. (1994). Street youth in substance abuse treatment: Characteristics and treatment compliance. *Adolescence*, *29*, 733–745.

Stanton, M. D., & Shadish, W. R. (1997). Outcome, attrition, and family-couples treatment for drug abuse: A meta-analysis and review of the controlled, comparative studies. *Psychological Bulletin*, *122*, 170–191.

Szapocznik, J., Perez-Vidal, A., Brickman, A. L., Foote, F. H., Santisteban, D. A., Hervis, O. E., & Kurtines, W. M. (1988). Engaging adolescent drug abusers and their families into treatment: A strategic structural systems approach. *Journal of Consulting and Clinical Psychology*, *56*, 552–557.

Teare, J. F., Furst, D. W., Peterson, R. W., & Authier, K. (1992). Family reunification following shelter placement: Child, family, and program correlates. *American Journal of Orthopsychiatry*, *62*, 142–146.

Waldron, H. B. (1997). Adolescent substance abuse and family therapy outcome: A review of randomized trials (pp. 199–234). In T. H. Ollendick & R. J. Prinz (Eds.), *Advances in clinical child psychology* (Vol. 19). New York: Plenum.

Yates, G. L., MacKenzie, R., Pennbridge, J., & Cohen, E. (1988). A risk profile comparison of runaway and non-runaway youth. *American Journal of Public Health*, *78*, 820–821.

Zimet, G. D., Sobo, E. J., Zimmerman, T., Jackson, J., Mortimer, J., Yanda, C. P., & Lazebnik, R. (1995). Sexual behavior, drug use, and AIDS knowledge among Midwestern runaways. *Youth and Society*, *26*, 450–462.

About the authors: Natasha Slesnick and Jillian Prestopnik are affiliated with The University of New Mexico, Center on Alcoholism, Substance Abuse and Addictions (CASAA).

Acknowledgment: This work was supported by a NIAAA and CSAT grant (R01 AA 12173).

Address correspondence to: Natasha Slesnick, The University of New Mexico, Center on Alcoholism, Substance Abuse and Addictions, 2650 Yale SE, Suite 200, Albuquerque, NM 87106. E-mail: tash@unm.edu

Distinguishing Features of Emerging Adulthood: The Role of Self-Classification As an Adult[1]

Until the late 1990s, researchers (e.g., Greene, Wheatley, & Aldava, 1992; Hogan & Astone, 1986) have specified events such as marriage, completion of education, and starting a career as markers of adulthood. However, recent research (e.g., Arnett, 1997), which employs self-report formats, reveals that those individuals who are actually in the process of making the transition to adulthood do not consider marriage and other events as important markers or criteria for adulthood. Instead, these studies of 18- to 25-year-olds have found that young people use more internal and individualistic qualities as their criteria for adulthood, which include taking responsibility for one's actions, independent decision making, and financial independence from parents. Besides having these criteria for adulthood, 18- to 25-year-olds (a) are becoming increasingly devoted to individualistic-oriented, rather than other-oriented, goals; (b) are experimenting with work, relationships, and worldviews; (c) lack specific transitional roles that prepare them for adult roles; (d) are entering into increasingly intimate, nonmarital relationships; and (e) are engaging in relatively high rates of risky behaviors, such as unprotected intercourse, illegal drug use, and driving while drunk (see Arnett, 2000). Given the length and changing nature of this part of young people's lives, Arnett (2000) has argued that this is a new and distinct developmental period that he has labeled emerging adulthood.

One of the most convincing pieces of evidence that emerging adulthood is a unique period in development is the ambivalence that emerging adults have about their own status as adults. When asked whether they have reached adulthood, young people between the ages of 18 and 25 tend to respond with "in some respects yes, in some respects no" (e.g., Arnett, 1997, 2001; Nelson, 2003). This reflects the transitional nature of this time of their lives; they know that they have left adolescence, but at the same time they do not yet feel that they have taken on adult roles. It is not until the late 20s and early 30s that a clear majority of people consider themselves to be adults (Arnett, 2000).

However, there are some 18- to 25-year-old individuals who do consider themselves to be adults (e.g., Arnett, 1997, 1998, 2001; Nelson, 2003). Although they are clearly the minority within this age group, they represent a unique group that is worthy of investigation. They stand out because they perceive themselves as adults at an age when the majority of their peers do not. This finding gives rise to the question of how they differ from their peers. Furthermore, it is unclear whether they have different criteria that they use to define themselves as adults. If these individuals are employing different criteria, it would be interesting to know what those criteria are. If these individuals are using the same criteria, it would be important to know if they indeed believe that they have achieved those criteria. Finally, questions exist as to whether these self-perceived adults differ from their emerging-adult peers in attitudes and behaviors that are characteristic of this developmental period (e.g., identity issues, risk-taking behaviors). Thus, this study sought to identify a subset of 18- to 25-year-old perceived adults and compare them to their emerging-adult peers to see whether they (a) use the same criteria for adulthood, (b) believe that they have achieved those criteria, and (c) are different on three significant emerging-adulthood issues (identity issues, risk-taking behaviors, and depression).

Defining Features of Emerging Adulthood
Criteria for Adulthood

The first question that may be asked of those 18- to 25-year-old individuals who consider themselves to be adults is whether they use the same criteria for adult status as their emerging-adult peers. As previously noted, recent research done primarily in the United States reveals that emerging adults do not consider marriage and other events as important markers or criteria for adulthood. Instead, young people use more internal and individualistic qualities as criteria for adulthood, which include taking responsibility for one's actions, independent decision making, and financial independence from parents (Arnett, 1997, 1998, 2001; Greene et al., 1992), (including in various cultural subgroups within the United States such as ethnic minority groups [Arnett, 2001] and religious subgroups) (Nelson, 2003). Taken together, studies of young people predominantly from individualistic cultures suggest that the theme of independence (e.g., financial independence, independent decision making) is a general feature in the process of becoming adults.

However, although investigators have repeatedly found these criteria to be mentioned as the measuring sticks for adulthood, most of the respondents in these past studies who have listed these current standards as their criteria for adulthood have been individuals who did not yet perceive themselves as adults (i.e., they perceived themselves as emerging adults). In other words, no study has systematically compared those young people who consider themselves to be adults with those who do not. It would be important to compare these groups to determine whether they use the same criteria for adulthood. Thus, the first purpose of the current study was to explore whether self-perceived adults (ages 18 to 25 years) differed from their emerging-adult peers on the criteria that they use to determine adult status. Given that these criteria have emerged repeatedly across studies as the important factors for determining the transition to adulthood, it was believed that there would be no differences between the groups in the criteria that they use to measure adult status.

Assuming adulthood criteria do not differ as a function of perceived adult status, the next question that arises is whether self-perceived adults believe that they have achieved those criteria. No study has actually examined the extent to which the current criteria for adulthood differentiate self-perceived adults from self-perceived emerging adults. Thus, the second purpose of this study was to examine whether self-perceived adults believe that they have achieved those criteria to a greater extent than have their emerging-adult peers. Given the consistent findings that these are the criteria that young people use to measure adulthood (e. g., Arnett, 1998), it was hypothesized that these individuals would perceive themselves as having reached these criteria to a greater extent than would their peers.

Identity Distinctions

Many theorists and researchers have identified identity formation as a defining feature of the transition to adulthood (see Schwartz, 2001, for a review). For example, Erikson (1950) believed that adolescents go through a period of exploration (possibly lasting into the early 20s; Erikson, 1968) during which they attempt to answer the following question: Who am I, and what is my place in society? After a period of exploration, those who successfully self-chose values and vocational goals achieve identity synthesis, whereas those who are unable to develop a working set of ideals on which to base their identity as adults remain in a state of identity confusion.

Based on Erikson's work, Marcia (1966, 1980, 1988) grouped individuals into four categories that are reflective of the progress they have made toward forming a mature identity. These categories are based on an individual's level of exploration and commitment to a specific set of goals, values, and beliefs, including identity achievement (a period of exploration followed by a commitment), identity moratorium (active exploration without much commitment), identity foreclosure (commitment with little exploration), and identity diffusion (lack of both exploration and commitment). In general, emerging adulthood tends to be characterized as a state of moratorium, extensive exploration with little commitment.

Additional work in this area has extended and expanded on the foundational work of Erikson (1950, 1968) and Marcia (1966, 1980, 1988), including (a) work focusing more specifically on the process of exploration (Grotevant, 1987); (b) conceptualizations of identity styles based on how individuals make decisions on a daily basis (Berzonsky, 1989); (c) the importance of individual skills and abilities in making decisions that influence identity (Kurtines, Azmitia, & Alvarez, 1992); and (d) the capital, or resources, that a person's identity gives him or her (Côté, 1997). Taken together, these perspectives underscore the processes involved in and the importance of acquiring a mature identity going into adulthood.

Exploration during this period of time tends to occur in multiple domains. For example, Côté (1996) identified three domain clusters including psychological (e.g., career choice), interactional (e.g., dating), and social-structural (e.g., politics, morality). Given that emerging adults, especially those in higher education, have few societal roles, responsibilities, and expectations placed on them during these years, they have an extended period of time to explore and try on various possible selves in each of these domains. First, explorations in work can be seen in emerging adults' tendencies to change majors, increasingly attend graduate school (often in fields different from undergraduate paths), participate in short-term volunteer jobs (e.g., Americorps, Peace Corps), and travel to various places in the country or the world as part of work or educational experiences (Arnett, 2000). Second, explorations in love can be observed in that romantic relationships during these years tend to last longer than in adolescence (but still tend not to be long-term relationships or include marriage), are likely to include sexual intercourse, and may include cohabitation (Michael, Gagnon, Laumann, & Kolata, 1995). Finally, research shows that emerging adults explore worldviews (Arnett, 1997; Pascarella & Terenzini, 1991) and religious beliefs (Arnett & Jensen, 2002; Hoge, Johnson, & Luidens, 1993), with many often changing from the views in which they were raised (Perry, 1970/1999).

Given the importance of identity exploration during emerging adulthood, the third purpose of this study was to compare perceived adults and perceived emerg-

ing adults in the extent to which they were exploring their identity. Specifically, the two groups were com-
200 pared in their progress toward identity resolution of values and beliefs, career, romantic partner, and an overall sense of self. Because identity exploration is 255 such a focus of emerging adulthood, it was expected that those individuals who feel a sense of instability in
205 regard to who they are would be less likely to consider themselves to be adults. Hence, it was expected that compared to perceived emerging adults, perceived 260 adults would have a stronger sense of their identity with respect to their values or beliefs, career, romantic
210 partner, and overall sense of self.

Depression

Because emerging adulthood is a time of experi-mentation and exploration, for some, it may also be a 265 time of instability and uncertainty. The lack of roles and responsibilities, coupled with the search for iden-
215 tity, may lead to a sense of ambivalence. Such instabil-ity and ambivalence may give rise to depression. In-deed, studies have found that depression is a growing 270 problem across college campuses in the United States (O'Conner, 2001). Whether this is because of in-
220 creased reporting of the problem or changing aspects of the age period is unclear, but it is possible that heightened instability and exploration may be related 275 to depression for some individuals.

According to adolescents, some of the perceived
225 causes of their depression include psychological harm to the self by others, separation from someone close, conflict with someone close, loneliness, and feelings 280 of incompetence (see Harter, 1999). Based on these potential causes of depression, there are several rea-
230 sons why depression may be an issue of concern dur-ing emerging adulthood, including those attending a university. First, by definition, emerging adulthood is 285 a time during which young people are trying to sepa-rate themselves from their parents. Although an impor-
235 tant process, this renegotiation of the parent–child rela-tionship can be a painful process, too. Furthermore, as emerging adults explore their identity, they often move 290 in and out (i.e., separation) of romantic relationships (Michael et al., 1995). Hence, separation is a recurring
240 theme of this time period, and the attachment literature (Bowlby, 1973) has documented that separation typi-cally fosters depression. Furthermore, separation could 295 very well lead to loneliness, which also could contrib-ute to the possibility of depression (Harter, 1999). Fi-
245 nally, as emerging adults attempt new things and try out possible identities, questions about one's own competence and failures are likely to occur, as seen in 300 research that shows that feelings of incompetence are typical during periods of transition (Wigfield, Eccles,
250 MacIver, Reuman, & Midgley, 1991).

Taken together, there are several aspects of emerging adulthood (e.g., separation, loneliness, ex-ploration, and failure) that lend themselves to the pos-sibility of depression during this time period. Hence, another purpose of this study was to compare per-ceived adults and perceived emerging adults in levels of depression. It was expected that perceived adults would be experiencing less depression because they are experiencing less instability and ambivalence in their lives compared to their emerging-adult peers.

Behavioral Distinctions

In addition to differences in identity development and depression that set emerging adults apart from others, there are numerous behavioral characteristics of emerging adults that distinguish them from adoles-cents and young adults. As described earlier, romantic relationships (nonmarital) tend to include sexual inter-course and often cohabitation (Michael et al., 1995). Furthermore, emerging adulthood (rather than adoles-cence) is the peak period for several risk behaviors, including unprotected sex; most types of substance use, including binge drinking; and risky driving behav-iors, such as driving at high speeds or while intoxi-cated (Arnett, 1992; Bachman, Johnston, O'Malley, & Schulenberg, 1996). Parental monitoring decreases during emerging adulthood, which may be one reason why risk behavior is consistently higher for emerging adults than for adolescents (Arnett, 1998; Bachman et al., 1996). However, research shows that parenting (Barnes & Farrell, 1992; Bogenschneider, Wu, Raf-faelli, & Tsay, 1998), peers (Berndt, 1996), school environment (Kasen, Cohen, & Brook, 1998), religios-ity (Wallace & Williams, 1997), and individual factors such as aggression (Donovan, Umlauf, & Salzberg, 1988) all contribute to risk behaviors in adolescence and emerging adulthood.

Regardless of the reasons why risk behaviors are common during emerging adulthood, they are impor-tant features of this developmental period. An interest-ing finding was that cessation of risk behaviors does not rank at the top of the criteria necessary for adult-hood. Therefore, given the prevalence of risk behav-iors for 18- to 25-year-olds and the relative lack of importance placed on the elimination of risk behaviors to become an adult, it would be useful to know whether perceived adults and emerging adults can be distinguished by their behavior. Because researchers to date have not examined this issue, the final purpose of this study was to examine whether 18- to 25-year-olds who consider themselves to be adults engage in less risk behaviors than do their emerging-adult peers. It was hypothesized that perceived adults would engage in fewer risk behaviors than would emerging adults because perceived maturity of adulthood would be reflected in perceived maturity of behavior.

305   In summary, emerging adulthood (i.e., 18 to 25 years of age) is a new and distinct developmental period defined by ambivalence concerning adult status, individualistic criteria for adulthood, identity exploration, and frequent participation in risk behaviors.

310   Given these unique features that occur between 18 and 25 years of age, it now may be considered atypical to consider oneself an adult during this period of the life span. Thus, there is a need to examine those individuals who do consider themselves to be adults during a

315   time period when it is not expected of them to do so. Therefore, the purpose of this study was to (a) attempt to identify individuals who consider themselves adults at an age when it is developmentally atypical to do so; (b) explore whether they differ from their emerging-

320   adult peers on the criteria that they use for adult status; (c) examine whether they believe they have achieved those criteria; and (d) compare them to their emerging-adult peers on identity development, depression, and risk behaviors (e.g., substance use, drunk driving). It

325   was expected that compared to emerging adults, perceived adults would (a) have the same criteria for adulthood; (b) perceive themselves as having reached those criteria (to a greater extent than their emerging-adult peers); and (c) achieve greater identity formation,

330   experience less depression, and engage in fewer risk behaviors.

References

Arnett. J. J. (1992). Reckless behavior in adolescence: A developmental perspective. *Developmental Review, 12*, 339–373.

Arnett, J. J. (1997). Young people's conceptions of the transition to adulthood. *Youth & Society, 29*, 1–23.

Arnett, J. J. (1998). Learning to stand alone: The contemporary American transition to adulthood in cultural and historical context. *Human Development, 41*, 295–315.

Arnett, J. J. (2000). Emerging adulthood: A theory of development from the late teens through the twenties. *American Psychologist, 55*, 469–480.

Arnett, J. J. (2001). Conceptions of the transition to adulthood: Perspectives from adolescence to midlife. *Journal of Adult Development, 8*, 133–143.

Arnett, J. J. (2001). Conceptions of the transition to adulthood among emerging adults in American ethnic groups. *Journal of Adult Development, 8*, 133–143.

Arnett, J. J., & Jensen, L. A. (2002). A congregation of one: Individualized religious beliefs among emerging adults. *Journal of Adolescent Research, 17*, 451–467.

Bachman, J. G., Johnston, L. D., O'Malley, P., & Schulenberg, J. (1996). Transitions in drug use during late adolescence and young adulthood. In J. A. Graber, J. Brooks-Gunn, & A. C. Petersen (Eds.), *Transitions through adolescence: Interpersonal domains and context*. Mahwah, NJ: Lawrence Erlbaum.

Barnes, G. M., & Farrell, M. P. (1992). Parental support and control as predictors of adolescent drinking, delinquency, and related problem behaviors. *Journal of Marriage and the Family, 54*, 763–776.

Berndt, T. J. (1996). Exploring the effects of friendship quality on social development. In W. M. Bukowski, A. G. Newcomb, & W. W. Hartup (Eds.), *The company they keep*. Cambridge, UK: Cambridge University Press.

Berzonsky, M. D. (1989). Identity style: Conceptualization and measurement. *Journal of Adolescent Research, 4*, 267–281.

Bogenschneider, K., Wu, M., Raffaelli, M., & Tsay, J. C. (1998). Parent influences on adolescent peer orientation and substance use: The interface of parenting practices and values. *Child Development, 69*, 1672–1688.

Bowlby, J. (1973). *Attachment and loss: Separation* (Vol. 2). New York: Basic Books.

Côté, J. E. (1996). An empirical test of the identity capital model. *Journal of Adolescence, 20*, 421–37.

Donovan, D. M., Umlauf, R. L., & Salzberg, P. M. (1988). Derivation of personality subtypes among high risk drivers. *Alcohol, Drugs, and Driving, 4*, 233–244.

Erikson, E. H. (1950). *Childhood and society*. New York: Norton.

Erikson, E. H. (1968). *Identity: Youth and crisis*. New York: Norton.

Greene, A. L., Wheatley, S. M., & Aldava, J. F., IV. (1992). Stages on life's way: Adolescents' implicit theories of the life course. *Journal of Adolescent Research, 7*, 364–381.

Grotevant, H. D. (1987). Toward a process model of identity formation. *Journal of Adolescent Research, 2*, 203–222.

Harter, S. (1999). *The construction of the self*. New York: Guilford.

Hogan, D. P., & Astone, N. M. (1986). The transition to adulthood. *American Sociological Review, 12*, 109–130.

Hoge, D. R., Johnson, B., & Luidens, D. A. (1993). Determinants of church involvement of young adults who grew up in Presbyterian churches. *Journal of the Scientific Study of Religion, 32*, 242–255.

Kasen, S., Cohen, P., & Brook, J. S. (1998). Adolescent school experiences, and dropout, adolescent pregnancy, and young adult deviant behavior. *Journal of Adolescent Research, 13*, 49–72.

Kurtines, W. M., Azmitia, M., & Alvarez, M. (1992). Science, values, and rationality: Philosophy of science from a co-constructivist perspective. In W. M. Kurtines, M. Azmitia, & J. L. Gewirtz (Eds.), *The role of values in psychology and human development* (pp. 3–29). New York: John Wiley.

Marcia, J. E. (1966). Development and validation of ego identity status. *Journal of Personality and Social Psychology, 5*, 551–558.

Marcia, J. E. (1980). Identity in adolescence. In J. Adelson (Ed.), *Handbook of adolescent psychology*. New York: John Wiley.

Marcia, J. E. (1988). Common processes underlying ego identity, cognitive or moral development, and individuation. In D. K. Lapsley & F. C. Power (Eds.), *Self ego, and identity: Integrative approaches* (pp. 211–266). New York/Berlin: Springer-Verlag.

Michael, R. T., Gagnon, J. H., Laumann, E. O., & Kolata, G. (1995). *Sex in America: A definitive survey*. New York: Warner Brooks.

Nelson, L. J. (2003). Rites of passage in emerging adulthood: Perspectives of young Mormons. *New Directions in Child and Adolescent Development, 100*, 33–49.

O'Conner, E. M. (2001). Student mental health: Secondary education no more. *Monitor on Psychology, 32*, 44–47.

Pascarella, E., & Terenzini, P. (1991). *How college affects students: Findings and insights from twenty years of research*. San Francisco: Jossey-Bass.

Perry, W. G. (1999). *Forms of ethical and intellectual development in the college years: A scheme*. San Francisco: Jossey-Bass. (Original work published 1970)

Schwartz, S. J. (2001). The evolution of Eriksonian and neo-Eriksonian identity theory and research: A review and integration. *Identity: An International Journal of Theory and Research, 1*, 7–58.

Wallace, J. M., & Williams, D. R. (1997). Religion and adolescent health-compromising behavior. In J. Schulenberg, J. L. Maggs, & K. Hurrelmann (Eds.), *Health risks and developmental transitions in adolescence* (pp. 444–468). New York: Cambridge University Press.

Wigfield, A., Eccles, J., Mac Iver, D., Reuman, D., & Midgley, C. (1991). Transitions at early adolescence: Changes in children's domain-specific self-perceptions and general self-esteem across the transition to junior high school. *Developmental Psychology, 26*, 552–565.

About the authors: *Larry J. Nelson* is an assistant professor of marriage, family, and human development in the School of Family Life at Brigham Young University. He received his Ph.D. in 2000 from the University of Maryland, College Park. His major research interests are in social and self-development during early childhood and emerging adulthood. *Carolyn McNamara Barry* is an associate professor of psychology at Loyola College in Maryland. She received her Ph.D. in 2001 from the University of Maryland, College Park. Her major research interests are in social and self-development during adolescence and emerging adulthood.

Acknowledgments: The authors express appreciation to the human development and psychology instructors at the University of Maryland, College Park, for their assistance. We also extend our gratitude for the grant support of the College of Family, Home, and Social Sciences and the Family Studies Center at Brigham Young University.

Address correspondence to: Larry J. Nelson, Ph.D., Marriage, Family, and Human Development, School of Family Life, 924 SWKT, Brigham Young University, Provo, UT 84602. E-mail: larry_nelson@byu.edu

Mental Health Professionals' Contact with Family Members of People with Psychiatric Disabilities[1]

Background Literature

Studies drawn from the mental health practice literature called for increased contact with families of mental health consumers as avenues of improved consumer mental health status, decreased treatment costs, and increased family member coping skills (DeChillo, 1993; Falloon, McGill, Boyd, & Pederson, 1987; Hogarty et al., 1991; Lefley, 1994). Werrbach, Jenson, and Bubar (2002) reported that training mental health professionals in family strengths assessment and collaborative practice reduced parent and professional tensions and increased communication between the groups. Family inclusive interventions were developed and studied (i.e., family support groups, psychoeducation, collaboration, consultation, education, and involvement; Heller, Roccoforte, Hsieh, Cook, & Pickett, 1997; St-Onge & Morin, 1998). Family psychoeducation, consisting of a series of meetings with families to discuss mental illness, mental health treatment, community resources, and coping with stressors, showed particular promise. According to Falloon's (1998) research, 20 of 22 controlled studies, including 14 studies that used random assignment, demonstrated that adding family psychoeducation to mental health programs for people with psychiatric disabilities resulted in decreased consumer mental illness symptoms. Falloon (1998) offered further review of the outcomes of family psychoeducation in the mental health literature: "Major exacerbations of psychotic symptoms and admissions to hospitals are more than halved, social disability is reduced, and with increased employment rates, burdens on family caregivers are lowered, and their health improved" (Appendix, p. 1).

Family inclusive interventions incorporate a number of theoretical assumptions. Family members are viewed from a competence paradigm (Marsh, 1994). Competent family members are presumed to be potential sources of social and instrumental support for mental health consumers who are served by a biopsychosocial and cultural model of mental health treatment (Lefley, 1996; Spaniol & Zipple, 2000). At the same time, family members of people with serious mental illnesses are subject to the same stressors as those of individuals with serious physical illnesses; they may experience grief and loss as well as stress, coping, and adaptation responses (Hatfield, 1990). It is assumed that family inclusive interventions are part of effective mental health practice because they support and strengthen family caregivers of people with psychiatric disabilities. Families are strengthened by acquiring knowledge about mental illness, mental health treatment, community resources, and coping strategies. In turn, the process may offer positive outcomes for consumers because stronger social or family support networks may be associated with improved mental health.

Despite two decades of mental health literature recommending family contact and demonstrated positive outcomes reported within studies of family inclusive interventions, little is known about professionals' reported contact with families within today's community-based mental health practice. Several studies found that family relationship information was not collected by mental health agencies (Nicholson, 1994) or available within mental health agencies' family therapy billing records (Dixon et al., 1999). The studies discussed herein include the majority of the published mental health literature about mental health professionals' reported frequency of contact, patterns of contact, facilitators of contact, and barriers of contact with families of people with psychiatric disabilities.

Frequency of Contact

An early study by Smets (1982) found that a majority of staff in a psychiatric hospital reported spending 0 to 1 hour per week with family members. Bernheim and Switalski (1988) indicated that 82% of 350 community- and hospital-based mental health professionals reported spending less than 2 hours per week with family members. St-Onge and Morin (1998) surveyed 266 mental health professionals working in six community and hospital mental health treatment facilities; respondents reported spending about 1 hour per week engaged in interactions with family members (38.5%) or never contacting family members within the last 6 months (34.6%). Wright (1997) found that most of 184 mental health professionals reported a low total family involvement score ($M = 1.44$, $SD = 1.09$). Wright (1997) reported that this family involvement score meant mental health professionals "not very of-

---

[1] Literature review excerpt from: Riebschleger, J. (2005). Mental health professionals' contact with family members of people with psychiatric disabilities. *Families in Society: The Journal of Contemporary Social Services, 86,* 9–16. Copyright © 2005 by the Alliance for Children and Families. All rights reserved. Reprinted with permission.

ten to sometimes" interacted with family members of mental health consumers within a 6-month time period (e.g., listening to families, advocating for families). Dixon, Lucksted, Stewart, and Delhanty (2000) surveyed 36 community mental health center therapists who reported at least one past year contact with a family member for 61% of the mental health consumers they served.

Patterns of Contact

Questions about mental health professionals' reported patterns of contact with family members include the following:

- Who contacts whom?
- What is the most frequent contact mode?
- Which family roles are most involved in the contact interactions?
- What activities take place during the interactions between mental health professionals and family members?

Bernheim and Switalski (1988) reported that mental health professionals' contact with family members primarily consisted of "brief, informal chats and telephone calls" usually initiated by family members or mental health consumers. According to Dixon et al. (2000), 36 mental health professionals said that telephone contact with families was the most frequent mode of communication (87%); family members were most likely to be mothers (26%), siblings (13%), or other (34%). According to Atkinson and Coia (1995), parents and spouses are most likely to serve as primary supports and caregivers for people with serious mental illness. In addition, they noted that primary caregivers tend to be female.

Bernheim and Switalski (1988) asked mental health professionals to describe the types of interactive activities that should take place with family members of mental health consumers (e.g., involving family members in treatment planning, teaching family members coping skills, and getting information about consumers from family members). Wright (1997) built on the work of Bernheim and Switalski (1988); their research asked how frequently mental health professionals reported actually engaging in these specific activities with family members of mental health consumers. In the Wright study (1997), mental health professionals responded "less than sometimes" to the following items: (a) helping families understand the consumer's psychiatric illness, (b) encouraging family members to support the consumer emotionally, (c) helping family members "to set appropriate limits," (d) informing families of the consumer's progress, and (e) encouraging families to accept the consumer's independence. According to Wright (1997), mental health professionals' least frequently reported activities (less than not

very often) were conducting family therapy and advocating to help families obtain needed services. Dixon et al. (2000) found that therapists said their interactions with family members most frequently consisted of helping family members in solving a problem related to the consumer's behavior, providing the family members with emotional support, obtaining information about the consumer for assessment, providing education or information to the family members, and dealing with a crisis situation.

Facilitators of Contact

What factors may facilitate mental health professionals' contact with family members? Using ordinary least squares regression, Wright (1997) found that job and organizational factors were the strongest predictors of family involvement (i.e., working day or evening shifts, working as a therapist or social worker, working with consumers who had more severe psychiatric disabilities, and perceptions that the mental health treatment unit was "functioning more smoothly"). Dixon et al. (2000) reported that contact with families occurred most frequently during mental health consumer psychiatric crises; increased interactions with families were statistically associated with serving younger consumers, a consumer diagnosis of schizophrenia, and mental health services in the form of community outreach teams. Farhall et al. (1998) reported that mental health professionals who participated in an extended training program about family issues increased their contact with consumers' families. DeChillo (1993) developed a Collaboration with Families Scale with data drawn from a sample of 102 family members who had experienced at least one in-person meeting with a social worker. DeChillo (1993) found that increased collaboration among family members and mental health professionals was predicted by a higher number of in-person meetings.

Barriers to Contact

What factors may serve as barriers to family contact? According to Bernheim and Switalski (1988), mental health professionals responded that "sometimes to always" the largest barrier to working with families was lack of time (95%). In Dixon et al.'s (1999) report, mental health professionals listed barriers to the implementation of multifamily group psychoeducation in community-based treatment settings. The most frequent barriers included intense work pressure (95%), uncertainty about financing the interventions (71%), agency bureaucracy (68%), skepticism about the intervention (60%), and confidentiality concerns (45%). In a smaller study, Dixon et al. (2000) found the most frequently reported barrier to contact with families was that the therapist "perceived it would be of no benefit."

References

American Psychiatric Association. (1994). *Diagnostic and statistical manual of mental disorders* (4th ed.). Washington, DC: Author.

Atkinson, J. M., & Coia, D. A. (1995). *Families coping with schizophrenia.* New York: Wiley.

Bernheim, K. F., & Switalski, T. (1988). Mental health staff and patient's relatives: How they view each other. *Hospital and Community Psychiatry, 39,* 63–68.

DeChillo, N. (1993). Collaboration between social workers and families of patients with mental illness. *Families in Society, 74,* 104–115.

Dixon, L., Lucksted, A., Stewart, B., & Delhanty, J. (2000). Therapists' contacts with family members of persons with severe mental illness in a community treatment program. *Psychiatric Services, 51,* 1449–1451.

Dixon, L., Lyles, A., Scott, J., Lehman, A., Postrado, L., Goldman, H., & McGlynn, E. (1999). Services to families of adults with schizophrenia: From treatment recommendations to dissemination. *Psychiatric Services, 50,* 233–238.

Falloon, I. R. H. (1998). Cognitive-behavioural interventions for patients with functional psychoses and their caregivers. In *Families as partners in care* (pp. 1–14). Toronto: World Fellowship for Schizophrenia and Allied Disorders.

Falloon, I. R. H., McGill, C. W., Boyd, J. L., & Pederson, J. (1987). Family management in the prevention of morbidity of schizophrenia: Social outcome of a two-year longitudinal study. *Psychological Medicine, 17,* 59–66.

Farhall, J., Webster, B., Hocking, B., Leggatt, M., Riess, C., & Young, J. (1998). Training to enhance partnerships between mental health professionals and family caregivers: A comparative study. *Psychiatric Services, 49,* 1488–1490.

Hatfield, A. B. (1990). *Family education in mental illness.* New York: Guilford.

Heller, T., Roccoforte, J. A., Hsieh, K., Cook, J. A., & Pickett, S. A. (1997). Benefits of support groups for families of adults with severe mental illness. *American Journal of Orthopsychiatry, 67,* 187–198.

Hogarty, G. E., Anderson, C. M., Reiss, D. I., Kornblith, S. J., Greenwald, D. P., Ulrich, R. F., & Carter, M. (1991). Family psychoeducation, social skills training, and maintenance chemotherapy in the aftercare treatment of schizophrenia: II. Two-year effects of a controlled study on relapse and adjustment. *Archives of General Psychiatry, 48,* 340–347.

Lefley, H. P. (1994). Interventions with families: What have we learned? In A. B. Hatfield (Ed.), *Family interventions in mental illness* (Vol. 62, pp. 89–98). San Francisco: Jossey-Bass.

Lefley, H. P. (1996). Family caregiving in mental illness. In D. E. Biegel & R. Schulz (Series Eds.), *Family caregiver application series* (Vol. 7). Thousand Oaks, CA: Sage.

Marsh, D. T. (1994). Services for families: New modes, models, and interventions strategies. In J. A. Talbott (Series Ed.) & H. P. Lefley & M. Wasow (Vol. Eds.), *Chronic mental illness: Volume 2: Helping families cope with mental illness* (pp. 39–62). Chur, Switzerland: Harwood Academic.

Nicholson, J. (1994). Only sixteen states ask if you're a parent. *OMH News, 6,* 16.

Smets, A. C. (1982). Family and staff attitudes toward family involvement in the treatment of hospitalized chronic patients. *Hospital and Community Psychiatry, 33,* 573–575.

Spaniol, L., & Zipple, A. M. (2000). Changing family roles. In L. Spaniol, A. M. Zipple, D. T. Marsh, & L. Y. Finley (Eds.), *The role of the family in psychiatric rehabilitation* (pp. 29–42). Boston: Center for Psychiatric Rehabilitation, Boston University.

St-Onge, M., & Morin, G. (1998). *La collaboration entre le personnel clinique et les familles de personnes d'âge adulte ayant des incapacitiés: Rapport final.* Quebec: Institut de réadaption en déficience physique de Quebéc and École de service social, Université Laval.

Werrbach, G. B., Jenson, C. E., & Bubar, K. (2002). Collaborative agency training for parent employees and professionals in a new agency addressing children's mental health. *Families in Society, 83,* 457–464.

Wright, E. R. (1997). The impact of organizational factors on mental health professionals' involvement with families. *Psychiatric Services, 48,* 921–927.

About the author: Joanne Riebschleger, Ph.D., ACSW, is assistant professor, School of Social Work, Michigan State University.

Address correspondence to: Joanne Riebschleger, Michigan State University, School of Social Work, 254 Baker Hall, East Lansing, MI 48824-1118. E-mail: riebsch1@msu.edu

The Well-Being of Immigrant Latino Youth: A Framework to Inform Practice[1]

According to the 2000 census, the Latino population living in the United States increased by 58% over 10 years, growing from 22.4 million in 1990 to 35.3 million in 2000 (Schmidley, 2001). As their presence in the United States grows, Latinos are relocating in many areas of the country that have not been traditional destinations for new Latino immigrants, such as the South and the Midwest. As a result, health and social service providers, in both traditional and new receiving communities, are working with increasing numbers of Latino clients. To better serve these clients, helping professionals will need to develop an understanding of the risk and protective factors for Latino youth. In particular because the largest percentage of Latinos living in the United States are immigrants or children of immigrants (Hernandez, 1997; Suarez-Orozco & Suarez-Orozco, 2001), service providers will need to understand the risk and protective factors associated with migration and acculturation.

Research suggests that Latino youth face multiple threats to their well-being, including substance use, poor school functioning, and early adult role-taking. These risks may be particularly acute for children who immigrate later in childhood, especially during adolescence (Portes & Rumbaut, 2001). Despite these risks, additional research suggests that new immigrant Latino families possess certain cultural attitudes and norms that are protective against the many risks that accompany immigration.

In this article, we summarize findings regarding the well-being of Latino youth on domains important to functioning later in life. The summary is followed by a discussion of the psychosocial risks that threaten the successful adaptation of Latino youth in immigrant families and the protective factors that facilitate their adaptation. We argue that the understanding of risk and resiliency among Latino youth can be improved if it is embedded in an ecological framework that more fully accounts for the challenges of immigration. Based on this argument, a framework is proposed to guide helping professionals in assessing the needs of Latino youth.

Status of Latino Youth

Mental Health

Few investigations of the incidence and prevalence of specific mental health diagnoses for Latino youth exist. Most current research compares several ethnic groups on specific diagnostic categories or other measures of well-being. In a multistage probability sample, Shrout et al. (1992) found limited differences between Puerto Rican and mainland Hispanics on a variety of diagnoses. Kleykamp and Tienda (in press) found limited well-being differences between Latino and white youth in a nationally representative sample. In a study of 3,962 ethnic minority youth receiving outpatient mental health services in San Diego, Yeh, McCabe, Hurlburt, Hough, Hazen, Culver, Garland, and Landsverk (2002) found that Latinos were more likely to receive diagnoses of adjustment disorders, anxiety disorders, and psychotic disorders compared with non-Hispanic whites. The study sample was also less likely to be diagnosed with attention deficit disorder. Latino females appear to be at particular risk for depressive symptoms and suicidal behavior. The Commonwealth Fund reported that 27% of Latina girls enrolled in Grades 5 through 12 experienced depressive symptoms in the past 2 weeks; this percentage is higher than that for all other groups except Asian girls (Schoen et al., 1997). In 1999, more than 25% of Latina girls reported seriously considering suicide and nearly 1 in 5 Latina girls between the ages of 12 and 21 attempted suicide one or more times in the past 12 months (Centers for Disease Control [CDC], 2002). This percentage for Latina girls was more than double those reported by any other ethnic or racial group regardless of gender. However, more than 25% of Latino boys also reported feeling sad or hopeless almost every day for 2 weeks or longer in the past 12 months (CDC, 2002). Findings suggest that Hispanic adults and children living in New York City have developed higher rates of posttraumatic stress disorder symptoms in response to the World Trade Center disaster than members of other groups; the reasons for these findings are unclear (Galea et al., 2002).

Although detailed findings on Latino mental health are only now beginning to appear in the literature, other research indicates that these youth are en-

---

[1] Literature review excerpt from: Chapman, M. V., & Perreira, K. M. (2005). The well-being of immigrant Latino youth: A framework to inform practice. *Families in Society: The Journal of Contemporary Social Services*, *86*, 104–111. Copyright © 2005 by the Alliance for Children and Families. All rights reserved. Reprinted with permission.

gaged in behaviors and situations that either put them at increased risk for mental health difficulties or are often co-occurring with mental disturbance. In particular, a comparison of documentation of elevated rates of aggressive behavior, hate crimes based on race, school failure, and child sexual abuse between Latino youth and other groups may indicate the presence of un-measured mental health concerns (CDC, 2002; Kaufman et al., 2001; Tienda & Kleykamp, 2000).

Substance Use

Substance abuse of both illicit drugs and alcohol is problematic among Latino youth. Alcohol consumption is thought to act as a gateway to illicit substance use for Latino youth perhaps because its use is culturally accepted (Gil & Vasquez, 1996; Warheit, Vega, Khoury, Gil, & Elfenbein, 1996). For 1999, CDC reported that the percentage of Latino adolescents who had used marijuana, cocaine, heroin, and methamphetamines during their lifetime was higher than for either African Americans or non-Latino whites. In addition, the 1999 CDC report also noted that Latinos had the highest lifetime percentage of students who had injected illegal drugs (CDC, 2002). King, Gaines, Lambert, Summerfelt, and Bickman (2000) confirm that substance abuse disorders in adolescents are often comorbid with mental health diagnoses and are often missed by clinicians.

School Functioning and Early Adult Role-Taking

It is important to note that much of the existing data come from Latino youth who are attending school. Indeed, when one considers Freud's classic definition of mental health, "the ability to work and to love," adequate school functioning represents a full half of Freud's equation among adolescents (Erikson, 1950). In more practical terms, completion of high school predicts improved life chances. Many factors influence school functioning, including individual, family, and institutional characteristics, all of which have been linked to school performance among Latino youth (Fernandez & Velez, 1989; Kao & Tienda, 1995; Ogbu; 1987; Rumberger; 1995; Rumberger & Thomas, 2000; Velez, 1989). However, current data suggest that many Latino youth are falling below grade-level work or dropping out of school (CDC, 2002; U.S. Census Bureau, 1999). The National Center for Education Statistics (1995) reported that 38.2% of young adult Latinos did not have a high school diploma.

Furthermore, accelerated role-taking may be a particularly relevant variable for Latino youth and school success. Early childbearing is commonly correlated with school dropout (Leadbeater, 1996). Given that Latinas are less likely to use contraception before pregnancy or to terminate a pregnancy (Erickson, 1998), teen childbearing, and hence the early adoption of adult roles, likely relates to decreased educational attainment. For Latino boys, family monetary needs may push them into the workforce earlier than their non-Latino counterparts, again interfering with school performance.

Taken together, the literature suggests that, regardless of the presence of considerable cultural strengths, Latino youth are suffering. However, the context of the struggle is missing. These studies do not take into account the immigration experience of the child and family, the role of immigrant generation, acculturation levels, and family functioning. Without that context, practitioners and policymakers are poorly informed about which Latino youth are having difficulties and how the potential protective factors of Latino families interact with contextual risks. The potential results are inadequately informed theoretical or intervention models and inadequate clinical assessments.

Risk Factors for Latino Youth

The Migration Experience: Leaving Home and Entering the United States

Children and families immigrate for many reasons and in many ways. Some come to escape poverty or to expand their economic prospects; others come looking for sanctuary from violence; some come as whole families; others send a parent first with children following months or even years later. The reasons one immigrates and the events that happen during that process may shape both a parent's and a child's experience of entering a new country. In their studies of immigrant children, Suarez-Orozco and Suarez-Orozco (2001) along with Portes and Rumbaut (2001) have documented the stress inherent in immigration. Family separations and reunifications, traumatization before and during the journey, changing socioeconomic status, and changes in family rules and roles conspire to make the immigration process a threat to the well-being of both parents and children (Portes & Rumbaut, 2001; Suarez-Orozco & Suarez-Orozco, 2001).

In addition, parents and youth may experience immigration differently. For example, a parent may make the decision to immigrate and be grateful for the chance to work, no matter how hard, in a new land. For the parent in this example, immigration is a chosen stressor. Adolescents, in contrast, may not have participated in the decision to immigrate. When they are confronted with making new friends, planning for their adult life, and learning to operate in the world outside of home in a radically different culture and in another language, their appraisals may be much less positive than those of their parents. The voluntariness or degree of voluntary choice of a stressor is theorized to be related to how one copes with that stressor (Boss, 1988;

Rumbaut, 1991). Thus, those who have had immigration imposed on them may be less likely to adapt positively than those for whom immigration was a choice. In addition, Suarez-Orozco and Suarez-Orozco (1995) discuss a dual frame of reference, in which one's current circumstances, no matter how dire, are viewed positively compared with the difficult situations that prompted emigration from one's home country. This dual frame of reference may help parents who made the decision to immigrate endure their adjustment to life in a new country.

Conceptually and practically, it may be advantageous to extend the dual frame of reference concept to consider multiple frames of reference that may exist within families. For example, children and parents may view the same set of circumstances as positive or negative depending on their experience of both the current circumstances in the host country and past circumstances. Children and youth may be protected in their countries of origin from physical poverty or danger in a way that adults cannot be, creating a sense in children that what they gave up is not worth the hardships they endure as new immigrants.

On arrival in the new country, another group of factors is influential. The support found in coethnic communities and the attitudes of the native culture toward immigrants can create either powerful barriers or opportunities for success (Portes & Rumbaut, 2001; Zayas, Kaplan, Turner, Romano, & Gonzales-Ramos, 2000). Furthermore, work opportunities, the availability of adequate and affordable housing, and the general level of community wealth and support services create a climate that encourages either successful or less successful adaptation by new immigrants (Portes & Rumbaut, 2001).

Acculturation and Assimilation

The experience of immigration is, by definition, one of change. Immigrants leave their native land hoping for a better life in a new place. Yet learning a new language, navigating new systems, reestablishing social connections, and incorporating new norms require a substantial adjustment. Beginning in the 1920s, scholars began examining the process of assimilation (Alba & Nee, 1997). Before 1965, classic assimilation theorists proposed that adaptation to the United States was a gradual but inevitable process by which ethnic immigrants abandoned the culture of their homelands and adopted the cultural and behavioral patterns of the United States (Gordon, 1964). Thus, one was fully assimilated when he or she had given up her or his cultural identity, lost distinctive characteristics, and no longer differed significantly from European Americans.

Assimilation studies have challenged the classic assimilation perspective with findings that associate high levels of assimilation with outcomes that diverge from European American norms (Zhou, 1997). Some first- and second-generation children may have better health, education, and employment outcomes than their white or ethnic native counterparts, whereas others may have significantly worse outcomes (Gans, 1992; Perlmann & Waldinger, 1996; Portes, 1995; Zhou, 1999).

Currently, the term *acculturation* is defined as a process of assuming the values, language, and cultural practices of the new culture (Castro, Coe, Gutierres, & Saenz, 1996). Assimilation has traditionally been seen as the endpoint of this process. However, some literature has challenged acculturation and assimilation as positive goals for immigrants. Rather, both high and low levels of acculturation have been seen as risks for a variety of problematic behaviors, including substance abuse and mental health difficulties (Al-Issa & Tousignant, 1997; Delgado, 1998; Caetano & Clark, 2003; Szapocznik & Kurtines, 1980; Szapocznik, Kurtines, & Fernandez, 1980). In addition, the process of acculturation is assumed to be fraught with stress and anxiety, a scenario ripe for producing mental health symptoms. *Acculturation strain* is a term commonly used to describe the emotional difficulties experienced as immigrants adapt to their new environment (Gil & Vega, 1999). Combined with previous stressful experiences and recent life events, acculturation strain has been shown to impact depressive symptoms and other manifestations of distress (Cervantes & Castro, 1985; Miranda & Umhoefer, 1998).

Family Functioning and Attitudes

Caregivers, usually parents, must adapt to their own life changes while trying to help their children adapt and adjust. In this situation, the caregiver's mental and emotional health may be negatively affected. A number of scholars have hypothesized and documented the relationship between family functioning in Latino families and stresses associated with immigration and acculturation. In the United States, intergenerational stress is assumed to be normative. However, this experience can be exacerbated in immigrating families in which adolescent rebellion is unanticipated and compounded by children exposed to norms and expectations that are different from those in their home country (Szapocznik & Williams, 2000). Intergenerational conflict has been demonstrated to increase family stress in immigrant families (Szapocznik & Kurtines, 1980; Szapocznik, Santisteban, Kurtines, Perez-Vidal, & Harvis, 1984, 1986; Zayas, 1987). Younger family members who may have more exposure to the host culture through school and other social outlets may adopt norms and values that conflict with those of their elders, creating strained family relationships (Gil

& Vega, 1996; Gil et al., 1994; Szapocznik & Williams, 2000).

300 The link between caregiver mental health and child well-being is well-documented for both native and immigrant populations (Lovejoy, Graczyk, O'Hare, & Neuman, 2000). Parental depression and related symptoms of anxiety may affect youth in a 305 variety of ways. Genetic transmission or living with a depressed parent may predispose children to develop depressive symptoms of their own. The parent–child relationship may be further affected by less positive interactions because of the parent's depressive symptoms (Lovejoy et al., 2000). Combined with acculturative stress or symptoms that may follow traumatic events before, during, or after immigration, depressive and related symptoms in parents may be a particularly important issue when considering well-being among 315 new immigrant Latino youth.

School Context and Discrimination

Outside of the family, the school is the most important institutional environment in the socialization and adaptation of immigrant children. Within schools, immigrant youth become intensively exposed to the 320 native culture, experience discrimination from students or teachers, and as a result will form beliefs about what society and persons outside of their family expect from them. Investigations show that school characteristics, such as school size and student–teacher ratios, 325 predict half of the variance in student turnover regardless of ethnicity (Rumberger; 1995; Rumberger & Thomas, 2000). Teacher support and perceived meaningfulness of school have been related to student grades and level of educational investment (Bowen & 330 Bowen, 1998a, 1998b). For Latino youth, the percentage of Latino students in the school also appears to be a salient predictor of academic success or failure (Rumberger & Thomas, 2000). In areas that have not traditionally incorporated significant numbers of immigrants, school policies and procedures concerning 335 language use or classroom placement may place new immigrant students at academic risk.

Schools are often a place where students experience discrimination (Phinney & Tarver, 1988). For 340 new immigrant youth coming to the United States from a country that is much more racially homogenous, seeing themselves as an ethnic minority may be a new and deeply troubling experience (Romero & Roberts, 2003). Unlike racial groups who have experi- 345 enced discrimination across generations, new immigrant parents may not have the strategies for coping with racism that parents in other minority groups use to help their children cope. Research suggests that incorporating an externally imposed identity as an ethnic 350 minority with limited support for understanding and

coping with this task may pose risks to well-being (Smokowski, Chapman, & Bacallao, 2004).

Protective Factors in Latino Families

Three themes have emerged consistently as important to parenting and adolescent development 355 among Latinos in the United States: respect, familism, and biculturalism (Harwood, Leyendecker, Carlson, Asencio, & Miller, 2002; Buriel, 1993; Vega, 1990).

Respect

Respeto, in Latino families, refers to teaching 360 children courtesy and decorum in various social contexts with people of a particular age, sex, and social status. Among adolescents, emphasis on respect in Latino families is associated with greater deference to parental authority and more cooperative behavior 365 (Flanagan, 1996; Fuligni, 1997; Knight, Cota, & Bernal, 1993), cooperative behavior being that which enhances family relationships and precludes risk-taking that might be detrimental to health.

Familism

Familism, or *familismo*, refers to "feelings of loyalty, reciprocity, and solidarity towards members of 370 the family, as well as the notion of the family as an extension of self" (Cortes, 1995, p. 249). Familism has been associated with larger and more cohesive social networks composed of extended family systems (Miller & Harwood, 2001; Gamble & Dalla, 1997). It has also been associated with a normative emphasis on family solidarity and support that is reflected in a less child-centered approach to everyday activities, more 375 frequent contact between family members, more positive attitudes toward parents by their children, and greater levels of satisfaction with family life (Fuligni et al., 1999; Leyendecker et al., 2000; Suarez-Orozco 380 & Suarez-Orozco, 1995; Zayas & Solari, 1994). Finally, this strong sense of family orientation, obligation, and cohesion appears to improve the physical health, emotional health, and educational well-being of adolescent youth (Bird et al., 2001; Dumka, Roosa, & Jackson, 1997; Hill, Bush, & Roosa, 2003).

Biculturalism

The majority of immigrants successfully navigate becoming a part of a new culture. LaFromboise, Coleman, and Gerton (1993) propose a curvilinear 390 relationship between acculturation levels and problem behavior and symptoms. They posit that the ability to interact positively with the dominant culture while retaining one's cultural identity promotes optimal functioning. Both high and low levels of acculturation 395 are thus undesirable. A middle level of acculturation, in which one is able to interact comfortably with and enjoy aspects of the host culture yet retain one's cultural identity, appears optimal in terms of promoting

400 general well-being. This ability to move comfortably between two cultures is referred to as biculturalism. Individuals who are bicultural are believed to have less stress and anxiety because they are not choosing be- tween competing cultural loyalties; rather, they are

405 able to embrace both depending on the situations in which they find themselves (LaFromboise et al., 1993).

References

Alba, R., & Nee, V. (1997). Rethinking assimilation theory for a new era of immigration. *International Migration Journal, 31,* 826–873.

Al-Issa, I., & Tousignant, M. (Eds.). (1997). *Ethnicity, immigration, and psychopathology.* New York: Plenum.

Bird, H., Canino, G. J., Davies, M., Zhang, H., Ramirez. R., & Lahey, B. B. (2001). Prevalence and correlates of antisocial behaviors among three ethnic groups. *Journal of Abnormal Child Psychology, 29,* 465–478.

Boss, P. (1988). *Family stress management.* Newbury Park, CA: Sage.

Bowen, N. K., & Bowen, G. L. (1998a). The effects of home microsystem risk factors and school microsystem protective factors on student academic performance and affective investment in schooling. *Social Work in Education, 20,* 219–231.

Bowen, N. K., & Bowen, G. L. (1998b). The mediating role of educational meaning in the relationship between home academic culture and academic performance. *Family Relations, 47,* 45–51.

Buriel, R. (1993). Childrearing orientations in Mexican American families: The influence of generation and sociocultural factors. *Journal of Marriage and the Family, 55,* 987–1000.

Caetano, R., & Clark, L. (2003). Acculturation, alcohol consumption, smoking, & drug use among Hispanics. In K. M. Chum, P. B. Organizta, & G. Marin (Eds.) *Acculturation: Advances in theory, measurement and applied research* (pp. 223–239). Washington, DC: American Psychological Association.

Castro, F. G., Coe, K., Gutierres, S., & Saenz, D. (1996). Designing health promotion programs for Latinos. In P. M. Kato, & T. Mann (Eds.). *Handbook of diversity issues in health psychology* (pp. 319–346). New York: Plenum.

Cervantes, R. C., & Castro, F. G. (1985). Stress, coping, and Mexican-American mental health: A systematic review. *Hispanic Journal of Behavioral Sciences, 7,* 1–73.

Cortes, D. E. (1995). Variations in familism in two generations of Puerto Ricans. *Hispanic Journal of Behavioral Sciences, 17,* 249–255.

Delgado, M. (Ed.). (1998). *Alcohol use/abuse among Latinos: Issues and examples of culturally competent service.* New York: Haworth.

Dumka, L. E., Roosa, M. W., & Jackson, K. M. (1997). Risk, conflict, mothers' parenting, and children's adjustment in low-income Mexican immigrant and Mexican American families. *Journal of Marriage and the Family, 59,* 309–323.

Erickson, P. I. (1998). *Latina adolescent childbearing in East Los Angeles.* Austin: University of Texas Press.

Erikson, E. (1950). *Childhood and society.* New York: Norton.

Fernandez, R. R., & Velez, W. (1989). *Who stays: Who leaves? Findings from the ASPIRA five cities high school drop out study* (Working Paper No. 89-1). Washington, DC: ASPIRA.

Flannagan, D. (1996). Mothers' and kindergartners' talk about interpersonal relationships. *Merrill-Palmer Quarterly, 42,* 519–536.

Fuligni, A. I. (1999). Authority, autonomy, and parent–adolescent conflict and cohesion: A study of adolescents from Mexican, Chinese, Filipino, and European family backgrounds. *Developmental Psychology, 34,* 782–792.

Galea, S., Ahern, I., Resnick, H., Kilpatrick, D., Bucuvalas, M., Gold, I., & Vlahov, D. (2002). Psychological sequelae of the September 11 terrorist attacks in New York City. *New England Journal of Medicine, 346,* 982–987.

Gamble, W. C., & Dalla, R. L. (1997). Young children's perceptions of their social world in single- and two-parent Euro- and Mexican-American families. *Journal of Social and Personal Relationships, 14,* 357–372.

Gans, H. J. (1992). Second-generation decline: Scenarios for the economics and the futures of the post-1965 American immigrants. *Ethnic Racial Studies, 15,* 173–192.

Gil, A. G., & Vega, W. A. (1996). Two different worlds: Acculturation stress and adaptation among Cuban and Nicaraguan families. *Journal of Social and Personal Relationships, 13,* 435–456.

Gil, R. M., & Vasquez, C. (1996). *The Maria paradox.* New York: Putnam.

Gordon, H. J. (1964). Assimilation in American life: *The role of race, religion, and national origins.* New York: Oxford University Press.

Harwood, R., Leyendecker, B., Carlson, V., Asencio, M., & Miller, A. (2002). Parenting among Latino families in the U.S. In M. H. Bornstein (Ed.). *Handbook of parenting: Social conditions and applied parenting* (2nd ed., pp. 21–46). Mahwah, NJ: Erlbaum.

Hernandez, D. (1997). Child development and the social demography of childhood. *Child Development, 68,* 149–169.

Hill, N. E., Bush, K. R., & Roosa, M. W. (2003). Parenting and family socialization strategies and children's mental health: low-income Mexican-American and Euro-American mothers and children. *Child Development, 74,* 189–204.

Kao, G., & Tienda, M. (1995). Optimism and achievement: The educational performance of immigrant youth. *Social Science Quarterly, 76,* 1–19.

Kaufman, P., Chen, X., Choy, S. P., Peter, K., Ruddy, S. A., Miller, A. K. et al. (2001). *Indicators of school crime and safety: 2001* (NCES 2002-113NCI-190075). Washington, DC: U.S. Department of Education and Justice.

King, R. D., Gaines, L. S., Lambert, E. W., Summerfelt, T., & Bickman, L. (2000). The co-occurrence of psychiatric and substance use diagnoses in adolescents in different service systems: Frequency, recognition, cost, and outcomes. *Journal of Behavioral Health Services and Research, 27,* 417–430.

Knight, G. P., Cota, M. K., & Bernal, M. E. (1993). The socialization of cooperative, competitive, and individualistic preferences among Mexican American children: The mediating role of ethnic identity. *Hispanic Journal of Behavioral Sciences, 15,* 291–309.

LaFromboise, T., Coleman, H. L., & Gerton, J. (1993). Psychological impact of biculturalism: Evidence and theory. *Psychological Bulletin, 114,* 395–412.

Leadbeater, B. I. (1996). School outcomes for minority-group adolescent mothers at 28 to 36 months postpartum: A longitudinal follow-up. *Journal of Research on Adolescence, 6,* 629–648.

Lovejoy, M. C., Graczyk, P. A., O'Hare, E., & Neuman, G. (2000). Maternal depression and parenting behavior: A meta-analytic review. *Clinical Psychology Review, 20,* 561–592.

Leyendecker, B., Lamb, M. E., Scholmerich, A., & Fracasso, M. P. (1995). The social worlds of 8- and 12-month-old infants: Early experiences in two subcultural contexts. *Social Development, 4,* 194–208.

Miller, A. M., & Harwood, R. L. (2001). Long-term socialization goals and the construction of infants' social networks among middle-class Anglo and Puerto Rican mothers. *International Journal of Behavioral Development, 25,* 450–457.

Miranda, A., & Umhoefer, D. (1998). Depression and social interest differences between Latinos in dissimilar acculturation stages. *Journal of Mental Health Counseling, 20,* 159–171.

National Center for Education Statistics. (1995). *Trends among high school seniors, 1972–1992.* Washington, DC: U.S. Government Printing Office.

Ogbu, J. U. (1987). Variability in minority school performance: A problem in search of an explanation. *Anthropology and Education Quarterly, 18,* 312–334.

Perlmann, J., & Waldinger, R. (1996). *Second generation decline? Immigrant children past and present: A reconsideration.* Paper presented at the Conference on Becoming American/American Becoming: International Migration to the United States. Sanibel Island, FL.

Phinney, J. S., & Tarver, S. (1988). Ethnic identity search and commitment in black and white eighth graders. *Journal of Early Adolescence, 8,* 265–277.

Portes, A. (1995). Children of immigrants: Segmented assimilation and its determinants. In A. Portes (Ed.), *The economic sociology of immigration* (pp. 248–279). New York: Russell Sage Foundation.

Portes, A., & Rumbaut, R. G. (2001). *Ethnicities: Children of immigrants in America.* Berkeley: University of California Press.

Romero, A. J., & Roberts, R. E. (2003). Stress within a bicultural context for adolescents of Mexican descent. *Cultural Diversity and Ethnic Minority Psychology, 9,* 171–184.

Rumbaut, R. (1991). Migration, adaptation, and mental health: The experience of Southeast Asian refugees in the United States. In H. Alderman (ED.). *Refugee Policy: Canada and the United States* (pp. 383–427). Toronto, Ontario, Canada: York Lanes.

Rumberger, R. W. (1995). Dropping out of middle school: A multilevel analysis of students and schools. *American Educational Research Journal, 32,* 583–625.

Rumberger, R. W., & Thomas, S. L. (2000). The distribution of dropout and turnover rates among urban and suburban high schools. *Sociology of Education, 73,* 39–67.

Schmidley, D. A. (2001). Profile of the foreign-born population of the United States. *U.S. Census Bureau current population reports* (Series p 23–206). Washington, DC: U.S. Government Printing Office.

Schoen, C., Davis. K., Collins, K., Greenberg, L., Des Roches, C., & Abrams, M. (1997). The Commonwealth Fund Survey of the health of adolescent girls. *Women's Health.* Retrieved December 21, 2004, from http://www.cmwf.org/publications/publications_show.htm?doc_id=221230

Shrout, P. E., Canino, G. J., Bird, H. R., Rubio-Stipec, M., Bravo, M., & Burnam, M. A. (1992). Mental health status among Puerto Ricans, Mexican Americans, and non-Hispanic whites. *American Journal of Community Psychology, 20,* 729–753.

Smokowski, P., Chapman, M. V., & Bacallao, M. (2004). *Discrimination and mental health in new immigrant youth.* Manuscript submitted for publication.

Suarez-Orozco, C., & Suarez-Orozco, M. M. (1995). *Transformations: Migration, family life, and achievement motivation among Latino adolescents.* Stanford. CA: Stanford University Press.

Suarez-Orozco, C., & Suarez-Orozco, M. M. (2001). *Children of immigration.* Cambridge. MA: Harvard University Press.

Szapocznik, J., & Kurtines, W. (1980). Acculturation, biculturalism and adjustment among Cuban Americans. In A. Padilla (Ed.). *Acculturation: Theory, models, and some new findings* (pp. 139–159). Boulder. CO: Praeger.

Szapocznik, J., Kurtines, W., & Fernandez, T. (1980). Biculturalism involvement and adjustment in Hispanic American youths. *International Journal of Intercultural Relations, 4,* 353–365.

Szapocznik, J., Santisteban, D., Kurtines, W., Perez-Vidal, A., & Harvis, O. (1984). Bicultural effectiveness training: A treatment intervention for enhancing intercultural adjustment in Cuban American families. *Hispanic Journal of Behavioral Sciences, 6,* 317–344.

Szapocznik, J., Santisteban, D., Kurtines, W., Perez-Vidal, A., & Harvis, O. (1986). Bicultural Effectiveness Training (BET): An experimental test of an intervention modality for families experiencing intergenerational/intercultural conflict. *Hispanic Journal of Behavioral Sciences, 4,* 303–330.

Szapocznik, J., & Williams, R. A. (2000). Brief strategic family therapy: Twenty-five years of interplay among theory, research and practice in adolescent behavior problems and drug abuse. *Clinical Child and Family Psychology Review, 3,* 117–134.

Tienda, M., & Kleykamp, M. (2000). *Physical and mental health status of Hispanic adolescent girls: A comparative perspective.* Office of Population Research, Princeton University.

U.S. Census Bureau. (1999). *School enrollment in the United States: Social and economic characteristics of students.* Available from http://www.census.gov

Vega, W. (1990). Hispanic families in the 1980s: A decade of research. *Journal of Marriage and the Family, 52,* 1015–1024.

Velez, W. (1989). High school attrition among Hispanic and non-Hispanic white youths. *Sociology of Education, 62,* 119–133.

Yeh, M., McCabe, L., Hurlburt, M., Hough, R., Hazen, A. L., Culver, S., Garland, A., & Landsverk, J. (2002). Referral sources, diagnoses, and service types of youth in public outpatient mental health care: A focus on ethnic minorities. *Journal of Behavioral Health Services and Research, 29,* 45–60.

Zayas, L. H. (1987). Toward an understanding of suicide risks in young Hispanic females. *Journal of Adolescent Research, 2,* 1–11.

Zayas, L. H., Kaplan, C., Turner, S., Romano, K., & Gonzales-Ramos, G. (2000). Understanding suicide attempts by adolescent Hispanic females. *Social Work, 45,* 53–63.

Zayas, L. H., & Solari, F. (1994). Early childhood socialization in Hispanic families: Context, culture, and practice implications. *Professional Psychology: Research and Practice, 25,* 200–234.

Zhou, M. (1997). Growing up American: The challenge confronting immigrant children and children of immigrants. *Annual Review of Sociology, 23,* 63–95.

Zhou, M. (1999). Segmented assimilation: Issues, controversies, and recent research on the new second generation. In C. Hirschman, P. Kasinitz, & J. Dewind (Eds.). *The handbook of international migration: The American experience* (pp. 196–211). New York: Russell Sage Foundation.

About the authors: *Mimi V. Chapman,* MSW, Ph.D., is assistant professor, School of Social Work, The University of North Carolina at Chapel Hill. *Krista M. Perreira,* Ph.D., is assistant professor, Department of Public Policy, The University of North Carolina at Chapel Hill.

Address correspondence to: Mimi V. Chapman, The University of North Carolina at Chapel Hill, 307 Pittsboro St., #3550, Chapel Hill, NC 27599-3550. E-mail: mimi@email.unc.edu

Early Intervention in Autism[1]

ABSTRACT. We now know that professionals can diagnose children with autism when they are as young as 2 years of age (Lord, 1995). Screening and the role of the pediatrician have become even more critical as we have recognized the stability of early diagnosis over time and the importance of early intervention. At this point, experts working with children with autism agree that early intervention is critical. There is professional consensus about certain crucial aspects of treatment (intensity, family involvement, focus on generalization) and empirical evidence for certain intervention strategies. However, there are many programs developed for children with autism that differ in philosophy and a lack of research comparing the various intervention programs. Most of the programs for children with autism that exist are designed for children of preschool age, and not all are widely known or available. While outcome data are published for some of these programs, empirical studies comparing intervention programs are lacking. In this review, existing intervention programs and empirical studies on these programs will be reviewed, with a particular emphasis on the birth to 3 age group.

Background

Autism is a developmental disorder that was first described by Leo Kanner in 1943, in a classic article that included case studies of 11 children. Since that time, the diagnostic criteria have evolved based on continued observations and research, resulting in the current criteria in the *Diagnostic and Statistical Manual of Mental Disorders, Fourth Edition or DSM-IV* (American Psychiatric Association, 1994) and the *International Classification of Diseases or ICD-10* (World Health Organization, 1993). At the present time, *autistic disorder* is defined in terms of qualitative impairments in social interaction and communication, and restricted, repetitive, and stereotyped patterns of behaviors, interests, and activities, with impairments in one of these areas prior to the age of 3 years.

In addition to autistic disorder, there are 4 other specific diagnoses included within the autistic spectrum disorders (ASD) category, which is a term now preferred by most parents and professional organizations (Filipek et al., 2000; Lord & McGee, 2001). Included among them are 2 disorders that are defined by a regression in skills: Rett syndrome and childhood disintegrative disorder. These will not be the focus of this article. Recently, a specific gene has been linked

with Rett syndrome (Cheadle et al., 2000). Childhood disintegrative disorder is a very rare disorder, with reported prevalence rates of 0.6 per 100,000 (Chakrabarti & Fombonne, 2001). This disorder involves a period of normal development in the first 2 years of life, followed by a regression in a number of skill areas prior to the age of 4 years, resulting in autistic symptoms.

The other 2 ASD diagnoses are Asperger's disorder and pervasive developmental disorder—not otherwise specified (PDD-NOS). Asperger's disorder, like autistic disorder, includes qualitative impairments in reciprocal social interactions, and restricted, repetitive, and stereotyped patterns of behaviors, interests, and activities. However, unlike autistic disorder, it does not require qualitative impairments in communication. In addition, this diagnosis requires that there is no clinically significant language delay prior to 3 years of age, no cognitive delays, and that the criteria for another specific PDD have not been met. If children who have ever met criteria for autistic disorder are ruled out, the diagnosis of Asperger's disorder is very rare (Miller & Ozonoff, 1997). Nevertheless, the diagnosis of Asperger's disorder is often used for milder cases of high-functioning autism. The final diagnosis within this general category is PDD-NOS. This disorder is characterized by qualitative impairments in social interaction, accompanied by either qualitative impairments in communication or restricted, repetitive, and stereotyped patterns of behaviors, interests, and activities. There is still controversy about this diagnosis, including whether it is "almost autism" or "atypical autism" (Towbin, 1997).

Recent epidemiological studies have reported rates of ASDs as high as 66 per 10,000 (Fombonne, 2002), which is a surprising increase over rates reported in the past. Early identification has increased in importance, as many studies have found that children with ASDs who receive services prior to 48 months of age make greater improvements than those who enter programs after 48 months of age (Harris & Weiss, 1998; Sheinkopf & Siegel, 1998).

Over the past 10 to 15 years, there has been evidence that children with ASDs can be reliably diagnosed as young as 2 years of age (Lord, 1995). One of the largest errors in diagnoses of 2-year-olds referred for autism is underdiagnosing children on the basis of

---

[1] Literature review excerpt from: Corsello, C. M. (2005). Early intervention in autism. *Infants & Young Children, 18,* 74–85.

Table 1
Intervention Studies

Method	Authors	Subjects/groups	Age, mo	Outcome measure	Findings
TEACCH home program	Ozonoff & Cathcart (1998)	11 TEACCH 11 control	31–69	PEP-R	TEACCH had significant gains in PEP-R scores when compared with controls
Discrete trial	Lovaas (1987)	19 for 40 h 19 for 10 h 21 no treatment	$M = 32$ $M = 35$	IQ score Educational placement Educational support	Intense intervention group: 47% in regular education 31 point IQ gain
Discrete trial	McEachin, Smith, & Lovaas (1993)	19 for 40 h 19 for 10 h	$M = 32$ $M = 35$	IQ score Adaptive behavior score	Intense intervention group: IQ higher Vineland score higher
Discrete trial	Smith, Groen, & Wynn (2000)	15 for 30 h 13 for 5 h by parents, 15 h special cases	18–42	IQ Language Behavioral measure Adaptive measure Class placement	27% in regular education 16 point gain Little difference in behavior Little difference in adaptive scores
Discrete trial & incidental teaching	Luiselli, Cannon, Ellis, & Sisson (2000)	8 younger than 3 y 8 older than 3 y	$M = 2.63$ y $M = 3.98$ y	ELAP or LAP	Duration of treatment was only predictor of change
Applied behavior analysis	Harris & Handleman (2000)	27 subjects No control group	31–65	Class placement	IQ and age predicted class placement
Incidental teaching	McGee, Morrier, & Daly (1999)	28 subjects No control group	29	Verbal sample Peer proximity	82% using meaningful words 71% improved in peer proximity
LEAP	Strain & Hoyson (2000)	6 subjects No control group	30–53	Class placement LAP CARS	Improvements in all areas

* PEP-R, Psychoeducational Profile—Revised; *M*, mean; ELAP, Early Learning Accomplishment Profile; LAP, Learning Accomplishment Profile; IQ, intelligence quotient; LEAP, Lifeskills and Education for Students with Autism and other Pervasive Developmental Disorders; CARS, Childhood Autism Rating Scale; mo, months; h, hours; and y, years.

clinical impression when their scores on standardized measures are consistent with a diagnosis of autism (Lord & Risi, 1998). Possible contributors to this bias are the variability in behaviors of 2-year-olds who have ASDs (Lord, 1995) and the lack of repetitive behaviors in autism that are often present in 3-year-olds, but may not be present in 2-year-olds with autism (Cox et al., 1999; Lord, 1995; Stone et al., 1999).

In this review, early intervention programs and empirical studies available on each of the programs (Table 1) will be reviewed, with a specific focus on the birth to 3 age group. When reviewing empirical support and programs, it is important to differentiate program outcome studies, which are designed to determine if a program is having the desired effect, from controlled empirical studies, which are designed to determine if the program or specific aspects of the program are clearly responsible for the changes observed.

When reviewing research on intervention for children with ASDs, there are several important considerations. These include the age groups included in the study, the control group, the control condition, and the outcome measures (Table 1). When reviewing programs, there are several components to cover, including method of intervention, the format, the setting, who implements the program, and whether it is child- or adult-directed (Table 2). Within this review, we will first focus on issues relevant to early intervention, followed by a review of programs and empirical support for programs, and suggested next steps with regard to intervention with very young children.

Interventions

Over the years, there have been many treatments developed for children with autism, evolving from different philosophies. These include behavioral interventions, developmental interventions, and cognitive–behavioral interventions. While each program is based on a different philosophy and uses unique intervention strategies, there is also considerable overlap in components of the programs.

Two aspects of intervention that are common to most intervention programs designed for ASDs and have empirical support include the intensity of the program and the age at which children should begin intervention. Dawson and Osterling (1997), based on a

Table 2
Intervention Programs

Method	Authors/program	H/wk	Format	Setting	Implementer	Adult- or child-directed
Incidental teaching	Walden Infant Toddler Program	30+	Group 1 to 1	Childcare center Home	Parents Educational staff	Child
Social pragmatic developmental approach	Wetherby & Prizant	Variable	1 to 1	Home	Parent Therapist Teacher	Child
Structured teaching	TEACCH	Variable	Group	Classroom Home	Parents School staff	Adult
Discrete trial	Lovaas (1987)	40	1 to 1	Home	Student therapists Trained consultants	Adult
Discrete trial	Douglass Developmental Disabilities Center	35–45	1 to 1 Small group	Class Home	School staff Parents Student therapists	Adult
Pivotal response intervention	Koegel, Koegel, & Harrows (1999)	Variable	1 to 1 Group	Inclusive setting	Highly skilled specialists Family Consultants	Child
				Home Preschool	School staff	
Behavioral and inclusion	LEAP*	15	Group	Integrated classroom	Teacher	Adult and child
Developmental	Greenspan	Variable	1 to 1	Home	Parents Educational staff	Child
Developmental	Denver Model	22	Group	Classroom	Trained staff	Child

* LEAP indicates Lifeskills and Education for Students with Autism and other Pervasive Developmental Disorders

review of programs for children with autism, report that most programs involve 15 to 25 hours of intervention a week. There is also empirical evidence that children who enter programs at younger ages make greater gains than those who enter programs at older ages (Harris & Handleman, 2000; Sheinkopf & Siegel, 1998). These studies generally compare children who are older than 4 or 5 years with those who are younger than 4 or 5 years. One study comparing children younger than 3 years with those older than 3 years did not find age differences in improvement (Luiselli, Cannon, Ellis, & Sisson, 2000), which may suggest that 4 years of age is young enough to lead to significant gains. A potentially complicating factor is that children tend to make intelligence quotient (IQ) gains regardless of intervention at the younger ages (Gabriels, Hill, Pierce, Rogers & Wehner, 2001; Lord & Schopler, 1989). This also leads to difficulties in interpreting changes in IQ scores, which are often used as an outcome measure.

Most early intervention programs are designed for preschool-aged children, although they may include younger children in their programs as well. It is only more recently that we have been able to identify children with autism as young as 2 years of age. There

are a few programs that are specifically designed for children between birth and 3 years of age. We will first cover the programs designed specifically for the birth to 3 age group, followed by widely available preschool programs, and finally preschool programs that are less widely available.

Early Intervention Programs Designed for Toddlers

Walden Toddler Program

The Walden Toddler Program (McGee, Morrier, & Daly, 2001) is a program designed specifically for toddlers with autism. The program is based on a typical daycare model, with a focus on using incidental teaching and social inclusion. Incidental teaching is a method of applied behavior analysis (ABA) that uses behavioral principles within natural learning contexts. The environment includes toys and activities that are appealing to young children, and the adult expands on requests and activities that the child initiates. The program is very structured and works on individual goals within planned activities. The program includes typical toddlers and toddlers with autism, between the ages of 15 and 36 months. There are no controlled empirical studies of this program, but program evaluation data found that 82% of the toddlers used meaningful words when they left the program and 71% of the children showed improvements in their proximity to other children.

Social Pragmatic Communication Approach

Amy Wetherby (Wetherby & Prizant, 1999) has also developed strategies for teaching communication to young children with ASDs, based on a pragmatic communication developmental approach. She has not developed a comprehensive intervention program; however, she has focused her intervention strategies on social pragmatic communication development for children younger than 3 years. Within this approach, the importance of teaching in naturalistic contexts, using a facilitative rather than a directive style, providing opportunities for communication, and consistently and contingently reinforcing communication attempts are emphasized (Wetherby & Prizant, 1999). Other strategies used in teaching communication to young children include incorporating environmental supports to create a predictable environment and teaching peers to initiate and respond to children with ASDs.

Comprehensive Programs

There are many comprehensive programs for children with ASDs; among the most widely known are the Developmental Intervention Model or Greenspan approach (Greenspan & Wieder, 1997), the TEACCH Model (Marcus, Lansing, Andrews, & Schopler, 1978; Mesibov, 1997; Schopler, Mesibov, & Baker, 1982), the UCLA Young Autism Project (Lovaas, 1987), the LEAP (Lifeskills and Education for Students with Autism and other Pervasive Developmental Disorders) Program, and the Denver Model. Most of these programs have been developed for children of preschool age or older. The Walden Toddler Program is an exception, as it was designed specifically for toddlers. Most of the research on the available models is descriptive rather than based on empirical studies. Currently, there is no empirical evidence that one program is superior to another.

There are many common elements of these programs, although they differ considerably in philosophy. All of these programs include young children (mean ages between 30 and 47 months), active family involvement, and are intensive in hours (12–36 hours a week). In addition, in most of the model programs, staff is well-trained and experienced in working with children with autism and the physical environment is supportive. It is important to note, however, that level of experience and training can vary considerably, particularly when adapting or incorporating model programs into the public domain. All of the programs focus on developmental skills and goals, and contain ongoing objective assessment of progress. The programs also use teaching strategies designed for the generalization and maintenance of skills, individualized intervention plans based on a child's strengths and needs, and planned transitions from preschool to school age. While there are many similarities, each program also has a different emphasis and defining features. Each of the programs will be reviewed below.

The TEACCH Program

The TEACCH program is a statewide, community-based intervention program that emphasizes environmental organization and visual supports, individualization of goals, and the teaching of independence and developmental skills. The setting in which the program is implemented varies, depending on the abilities and needs of each child (self-contained classroom, included classroom, home). Teaching strategies are designed to be meaningful to the child with autism, and are therefore taught within the natural environment and within context. The TEACCH program views ASDs as lifelong. From the beginning, it emphasizes skills that are important for future independence. One of the strengths of the TEACCH program is a focus on the lifespan and community-based intervention. One of the weaknesses is the lack of empirical studies of the program.

While the TEACCH program has been in existence for more than 30 years, there are relatively few empirical studies of the program. Two studies, comparing TEACCH interventions with only public education intervention, found significant differences in scores on the Psychoeducational Profile – Revised on follow-up testing (Ozonoff & Cathcart, 1998; Panerai, Ferrante, & Zingale, 2002). Only one of these studies focused on younger children (Ozonoff & Cathcart, 1998) and compared a TEACCH home program, involving 10 sessions, in addition to services provided by the public school, to solely public school services for children between 2 and 6 years of age. Children in the TEACCH group had significantly higher scores on the PEP-R than the children in the control group following 4 months of intervention. The groups in this study were small, but were matched on age, PEP-R pretest scores, and severity of autism and not randomly assigned.

Applied Behavioral Analysis Programs

One of the most widely known and sought-after types of intervention is applied behavior analysis (ABA). Parents and professionals frequently associate the name Ivar Lovaas and the discrete trial format of instruction with ABA intervention. The popularity of the Lovaas intervention is partly the result of his 1987 study (Lovaas, 1987) and Catherine Maurice's (Maurice, 1993) book, both of which provide accounts of remarkable improvements and use the term "normal functioning" in the best outcome group of children with autism who received discrete trial intervention.

In reality, discrete trials and the Lovaas method is only one specific type of ABA intervention. Applied behavior analysis includes a number of other intervention strategies and programs that are based on behavioral principles. Many treatment studies are based on behavioral interventions, which is the case not only in autism but also in psychology in general.

The UCLA Young Autism Project uses the Lovaas method of intervention, specifically discrete trial intervention, implemented in a one-to-one setting by trained ABA therapists, supervised by trained professionals. The focus of the first year is on imitation, interaction, play, and response to basic requests. In the second year, the focus shifts to continued work on language, descriptions of emotions, and preacademic skills. To teach generalization, the children practice the skills in other situations and with other people, once they have mastered them in a one-to-one setting.

The UCLA Young Autism Project has been empirically studied, and the most commonly cited article is Lovaas' article (Lovaas, 1987). At the time treatment began, the children had a mean age of 35 months in the experimental group and 41 months in the control group. The experimental group received one-to-one intervention 40 hours a week, and the control group received intervention 10 hours a week for 2 to 3 years. It was this article that started the belief that autistic children required intervention at least 40 hours a week. Lovaas (1987) used the term "normal functioning" in this article (p. 9), and he used IQ and class placement as outcome variables in this study. Understandably, parents have been quite influenced by this study. In a follow-up study of the children, between 9 and 19 years of age, the experimental group continued to have significantly higher IQs and Vineland scores than the control group (McEachin, Smith, & Lovaas, 1993).

There have been numerous criticisms of this study, including nonrandom selection of groups (the age restriction was lower for children without language and children had to achieve a certain mental age to be included), nonrandom assignment to groups, and a large discrepancy between the number of hours of intervention between the control and experimental groups. However, it was one of the first empirical studies of an intervention program for children with autism.

More recently, another study on the Lovaas method of intervention has been published and addresses some of the concerns of the original article (Smith, Groen, & Wynn, 2000). In this study, the experimental group received approximately 25 hours a week of intervention while the control group received 5 hours a week of parent training. In the parent-training condition, the parents were asked to work with the children 5 hours a week at home, and they were enrolled in special education classrooms for 10 to 15 hours a week. The children with ASDs in this study had IQ scores between 35 and 75, and an age range of 18 to 42 months at the time of enrollment in the program.

As in the Lovaas study, the experimental group had higher IQs than the control group on follow-up. At the time of follow-up, between the ages of 7 and 8 years, 27% of the children in the experimental group were in regular education and had made a 16-point IQ gain. There were little differences in Child Behavior Checklist (CBCL) scores and Vineland scores between the 2 groups. The outcome was not as impressive as in Lovaas' original study, as only 27% of the children in this study were defined as best outcome (IQ > 85 and in regular education without support) as opposed to 47% in the McEachin (McEachin et al., 1993) study. The average IQ gain was half that reported in the McEachin study, and the behavior and adaptive skills ratings were still reported as problematic in the experimental group in the Smith et al. study. Clearly, children made gains in this program, but not the same degree of progress described in the original Lovaas and McEachin studies. The Smith study, with better controls and design, suggests that children improve more than they would with early education and focused parent support or education, but do not recover when they receive approximately 25 hours a week of intensive one-to-one ABA intervention.

Another model ABA program is the Douglass Developmental Center at Rutgers in New Jersey. This program has different levels, starting with a one-to-one format for the youngest children, then moving to a small classroom with a 2:1 ratio and then to a class with typical peers, using a model similar to the LEAP program, which is described later in this article. A follow-up study of the children in the program reported that age and IQ predicted outcome (Harris & Handleman, 2000). Approximately 33% of the children had average IQs upon discharge from the program. It is important to note that 22% of the children (6 out of 27) had IQ changes from the range of mental retardation to average. Of these 6 children, 4 (67%) were between 3 and 4 years of age and 2 (33%) were between 4 and 5 years of age at the time they started the program. Upon exit from the program, 3 of these children were in special education, 2 were in integrated classrooms with support, and 1 child was fully included without support.

More recently, embedded trials, pivotal response training, and incidental teaching have emerged from the ABA literature. These techniques are less well-known and less widely available at the present time, but hold some promise for intervention for very young children with autism. Contemporary ABA strategies include naturalistic teaching methods, such as natural language paradigms (Koegel, O'Dell, & Koegel,

1987), incidental teaching (Hart, 1985; McGee, Krantz, & McClannahan, 1985; McGee, Morrier, & Daly, 1999), time delay and milieu intervention (Charlop, Schriebman, & Thibodeau, 1985; Charlop & Trasowech, 1991; Hwang & Hughes, 2000; Kaiser, 1993; Kaiser, Yoder, & Keetz, 1992), and pivotal response training or teaching core behaviors, with the idea that they will lead to changes in other behaviors and skills (Koegel, 1995; Koegel, Camarata, Koegel, Ben-Tall, & Smith, 1998). These methodologies have commonalities, including teaching within natural contexts (during play, snack, work, within the classroom, at home), the use of natural reinforcers (reinforcing children for requesting by giving them what they are asking for), and systematic trials that are initiated by the child (the child makes the initial attempt).

Contemporary behavioral approaches have resulted in good outcomes for teaching language content, including single word vocabulary, describing objects and pictures, responding to questions, and increasing the intelligibility of speech (Goldstein, 1999; Koegel et al., 1998; Krantz, Zalewski, Hall, Fenski, & McClannahan, 1981). McGee and colleagues (1999) also reported good outcomes through natural reinforcers of vocalization, speech shaping, and incidental teaching. Contemporary behavioral approaches have also been applied with some success to teach broader communication skills, such as functional communication, that may lead to decreases in challenging behaviors (Horner et al., 1990; Horner, Carr, Strain, Todd, & Reed, 2000; Koegel, Koegel, & Surratt, 1992). Spontaneous language is more difficult to teach and requires a number of naturalistic as well as developmental methods of instruction (Watson, Lord, Schaffer, & Schopler, 1989). Children who use more spontaneous language earlier in treatment have more favorable language outcomes.

Very few intervention strategies have demonstrated success using behavioral interventions in teaching skills, such as joint attention and symbolic abilities, that focus on what are considered core deficits to children with autism. However, there are a few studies that documented some success in teaching symbolic play skills through pivotal response training (Stahmer, 1995; Thorp, Stahmer, & Schreibman, 1995). Other studies that have demonstrated some improvements in these skills include increase in gaze to regulate social interactions, joint attention, shared positive affect, and the use of conventional gestures. Recently, there has also been documentation that naturalistic teaching of communication skills leads to improvements in joint attention in children with autism (Buffington, Krantz, McClannahan, & Poulson, 1998; Hwang & Hughes, 2000; Pierce & Schreibman, 1995).

The LEAP Program

There is an emphasis on including peers in intervention programs because children with autism have difficulty generalizing skills learned with adults to interactions with peers (Bartak & Rutter, 1973). Including typical peers is an essential component of both the LEAP program and the Walden Toddler Program. The LEAP program includes 10 typical children and 6 children with autism between the ages of 3 and 5 years in each classroom. The children are in class for 15 hours a week. The classroom is structured and incorporates incidental teaching and other ABA methods of intervention. Interventions are both child- and adult-directed. Peers are considered to be an essential element of the program (Harris & Handleman, 1994). Peer-mediated techniques for increasing interactions involve teaching peers to be "play organizers." These strategies have been shown to be effective in increasing social interactions, which have generalized to some extent and been maintained over time (Goldstein, Kaczmarek, Pennington, & Shafer, 1992; Hoyson, Jamison, & Strain, 1984; Strain, Kerr, & Ragland, 1979; Strain, Shores, & Timm, 1977).

Developmental Interventions

Developmental intervention is a specific term used to describe a philosophy and specific strategies for working with children with autism. One common feature of developmental interventions is that they are child-directed. In developmental interventions, the environment is organized to encourage or facilitate communicative and social interactions. The child initiates and the adult responds. There is limited empirical support for developmental approaches, but there is some support for language outcomes using such strategies (Hwang & Hughes, 2000; Lewy & Dawson, 1992; Rogers & Lewis, 1989) and many case studies (Greenspan & Wieder, 1997) using these approaches. Rogers and Lewis (1989) have documented improvements in symbolic play as a result of structured, development-based programs, and Lewy and Dawson (1992) also demonstrated improvements in gaze, turn taking, object use, and joint attention with a child-directed imitation strategy.

There are some limitations to developmental interventions. Because the intervention approach is child-directed, it requires that the child engage in behaviors to which the adult can respond. Many children with autism do not explore the environment in the way that typical children might. They may become stuck on certain activities or not play with the toys present in their environment. Developmental methods require considerable effort and skill on the part of the teacher or therapist, as she or he must know what child behaviors to respond to as well as how to respond. When the child engages in behaviors that the therapist can respond to, and the therapist is skilled, it may be an effective intervention.

The Greenspan Model

490 One of the most well-known developmental approaches is the Greenspan approach, also known as the Developmental Individual Difference (DIR) Model (Greenspan & Wieder, 1997). The Greenspan model is described as a "relationship-based model," in which 495 the goal is to help the child develop interpersonal connections that will lead to the mastery of cognitive and developmental skills, including (1) attention and focus, (2) engaging and relating, (3) nonverbal gesturing, (4) affect cuing, (5) complex problem solving, (6) sym-500 bolic communication, and (7) abstract and logical thinking. The program is based on following the child's lead and looking for opportunities to "close the circle of communication" or respond in a way that leads to expanding a skill or interaction. Within this 505 model, it is recommended that a child spend at least 4 hours a day in spontaneous play interactions with an adult, at least 2 hours a day in semistructured skill building activities with an adult, and at least 1 hour a day in sensory-motor play activities. The Greenspan 510 program is supplemented by time in an inclusive preschool program, speech and occupational therapy.

The DIR method of intervention is highly dependent on the skills of the parent or professional implementing the program. It requires that the adult rec-515 ognizes when and how to respond to a child's actions and behaviors, which can make it difficult to implement the program in the community. This differs from many behavioral approaches, which have a prescribed pattern of responses and adult-initiated teaching trials. 520 There are currently no controlled studies of this program.

The Denver Model

The Denver model (Rogers & Lewis, 1989) is also based on a developmental model of intervention. This program is delivered within a classroom setting 525 that is on a 12-month calendar and meets 4 to 5 hours a day, 5 days a week. The focus is on positive affect, pragmatic communication, and interpersonal interactions within a structured and predictable environment. Almost all activities and therapies are conducted 530 within a play situation. Goals of the program include using positive affect to increase a child's motivation and interest in an activity or person, using reactive language strategies to facilitate communication, and teaching mental representation.

535 There is outcome data available on the program, based on 31 children between 2 and 6 years of age with ASDs. Children demonstrated significant developmental improvements in cognition, language, social/emotional development, perceptual/fine motor 540 development, and gross motor development after 6 to

8 months in the program, after accounting for expected developmental progress. While only 53% of the children had functional speech when they entered the program, 73% had functional speech at follow-up.

Conclusion

The available evidence from a variety of programs and studies suggests that early intervention leads to better outcomes. As we have seen, a number of studies have demonstrated that children make greater gains when they enter a program at a younger age. It is important to keep in mind that most of the empirical support for the difference in gains is comparing children younger than 4 or 5 years to children older than 4–5 years of age. The preschool years are still considered "early" when it comes to early intervention.

There are many strategies for working with children with autism and not all of them are equally known or available. Most of the empirical studies have been conducted on ABA interventions. While there is evidence that certain strategies can be effective for teaching specific skills to children with autism, there is not currently evidence that one program is better than any other. Furthermore, most of the programs are developed for children aged 3 and older, and many interventionists are currently attempting to adapt their programs to better meet the needs of the 0 to 3 age group. This leads to complications when recommending intervention programs to parents of young children with autism. At this time, there is a great deal of interest in the common elements in the programs when making recommendations, including parent involvement, intensity, a predictable environment, incorporating the child's interests, actively engaging the child, and focusing on individualized developmental goals. It is important that professionals and parents are informed about the progress they can expect for their child, as well as remain aware that most research does not support a "cure" or "recovery" from autism. At this point, most of the programs focus on children of preschool age, and there is still much to learn about intervention for the birth to 3 age group.

References

American Psychiatric Association. (1994). *Diagnostic and statistical manual of mental disorders* (4th ed.) Washington, DC: Author.

Bartak, L., & Rutter, M. (1973). Special educational treatment of autistic children: A comparative study: I. Design of study and characteristics of units. *Journal of Child Psychology and Psychiatry and Allied Disciplines, 14,* 161–179.

Buffington, D. M., Krantz, P. J., McClannahan, L. E., & Poulson, C. L. (1998). Procedures for teaching appropriate gestural communication skills to children with autism. *Journal of Autism and Developmental Disorders, 28,* 535–545.

Chakrabarti, S., & Fombonne, E. (2001). Pervasive developmental disorders in preschool children. *JAMA, Special Issue, 285,* 3093–3099.

Charlop, M. H., Schreibman, L., & Thibodeau, M. G. (1985). Increasing spontaneous verbal responding in autistic children using a time delay procedure. *Journal of Applied Behavior Analysis, 18,* 155–166.

Charlop, M. H., & Trasowech, J. E. (1991). Increasing autistic children's daily spontaneous speech. *Journal of Applied Behavior Analysis, 24,* 747–761.

Cheadle, J. P., Gill, H., Fleming, N., Maynard, J., Kerr, A., Leonard, H., et al. (2000). Long-read sequence analysis of the MECP2 gene in Rett syndrome patients: Correlation of disease severity with mutation type and location. *Human Molecular Genetics, 9*, 1119–1129.

Cox, A., Klein, K., Charman, T., Baird, G., Baron-Cohen, S., Swettenham, J., et al. (1999). Autism spectrum disorders at 20 and 42 months of age: Stability of clinical and ADI-R diagnosis. *Journal of Child Psychology and Psychiatry and Allied Disciplines, 40*, 719–732.

Dawson, G., & Osterling, J. (1997). Early intervention in autism. In M. J. Guralnick (Ed.), *The effectiveness of early intervention* (pp. 307–326). Baltimore: Brookes.

Filipek, P. A., Accardo, P. J., Ashwal, S., Baranek, G. T., Cook, E. H., Jr., Dawson, G., et al. (2000). Practice parameter: Screening and diagnosis of autism: Report of the Quality Standards Subcommittee of the American Academy of Neurology and the Child Neurology Society. *Neurology, 55*, 468–479.

Fombonne, E. (2002). Epidemiological trends in rates of autism. *Molecular Psychiatry, 7*, S4–S6.

Gabriels, R. L., Hill, D. E., Pierce, R. A., Rogers, S. J., & Wehner, B. (2001). Predictors of treatment outcome in young children with autism: A retrospective study. *Autism, 5*, 407–429.

Goldstein, H. (1999). *Communication intervention for children with autism: A review of treatment efficacy.* Paper presented at the First Workshop of the Committee on Educational Interventions for Children with Autism, National Research Council, Department of Communication Sciences, Florida State University; December 13–14, 1999; Tallahassee, FL.

Goldstein, H., Kaczmarek, L., Pennington, R., & Shafer, K. (1992). Peer-mediated intervention: Attending to, commenting on, and acknowledging the behavior of preschoolers with autism. *Journal of Applied Behavior Analysis, 25*, 289–305.

Greenspan, S., & Wieder, S. (1997). Developmental patterns and outcomes in infants and children with disorders in relating and communicating: A chart review of 200 cases of children with autism spectrum diagnoses. *Journal of Developmental and Learning Disorders, 1*, 87–141.

Harris, S. L., & Handleman, J. S. (2000). Age and IQ at intake as predictors of placement for young children with autism: A four- to six-year follow-up. *Journal of Autism and Developmental Disorders, 30*, 137–142.

Harris, S. L., & Handleman, J. S. (Eds.). (1994). *Preschool education programs for children with autism.* Austin, TX: Pro-Ed.

Harris, S. L., & Weiss, M. J. (1998). *Right from the start: Behavioral intervention for young children with autism.* Bethesda, MD: Woodbine House.

Hart, B. (1985). Naturalistic language training strategies. In S. F. Warren & A. Rogers-Warren (Eds.), *Teaching functional language* (pp. 63–88). Baltimore: University Park Press.

Horner, R. H., Carr, E. G., Strain, P. S., Todd, A. W., & Reed, H. K. (2000). *Problem behavior interventions for young children with autism: A research synthesis.* Paper presented at the Second Workshop of the Committee on Educational Interventions for Children with Autism, National Research Council, Department of Special Education, University of Oregon; April 12, 2000; Eugene, OR.

Horner, R. H., Dunlap, G., Koegel, R. L., Carr, E. G., Sailor, W., Anderson, J. A., et al. (1990). Toward a technology of "nonaversive" behavioral support. *Journal of the Association for Persons with Severe Handicaps, 15*, 125–132.

Hoyson, M., Jamison, B., & Strain, P. S. (1984). Individualized group instruction of normally developing and autistic-like children: The LEAP curriculum model. *Journal of the Division for Early Childhood, 8*, 157–172.

Hwang, B., & Hughes, C. (2000). Increasing early social-communicative skills of preverbal preschool children with autism through social interactive training. *Journal of the Association for Persons with Severe Handicaps, 25*, 18–28.

Kaiser, A. (1993). Functional language. In M. Snell (Ed.), *Instruction of students with severe disabilities* (pp. 347–379). New York: Macmillan Publishing Co.

Kaiser, A. P., Yoder, P. J., & Keetz, A. (1992). Evaluating milieu teaching. In S. F. Warren & J. Reichle (Eds.), *Causes and effects in communication and language intervention* (Vol. 1 ed., pp. 9–47). Baltimore: Paul H. Brookes.

Koegel, L. K. (1995). Communication and language intervention. In *Teaching children with autism: Strategies for initiating positive interactions and improving learning opportunities* (pp. 17–32). Baltimore: Paul H. Brookes.

Koegel, R. L., Camarata, S., Koegel, L. K., Ben-Tall, A., & Smith, A. E. (1998). Increasing speech intelligibility in children with autism. *Journal of Autism and Developmental Disorders, 28*, 241–251.

Koegel, R. L., Koegel, L. K., & Surratt, A. (1992). Language intervention and disruptive behavior in preschool children with autism. *Journal of Autism and Developmental Disorders, 22*, 141–153.

Koegel, R. L., O'Dell, M. C., & Koegel, L. K. (1987). A natural language teaching paradigm for nonverbal autistic children. *Journal of Autism and Developmental Disorders, 17*, 187–200.

Krantz, P. J., Zalewski, S., Hall, L., Fenski, E., & McClannahan, L. E. (1981). Teaching complex language to autistic children. *Analysis & Intervention in Developmental Disabilities, 1*, 259–297.

Lewy, A. L., & Dawson, G. (1992). Social stimulation and joint attention in young autistic children. *Journal of Abnormal Child Psychology, 20*, 555–566.

Lord, C. (1995). Follow-up of two-year-olds referred for possible autism. *Journal of Child Psychology and Psychiatry and Allied Disciplines, 36*, 1365–1382.

Lord, C., & McGee, J. P. (2001). *Educating children with autism.* Washington, DC: National Academy Press.

Lord, C., & Risi, S. (1998). Frameworks and methods in diagnosing autism spectrum disorders. *Mental Retardation and Developmental Disabilities Research Reviews: Special Issue: Autism, 4*, 90–96.

Lord, C., & Schopler, E. (1989). The role of age at assessment, developmental level, and test in the stability of intelligence scores in young autistic children. *Journal of Autism and Developmental Disorders, 19*, 483–499.

Lovaas, O. I. (1987). Behavioral treatment and normal educational and intellectual functioning in young autistic children. *Journal of Consulting and Clinical Psychology, 55*, 3–9.

Luiselli, J. K, Cannon, B. O., Ellis, J. T., & Sisson, R. W. (2000). Home-based behavioral interventions for young children with autism/pervasive developmental disorder: A preliminary evaluation of outcome in relation to child age and intensity of service delivery. *Autism, 4*, 389–398.

Marcus, L. M., Lansing, M., Andrews, C. E., & Schopler, E. (1978). Improvement of teaching effectiveness in parents of autistic children. *Journal of the American Academy of Child Psychiatry, 17*, 625–639.

Maurice, C. (1993). *Let me hear your voice: A family's triumph over autism.* New York: Kopf.

McEachin, J. J., Smith, T., & Lovaas, O. I. (1993). Long-term outcome for children with autism who received early intensive behavioral treatment. *American Journal on Mental Retardation , 97*, 359–372.

McGee, G. G., Krantz, P. J., & McClannahan, L. E. (1985). The facilitative effects of incidental teaching on preposition use by autistic children. *Journal of Applied Behavior Analysis, 18*, 17–31.

McGee, G. G., Morrier, M. J., & Daly, T. (1999). An incidental teaching approach to early intervention for toddlers with autism. *Journal of the Association for Persons With Severe Handicaps, 24*, 133–146.

McGee, G. G., Morrier, M. J., & Daly, T. (2001). The Walden Early Childhood Program. In J. Handleman & S. L. Harris (Eds.). *Preschool education programs for children with autism* (2nd ed., pp. 157–190). Autism: Pro-ed.

Mesibov, G. B. (1997). Formal and informal measures on the effectiveness of the TEACCH program. *Autism, 1*, 25–35.

Miller, J. N., & Ozonoff, S. (1997). Did Asperger's cases have Asperger disorder? A research note. *Journal of Child Psychology and Psychiatry and Allied Disciplines, 38*, 247–251.

Ozonoff, S., & Cathcart, K. (1998). Effectiveness of a home program intervention for young children with autism. *Journal of Autism and Developmental Disorders, 28*, 25–32.

Panerai, S., Ferrante, L., & Zingale, M. (2002). Benefits of the Treatment and Education of Autistic and Communication Handicapped Children (TEACCH) programme as compared with a non-specific approach. *Journal of Intellectual Disability Research, 46*, 318–327.

Pierce, K., & Schreibman, L. (1995). Increasing complex social behaviors in children with autism: Effects of peer-implemented pivotal response training. *Journal of Applied Behavior Analysis, 28*, 285–295.

Rogers, S. J., & Lewis, H. (1989). An effective day treatment model for young children with pervasive developmental disorders. *Journal of the American Academy of Child and Adolescent Psychiatry, 28*, 207–214.

Schopler, E., Mesibov, G., & Baker, A. (1982). Evaluation of treatment for autistic children and their parents. *Journal of the American Academy of Child Psychiatry, 21*, 262–267.

Sheinkopf, S. J., & Siegel, B. (1998). Home based behavioral treatment of young children with autism. *Journal of Autism and Developmental Disorders, 28*, 15–23.

Smith, T., Groen, A. D., & Wynn, J. W. (2000). Randomized trial of intensive early intervention for children with pervasive developmental disorder. *American Journal on Mental Retardation, 105*, 269–285.

Stahmer, A. C. (1995). Teaching symbolic play skills to children with autism using pivotal response training. *Journal of Autism and Developmental Disorders, 25*, 123–141.

Stone, W. L., Lee, E. B., Ashford, L., Brissie, J., Hepburn, S. L., Coonrod, E. E., et al. (1999). Can autism be diagnosed accurately in children under 3 years? *Journal of Child Psychology and Psychiatry and Allied Disciplines, 40*, 219–226.

Strain, P. S., Kerr, M. M., & Ragland, E. U. (1979). Effects of peer-mediated social initiations and prompting/reinforcement procedures on the social behavior of autistic children. *Journal of Autism and Developmental Disorders, 9*, 41–54.

Strain, P. S., Shores, R. E., & Timm, M. A. (1977). Effects of peer social initiations on the behavior of withdrawn preschool children. *Journal of Applied Behavior Analysis, 10*, 289–298.

Thorp, D. M., Stahmer, A. C., & Schreibman, L. (1995). Effects of sociodramatic play training on children with autism. *Journal of Autism and Developmental Disorders, 25*, 265–282.

Towbin, K. E. (1997). Pervasive developmental disorder not otherwise specified. In D. J. Cohen & F. R. Volkmar (Eds.), *The handbook of autism and other pervasive developmental disorders* (2nd ed., pp. 123–147). New York: Wiley.

Watson, L. R., Lord, C., Schaffer, B., & Schopler, E. (1989). *Teaching spontaneous communication to autistic and developmentally handicapped children.* New York: Irvington Publishers Inc.

Wetherby, A. M., & Prizant, B. M. (1999). Enhancing language and communication development in autism: Assessment and intervention guidelines. In D. B. Zager (Ed.), *Autism: Identification, education, and treatment* (2nd ed., pp. 141–174). Mahwah, NJ: Erlbaum.

World Health Organization. (1992). *The ICD 10 Classification of Mental and Behavioral Disorders: Clinical Descriptions and Diagnostic Guidelines.* Geneva, Switzerland: World Health Organization.

About the author: Dr. Christina Corsello is the Associate Director of The University of Michigan Autism & Communications Disorders Center. Dr. Corsello is a Licensed Clinical Psychologist and an adjunct clinical instructor in the University of Michigan Psychiatry Department. Dr. Corsello specializes in diagnosis and intervention of children with autism. Dr. Corsello is responsible for the clinical training of psychology graduate students, interns, and postdoctoral students. Dr. Corsello also conducts evaluations and clinical intervention programs, collaborates in research, and conducts training seminars nationally and internationally on the leading standardized diagnostic instruments. Dr. Corsello previously worked at The University of North Carolina and The University of Chicago.

Address correspondence to: Dr. Christina M. Corsello, UMACC, University of Michigan, 1111 East Catherine Street, Ann Arbor, MI 48109-2054.

Effects of Viewing the Television Program *Between the Lions* on the Emergent Literacy Skills of Young Children[1]

One of the most compelling findings from recent evaluations of reading research is that children who have an inadequate start in reading rarely catch up (National Reading Panel, 2000; National Research Council, 1998). For example, in Juel (1988), 88% of children identified as poor readers at the end of first grade were still identified as poor readers at the end of the fourth grade. Reading trajectories are established early and are difficult to change. Johnson and Allington (1991) observed that "remedial reading is generally not very effective in making children more literate" (p. 1001). Therefore, eliminating the need for remedial reading in the first place may be the most sensible alternative. Finding ways that all children can bolster their early literacy experiences, sustain those gains, and become successful, fluent readers is an important challenge that demands attention.

Whitehurst and Lonigan (1998, 2001) proposed that adequate early reading instruction includes opportunities for children to acquire knowledge of two interdependent domains of information. First, children need sources of information that directly support their understanding of the meaning of print (i.e., outside-in processes: vocabulary knowledge, conceptual knowledge, story schemas, comprehension). Children also need to be able to translate print into sounds and sounds into print (i.e., inside-out: phonemic awareness, letter-sound correspondence). Recent intervention research designed to provide young children with the necessary early literacy skills to succeed in school has reported that changes in preschool emergent literacy environments (see, e.g., Neuman & Roskos, 1997) and teacher-directed (see, e.g., O'Connor, 2000; O'Connor, Jenkins, & Slocum, 1995), parent-led (Whitehurst & Lonigan, 1998), and peer-mediated strategies (Mathes, Howard, Allen, & Fuchs, 1998) help children acquire these skills. However, the ability to widely implement such programs will be difficult and costly, and, as a result, the scale of impact on the nation's population of young children learning to read may be slow and small.

Building on their success teaching preschoolers school readiness skills via television (i.e., *Sesame Street*), the producers of a new television program for young children, in collaboration with leading reading experts, created a program that incorporated both outside-in and inside-out emergent literacy processes (Strickland & Rath, 2000). Their goal was to reach all segments of society, especially children who might have little or no access to print resources or few informal literacy opportunities in their homes. The pervasiveness of television (e.g., over 99% of U.S. homes have a television set; *Statistical Abstracts,* 2000) offers a powerful way to address the literacy needs of children who have "low redundancy of educational opportunity" (Mielke, 1994, p. 126).

Models of Learning from Television

The process of acquiring new information from television is complex, involving attention to and subsequent comprehension of program stimuli. When children interact with television, they integrate the various stimuli into meaningful, comprehensible bits of information by attending to important or interesting aspects of the stimuli (Huston & Wright, 1989). Although a great deal of knowledge about young children has been gained from past research on traditional print and television, the obvious step of merging print and television to enhance early literacy development is a more recent phenomenon (Linebarger, 2001). Models from the television literature provide the most useful framework for developing testable hypotheses about how print on screen might affect children's attention and learning through television.

Huston, Wright, and their colleagues (Huston & Wright, 1983; Rice, Huston, & Wright, 1982) proposed a model of attention to television where perceptually salient features of the stimulus initially draw a child's attention to the screen. When a child has little experience with television, sounds and unusual visual effects trigger the basic orienting mechanisms of the perceptual system (Miron, Bryant, & Zillman, 2001). These salient features or formal features provide structure and give meaning to the sensory images contained in the programs (Calvert, Huston, Watkins, & Wright, 1982; Campbell, Huston, & Wright, 1987). Comprehension is then improved when formal features are used to denote key moments and critical content for young children's focal attention.

---

[1] Literature review excerpt from: Linebarger, D. L., Kosanic, A. Z., Greenwood, C. R., & Doku, N. S. (2004). Effects of viewing the television program *Between the Lions* on the emergent literacy skills of young children. *Journal of Educational Psychology*, *96*, 297–308. Copyright © 2004 by the American Psychological Association. All rights reserved. Reprinted with permission.

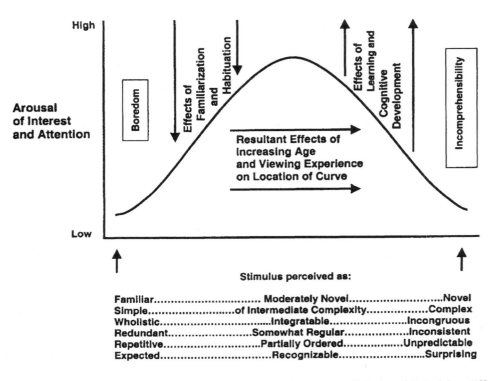

Figure 1. Traveling lens model. Reprinted from "The Forms and Codes of Television: Effects of Children's Attention, Comprehension, and Social Behavior," by M. L. Rice, A. C. Huston, and J. C. Wright, p. 32, in *Television and Behavior: Ten Years of Scientific Progress and Implications for the Eighties,* edited by D. Pearl, L. Bouthilet, and J. Lazar, 1982, Washington, DC: U.S. Government Printing Office. In the public domain.

Huston and Wright (1989; Rice et al., 1982) further elaborated this model of attention (see Figure 1). At various points while viewing a program, children make a series of attentional decisions. These decisions are based on cues of perceptual salience, comprehensibility of the program, and interpretability of the content. This model also predicts that attention is a joint function of the stimulus features, both form and content, and the dispositions of the viewer, including experience with the material, experience with the medium, and general world knowledge. Interest and attention are a function of the stimulus characteristics. A stimulus perceived as "moderately novel, of intermediate complexity, integratable, somewhat regular, partially ordered, and recognizable" (Huston & Wright, 1989, p. 117) should elicit the greatest amounts of interest and attention. When the stimulus characteristics no longer arouse interest or attention because of familiarization and habituation (i.e., familiar, simple, wholistic, redundant, repetitive, and expected), children no longer attend to them. Likewise, if the stimulus characteristics fall at the incomprehensible end of these continua (i.e., novel, complex, incongruous, inconsistent, unpredictable, and surprising), children do not attend because the stimulus is immediately perceived as incomprehensible. High-end stimuli become more familiar and hence more comprehensible with repetition and thus gain attention, whereas the low-end stimuli undergo further habituation with repetition and thus lose attention. The resultant of these two kinds of changes over time is that the high points of interest and attention slowly migrate toward the higher end. With age and viewing experience, the child's focus continually moves toward more cognitively challenging stimuli; hence, the stimuli that are initially incomprehensible "gradually move toward and through the child's focal lens of maximum interest, and then lose attention as they are habituated and become old hat" (Huston & Wright, 1989, p. 118).

Wright (2001) introduced an adjunct theoretical approach where the influence of an early condition, intervention, or other basis for predicting diverging individual differences over time will be greater if it produces differences opposite in direction from the developmental changes expected normatively for that outcome. Conversely, if the antecedent produces differences favoring the developmental direction that is normatively expected, its effects will be attenuated, and harder to detect. (Wright, 2001, p. 1)

For instance, in the literature for television viewing and aggression, interventions that would make boys less aggressive and more prosocial (e.g., educational
140 television) or that would make girls less prosocial or more aggressive (e.g., violent television) would be easier to detect than would an intervention that moves the child in a direction he or she is already progressing toward developmentally.

Application to Literacy

145   These two theoretical models of learning from television suggest that children with little print experience and, subsequently, poor reading skills may find print overly challenging and not attend to it, whereas children who are fluent readers may ignore print be-
150 cause they have habituated to it. When the curricular content of the program falls into the children's focus because it is appropriately interesting and cognitively challenging (i.e., as described in Figure 1), it would be predicted that this group of children would benefit
155 most from the content. Therefore, those children who are most at risk because they have no or very little familiarity with print are not able to benefit initially from exposure to it via television. Only through repeated exposure (either on or off television, or both)
160 would the print stimuli become accessible for these children. Similarly, children who are fluent readers also might not benefit from print exposure because they already have these skills in their repertoire and are progressing along a positive reading trajectory. The
165 group in the middle, emerging readers who are not yet fluent but do have modest levels of print exposure and reading skill, would then be the group evidencing the greatest gains in reading skill development because print is within their traveling lens; however, they may
170 still need significant instruction to attain reading fluency.

Most of the work supporting these models to date has been about comprehension of television content and not about acquisition of literacy skills or the appli-
175 cation of reading risk status to learning associated with viewing television. In addition, descriptions of the children's home media environments and subsequent relations to literacy skill acquisition are a new facet of what is known in the literature. Thus, the purposes of
180 this article are to describe the home media environments of young children, to determine whether watching an educational television series featuring literacy content for young children could improve these children's emergent literacy skills, and to examine
185 whether home media environments and emergent literacy skill improvements varied as a function of reading risk status.

References

Calvert, S. L., Huston, A. C., Watkins, B. A., & Wright, J. C. (1982). The relation between selective attention to television forms and children's comprehension of content. *Child Development, 53*, 601–610.

Campbell, T. A., Huston, A. C., & Wright, J. C. (1987). Form cues and content difficulty as determinants of children's cognitive processing of televised educational messages. *Journal of Experimental Child Psychology, 43*, 311–327.

Huston, A. C., & Wright, J. C. (1983). Children's processing of television: The informative functions of formal features. In J. Bryant & D. R. Anderson (Eds.), *Children's understanding of TV: Research on attention and comprehension* (pp. 37–68). New York: Academic Press.

Huston, A. C., & Wright, J. C. (1989). The forms of television and the child viewer. In G. Comstock (Ed.), *Public communication and behavior* (Vol. 2, pp. 103–158). San Diego, CA: Academic Press.

Johnson, P., & Allington, R. (1991). Remediation. In R. Barr, M. Kamil, P. Mosenthal, & P. D. Pearson (Eds.), *Handbook of reading research* (Vol. 2, pp. 984–1012). New York: Longman.

Juel, C. (1988). Learning to read and write: A longitudinal study of 54 children from first through fourth grades. *Journal of Educational Psychology, 80*, 437–447.

Linebarger, D. L. (2001). Learning to read using television: The effects of captions and narration. *Journal of Educational Psychology, 93*, 288–298.

Mathes, P. G., Howard, J. K., Allen, S. H., & Fuchs, D. (1998). Peer-assisted learning strategies for first-grade readers: Responding to the needs of diverse learners. *Reading Research Quarterly, 33*, 62–94.

Mielke, K. (1994). *Sesame Street* and children in poverty. *Media Studies Journal, 8*, 125–134.

Miron, D., Bryant, J., & Zillman, D. (2001). Creating vigilance for better learning from television. In D. G. Singer & J. L. Singer (Eds.), *Handbook of children and the media* (pp. 153–181). Thousand Oaks, CA: Sage.

National Reading Panel (2000). *Teaching children to read: An evidence-based assessment of the scientific research literature on reading and its implications for reading instruction.* Retrieved February 24, 2004, from http://www.nichd.nih.gov/publications/nrp/smallbook.htm

National Research Council (1998). *Preventing reading difficulties in young children.* Washington, DC: National Academy Press.

Neuman, S., & Roskos, K. (1997). Literacy knowledge in practice: Contexts of participation for young writers and readers. *Reading Research Quarterly, 32*, 10–32.

O'Connor, R. E. (2000). Increasing the intensity of intervention in kindergarten and first grade. *Learning Disabilities Research and Practice, 15*, 43–54.

O'Connor, R. E., Jenkins, J. R., & Slocum, T. A. (1995). Transfer among phonological tasks in kindergarten: Essential instructional content. *Journal of Educational Psychology, 87*, 202–217.

Rice, M. L., Huston, A. C., & Wright, J. C. (1982). The forms and codes of television: Effects of children's attention, comprehension, and social behavior. In D. Pearl, L. Bouthilet, & J. Lazar (Eds.), *Television and behavior: Ten years of scientific progress and implications for the eighties* (pp. 24–38). Washington, DC: U.S. Government Printing Office.

Statistical Abstracts. (2000). Washington, DC: Government Publishing Office.

Strickland, D. S., & Rath, L. K. (2000, August). *Between the Lions:* Public television promotes early literacy. *Reading Online, 4.* Retrieved February 24, 2004, from http://www.readingonline.org/articles/art_index.asp?HREF=/articles/strickland/index.html

Whitehurst, G. J., & Lonigan, C. J. (1998). Child development and emergent literacy. *Child Development, 69*, 848–872.

Whitehurst, G. J., & Lonigan, C. J. (2001). Emergent literacy: Development from prereaders to readers. In S. B. Neuman & D. K. Dickinson (Eds.), *Handbook of early literacy research* (pp. 11–29). New York: Guilford Press.

Wright, J. C. (2001, April). Demographic influences on long-term effects of television: A theoretical approach. In S. M. Fisch (Chair), *Theoretical approaches to the long-term effects of television viewing.* Symposium conducted at the meeting of the Society for Research in Child Development, Minneapolis, MN.

About the authors: *Deborah L. Linebarger,* Annenberg School for Communication, University of Pennsylvania. *Anjelika Z. Kosanic, Charles R. Greenwood,* and *Nii Sai Doku,* Juniper Gardens Children's Project, University of Kansas.

Acknowledgments: We thank Rhett Larsen, Patty Eskrootchi, and Denise Chowning, who collected the data for this project. We are especially thankful to Beth Kirsch, Linda K. Rath, other WGBH Boston staff, and Sirius Thinking, Ltd. staff, who provided valuable assistance and feedback in the completion of this project. Thanks are also extended to those schools, families, and children from the greater Kansas City metropolitan area who kindly volunteered to participate in this study.

Address correspondence to: Deborah L. Linebarger, Annenberg School for Communication, University of Pennsylvania, 3620 Walnut Street, Philadelphia, PA 19104. E-mail: dlinebarger @asc.upenn.edu

APPENDIX A

Sample *ERIC* Search

1. *Title*: Bright Beginnings for Babies
   Abstract: Notes the importance of positive human interactions and experiences on child development, and describes seven developmental areas crucial to early brain development. Suggests ways to enhance young children's development of emotional intelligence, social skills, motor skills, vision, language acquisition, vocabulary, and thinking skills.

2. *Title*: Diminutivization Supports Gender Acquisition in Russian Children
   Abstract: Gender agreement elicitation was used with Russian children to examine how diminutives common in Russian child-directed speech affect gender learning. Children were shown pictures of familiar and novel animals and asked to describe them after hearing their names, which contained regular morphophonological cues to masculine or feminine gender. Results indicate regularizing features of diminutives....

3. *Title*: Subject Realization and Crosslinguistic Interference in the Bilingual Acquisition of Spanish and English: What Is the Role of the Input?
   Abstract: Investigated whether crosslinguistic interference occurs in the domain of subject realization in Spanish in a bilingual (Spanish–English) acquisition context. Also explored whether the source of the interference is due to child-internal crosslanguage contact between English and Spanish or due to the nature of the language input in a bilingual family.

4. *Title*: Spanish Diminutives in Mother–Child Conversations
   Abstract: Examined gender and age patterns of diminutive use in conversations between Spanish-speaking Peruvian mothers and their 3- and 5-year-old children. Results confirm previous findings concerning both parents' greater use of diminutives with younger children and children's early acquisition of this aspect of morphology. Findings do not support studies on gender differences in parental use of diminut....

5. *Title*: Teaching Children with Autism Self-Initiations As a Pivotal Response
   Abstract: A study assessed whether two children (ages 4–6) with autism could be taught a child-initiated query as a pivotal response to facilitate the use of grammatical morphemes. Children learned the strategy and acquired and generalized the targeted morpheme. Children also showed increases in mean length of utterance and verb acquisition.

6. *Title*: Economy and Word Order Patterns in Bilingual English–Dutch Acquisition
   Abstract: Reports on bilingual acquisition of syntax. Draws on data from a bilingual English–Dutch child whose word order patterns testify to the fact that movement never occurs beyond the target and when deviant word orders are attested they result from lack of raising....

7. *Title*: Let's Change the Subject: Focus Movement in Early Grammar
   Abstract: Reanalyzes what the literature has taken to be children's productions of Gen subjects and argues that Gen subjects do not exist in child English. Suggests that what look like Gen subjects appear only in specific discourse contexts: contexts of contrastive focus or contexts of emphatic focus.

8. *Title*: Partial Constraint Ordering in Child French Syntax
   Abstract: Reanalyzes production data from three French children to make two basic points. Shows that tense and agreement inflection follow independent courses of acquisition (in child French). Using a mechanism of grammatical development based on partial rankings of constraints, analysis successfully models over three stages the frequency with which children use tensed, agreeing, and nonfinite verbs.

9. *Title*: Negative DPs and Elliptical Negation in Child English
   Abstract: Presents a new syntactical analysis of the negative marker "no" in child English. Claims that the majority of "no" constructions in early child English are determiner phrases in which "no" appears as a determiner. The claim is supported on the basis of distributional and morphosyntactic tests, a discourse analysis of children's elliptical negatives, and a comparison of "no" constructions in child....

10. *Title*: Young Children's Acquisition of Wh-Questions: The Role of Structured Input
    Abstract: Examined young children's acquisition of wh-questions. Children heard a wh-question and attempted to repeat it; a "talking bear" answered. The same format was used for two intervention sessions for children in a quasicontrol condition. Suggests very little input—if concentrated and varied and presented so the child attends to it and attempts to parse it—is sufficient for rapid extraction and....

11. *Title*: Lexically Specific Constructions in the Acquisition of Inflection in English
Abstract: Investigates the acquisition of elements that instantiate the grammatical category of "inflection"—copula "be," auxiliary "be" and 3sg present agreement—in longitudinal transcripts from five children, aged from 1 year and 6 months to 3 years and 5 months in the corpora examined. Aimed to determine whether inflection emerges as a unitary category, as predicted by recent generative accounts, or....

12. *Title*: The Role of Output Speech in Literacy Acquisition: Evidence from Congenital Anarthria
Abstract: Examines literary acquisition in a congenitally speechless child. Explains that in spite of a complete oral apraxia, the child developed normal intelligence and acquired complete mastery of reading and writing skills. Notes that though both his verbal memory and metaphonological skills were surprisingly preserved, he showed relative impairment in writing nonwords. Discusses the implications of....

13. *Title*: Acquisition of Multiple Languages among Children of Immigrant Families: Parents' Role in the Home-School Language Pendulum
Abstract: This study examined immigrant parents' role in young children's language learning in various linguistic contexts, focusing on how parents helped their children learn English while maintaining their mother tongue. Findings of questionnaires, observations, and interviews indicated factors supporting children's learning, including parents' interest in the two languages, joint parent–child activities....

14. *Title*: The Status of Functional Categories in Child Second Language Acquisition: Evidence from the Acquisition of CP
Abstract: Examines the status of the functional categories in child second language (L2) acquisition of English. Results from longitudinally collected data are reported, presenting counterevidence for recent hypotheses on early L2 acquisition that assume the following: (1) structure building approach according to which the acquisition of functional categories follows an implicational sequence of....

15. *Title*: The Role of Writing in Classroom Second Language Acquisition
Abstract: Argues that writing should play a more prominent role in classroom-based studies of second language acquisition. Contends that an implicit emphasis on spoken language is the result of the historical development of the field of applied linguistics and parent disciplines of structuralist linguistics, linguistic anthropology, and child language development.

16. *Title*: Children's Acquisition of Early Literacy Skills: Examining Family Contributions
Abstract: Examined the relationship between the family environment and children's language and literacy skills, guided by the three models of: (1) Family as Educator; (2) Resilient Family; and (3) Parent–Child Care Partnership. Found that only the Family as Educator model was significantly related to child language and literacy outcomes.

17. *Title*: Babytalk: Developmental Precursors to Speech
Abstract: Examines the process of language acquisition as well as scientists' understanding of the intricate process of learning to talk. Specifically addresses: (1) foundations of language; (2) prenatal period; (3) first month after birth; and (4) conversation. Also discusses adult–child activities that stimulate language learning.

18. *Title*: Learning English and Losing Chinese: A Case Study of a Child Adopted from China
Abstract: Looked at the acquisition of English and the loss of Chinese by a child adopted from China into an English-speaking Canadian family at the age of 17 months. The child's production and comprehension of Chinese were observed from 4 weeks after her arrival. Both acquisition of Chinese and loss of English were remarkably fast. Data suggest that the child's language acquisition was founded on already....

19. *Title*: Getting Started without a System: From Phonetics to Phonology in Bilingual Development
Abstract: Argues that the question of whether bilinguals initially have one or two phonetic systems is out of place because before the child develops a fairly substantial vocabulary of about 100 words, there is no system at all. This is supported by analyses of early word patterns drawn from three bilingual children.

20. *Title*: The Early Phonological Development of a Farsi–English Bilingual Child
Abstract: Addresses the issue of whether bilingual children begin phonological acquisition with one phonological system or two. Five hypotheses are suggested for the possible structure of the bilingual child's phonological system. Analyses from a longitudinal study of a Farsi–English bilingual infant supported the hypothesis that the child had acquired two separate phonologies with mutual influence.

21. *Title*: Morphological and Syntactic Transfer in Child L2 Acquisition of the English Dative Alternation
Abstract: Compares the acquisition of the English to- and for-dative alternation by native-speaking English, Japanese, and Korean children. Investigates whether second language learners (L2) like native language learners overextend the double-object variant and whether L2 learners, like L2 adults, transfer properties of the native language grammar.

22. *Title*: Is There Primacy of Aspect in Child L2 English?
    Abstract: Investigates whether the aspect-before-tense hypothesis accounts for the acquisition of tense-aspect morphology in child second language English. Addressed whether early uses of tense-aspect inflections can be analyzed as a spell-out of semantic/aspectual features of verbs. Data are from a longitudinal study of an 8-year-old Russian-speaking child who was learning English in the United States.

23. *Title*: Development of Academic Skills from Preschool through Second Grade: Family and Classroom Predictors of Developmental Trajectories
    Abstract: Relates children's experiences with parents and teachers to the acquisition of academic skills from preschool through second grade. Children tended to show better academic skills across time if their parents had more education and reported progressive parenting beliefs. Family background and teacher–child relationships indicated that a closer relationship with the teacher was positively related....

24. *Title*: Implications of Child Errors for the Syntax of Negation in Korean
    Abstract: Reviews the existing record pertaining to the acquisition of negation in Korean and juxtaposing it with current research in cross-linguistic child language acquisition.

25. *Title*: Multilanguage Programs. Beginnings Workshop
    Abstract: Presents five articles on multilanguage programs in early childhood education: "Bilingualism/Multilingualism and Language Acquisition Theories" (Evienia Papadaki-D'Onofrio); "Training and Supporting Caregivers Who Speak a Language Different from Those in Their Community" (Joan Matsalia and Paula Bowie); "Language Immersion Programs for Young Children" (Francis Wardle); and "Hearing Parents in....

26. *Title*: Determinant of Acquisition Order in Wh-Questions: Re-Evaluating the Role of Caregiver Speech
    Abstract: Analyzed naturalistic data from 12 2- to 3-year-old children and their mothers to assess the relative contribution of complexity and input frequency to wh-question acquisition. Results suggest that the relationship between acquisition and complexity may be a by-product of the high correlation between complexity and the frequency with which mothers use particular wh-words and verbs.

27. *Title*: French–English Bilingual Acquisition of Phonology: One Production System or Two?
    Abstract: Examines onset, atrophy, and possible interaction of a set of patterns in the speech of a child acquiring French and English. Examines how data bear on the question of whether the bilingual child has two distinct production phonologies from the earliest stage. Tests recent claims consonant harmony patterns.

28. *Title*: The Use and Function of Nonfinite Root Clauses in Swedish Child Language
    Abstract: Examines the use and structure of so-called nonfinite root clauses, including root infinitives and root supines, in Swedish child language. Investigation of four Swedish child language corpora shows that children use nonfinite root clauses in a systematic way. Also shows that children's use of root infinitives is closely associated with a particular speech act or speech function called the....

29. *Title*: Tense and Aspect in Early Child Russian
    Abstract: Observed child–parent interaction to investigate the early temporal and aspectual morphology in four monolingual Russian-speaking children. Analysis of data obtained in weekly videotaped sessions shows early mastery of all tenses as well as grammatical aspect at an early age.

30. *Title*: Why Is "Is" Easier than "-s"?: Acquisition of Tense/Agreement Morphology by Child Second Language Learners of English
    Abstract: This study of first-language-Russian children acquiring English as a second language investigates the reasons behind omission of verbal inflection in second language (L2) acquisition and argues for presence of functional categories in second-language grammar. Shows that child L2 learners, while omitting inflection, almost never produce incorrect tense/agreement morphology.

31. *Title*: Age and Language Skills of Deaf Children in Relation to Theory of Mind Development
    Abstract: A study examined theory of mind acquisition in 34 children (ages 5–10) with deafness using four traditional false-belief tasks. Results indicate the age of the child was strongly related to theory of mind development and that the children were delayed by approximately 3 years in this cognitive developmental milestone.

32. *Title*: Promoting Language and Literacy Development through Parent–Child Reading in Hong Kong Preschoolers
    Abstract: Evaluated Hong Kong Chinese kindergarten children's literacy development through dialogic reading, typical reading, and control groups. Found that early literacy-related activities in the home have strong effects on literacy growth and language development in Chinese. Concluded that success of the dialogic reading technique contributes to the goal of raising global literacy standards and....

33.   *Title*: Approache Pluraliste du Developpement et Etude des Variations Procedurals en Production D'Orthographes Inventees [A Pluralistic Approach to the Development and Study of Procedural Variations in the Production of Invented Spelling]
Abstract: This study used a pluralistic model to examine the procedures used by two preschoolers to achieve written productions using invented orthographies. The model allows children's procedural variations to be taken into consideration by understanding the hierarchy of different processing modes available to children in completing the task and incorporates children's procedural variations at the origin....

34.   *Title*: Phonological Neighborhoods in the Developing Lexicon
Abstract: Phonological neighborhood analyses of how children's expressive lexicons, maternal input, and an adult lexicon were conducted. In addition to raw counts and frequency-weighted counts, neighborhood size was calculated as the proportion of the lexicon to which each target word is similar, to normalize for vocabulary size differences. Analyses revealed children's lexicons contain more similar....

35.   *Title*: Opposites Attract: The Role of Predicate Dimensionality in Preschool Children's Processing of Negations
Abstract: Three experiments investigated the role of oppositional predicate dimensionally in 4- and 5-year-old children's processing of negation. Children often recalled negated items as affirmations, which suggests that children's use of predicate dimensionally contributes to nonclassical processing.

36.   *Title*: Morphosyntactic Constructs in the Development of Spoken and Written Hebrew Text Production
Abstract: Examined the distribution of two Hebrew nominal structures in spoken and written texts of two genres produced by 90 native-speaking participants. Written texts were found to be denser than spoken texts lexically and syntactically as measured by the number of novel N-N compounds and denominal adjectives per clause; in older age groups this difference was found to be more pronounced.

37.   *Title*: Early Syntactic Creativity: A Usage-Based Approach
Abstract: Determined the degree to which a sample of one child's creative utterances related to utterances that the child previously produced. Utterances were intelligible, multiword utterances produced by the child in a single hour of interaction with her mother. Results suggest the high degree of creativity in early English child language could be partially based upon entrenched schemas and a small....

38.   *Title*: A Connectionist Account of Spanish Determiner Production
Abstract: Investigates phonological cues available to children and explores the possibility that differential frequency in the linguistic input explains the priority given to masculine forms when children are faced with ambiguous novel terms. A connectionist model of determiner production was incrementally trained on a lexicon of determiner-noun phrases taken from parental speech in a longitudinal study.

39.   *Title*: Early Words, Multiword Utterances and Maternal Reading Strategies As Predictors of Mastering Word Inflections in Finnish
Abstract: Reports how children's language skills and mothers' book-reading strategies predict mastery of word inflections in a sample of Finnish children. Three theoretical models were tested on the longitudinal data using path analyses. Suggests direct developmental continuity from producing words and multiword utterances on later inflectional growth, but indirect effects of maternal strategies on....

40.   *Title*: Outcomes of Early Language Delay: II. Etiology of Transient and Persistent Language Difficulties
Abstract: A study involving 356 twin pairs with early language delay found environmental influences shared by both twins were more substantial than genetic factors. Heritability was significantly higher in those with persisting difficulties but only when assessed in terms of parental concern at 3 years or professional involvement at 4 years.

41.   *Title*: Outcomes of Early Language Delay: I. Predicting Persistent and Transient Language Difficulties at 3 and 4 Years
Abstract: Parent-based assessments of vocabulary, grammar, nonverbal ability, and use of language to refer to past and future were obtained for 8,386 twins at age 2. Of the children who had early language delay, 44.1% had persisting language difficulties at 3 years and 40.2% had persisting language difficulties at 4 years.

42.   *Title*: Designing an Outcome Study to Monitor the Progress of Students with Autism Spectrum Disorders
Abstract: The Autism Spectrum Disorders Outcome Study is tracking the educational progress of 67 students (ages 2–6) with autism. Initial results, based on the first 16 months of the study, indicate the majority of children have made significant progress in social interaction, expressive speech, and use of language concepts.

43.   *Title*: A Developmental Perspective on Language Assessment and Intervention for Children on the Autistic Spectrum
Abstract: This article presents a developmental perspective on language acquisition that can serve as a framework for understanding and treating the language and communication challenges faced by children with

autism. Profiles of five children (ages 3–7) with autism spectrum disorders are discussed to illustrate the application of a Developmental Social–Pragmatic Model.

44. *Title*: Out of the Mouths of Babes: Unlocking the Mysteries of Language and Voice
     Abstract: Summarizes three studies that have revolutionized child psychology by teaching us that children are biologically programmed to learn language; children's language development is orderly and pragmatic, but grammatically mysterious; and children's linguistic self-expression reveals some disturbing ways in which they have been socialized. Presents nine ways this information can be useful at camp.

45. *Title*: "Want That" Is Understood Well before "Say That," "Think That," and False Belief: A Test of de Villiers's Linguistic Determinism on German-Speaking Children
     Abstract: Two experiments with monolingual German-speaking 2.5- to 4.5-year-olds showed a consistent developmental gap between children's memory/inference of what someone wanted and what someone wrongly said or thought. Correct answers emerged with mastery of the false-belief task. It was concluded that the observed gap constrains de Villiers's linguistic determinism, which claims that acquisition of....

46. *Title*: Beginning to Communicate after Cochlear Implantation: Oral Language Development in a Young Child
     Abstract: This longitudinal case study examined the emergence of oral language skills in a child with deafness whose cochlear implant was activated at 20 months. Normal or above-normal rates of development were observed in decreased production of nonwords, increased receptive vocabulary, type-token ratio, regular use of word combinations, and phrase comprehension.

47. *Title*: Parent-Reported Language Skills in Relation to Otitis Media during the First 3 Years of Life
     Abstract: A study investigated the degree of association between parent-reported language scores at ages 1, 2, and 3 years, and the cumulative duration of middle-ear effusion (MEE) during the first 3 years in 621 children. At age 3, the cumulative duration of MEE significantly contributed to the variance in parent-reported scores.

48. *Title*: A Prospective Longitudinal Study of Phonological Development in Late Talkers
     Abstract: Free play and elicited language samples were obtained monthly for 10 to 12 months from five late-talking children. Analysis indicated that three of the children resolved their late onset of speech by 33 to 35 months of age. Both quantitative factors (e.g., limited phonetic inventory) and qualitative factors (e.g., atypical error patterns) were potential markers of long-term phonological delay.

49. *Title*: Drawing Insight from Pictures: The Development of Concepts of False Drawing and False Belief in Children with Deafness, Normal Hearing, and Autism
     Abstract: Three studies examined theory-of-mind concepts among children ages 6–13 years with deafness or autism, and 4-year-olds with normal development. Findings indicated that while the children with deafness or autism scored significantly lower on standard tests of false belief understanding, they scored higher on even the most challenging drawing-based tests.

50. *Title*: Cross-Cultural Similarities in the Predictors of Reading Acquisition
     Abstract: Compared reading development among kindergartners in Hong Kong and the United States using measures of word recognition, phonological awareness, speeded naming, visual spatial skill, and processing speed. Found that models of early reading development were similar across cultures. The strongest predictor of reading was phonological awareness. Speed of processing strongly predicted speeded naming....

51. *Title*: Reorganizing the Lexicon by Learning a New Word: Japanese Children's Interpretation of the Meaning of a New Word for a Familiar Artifact
     Abstract: Three studies investigated how 3-year-old Japanese children interpret the meaning of a new word associated with a familiar artifact. Findings suggest that children flexibly recruit clues from multiple sources, including shape information and function familiarity, but the clues are weighed in hierarchical order so children can determine the single most plausible solution in a given situation when....

52. *Title*: Understanding Child Bilingual Acquisition Using Parent and Teacher Reports
     Abstract: Examined the extent to which years of exposure to a language, amount of language input at home and at school, and amount of exposure to reading and other literacy activities in a language relate to observed bilingual performance in young children as obtained from teacher and parent reports.

53. *Title*: Caregivers' Contingent Comments to 9-Month-Old Infants: Relationships with Later Language
     Abstract: Examined the relationship between caregiver input to 9-month-old infants and their subsequent language. Mother–infant dyads were videotaped at ages 9, 12, and 30 months. Language comprehension was measured by parent report and correlated with an independent language measure. Found that the total number of words mothers used when their infants were 9 months predicted vocabulary.

54. *Title*: Minding the Absent: Arguments for the Full Competence Hypothesis
     Abstract: Suggests that the systematic omission of functional material by young children, contrary to current

beliefs, argues for the presence of functional structure because in the absence of such structure what is expected is not a systematic omission of functional material but rather its random use.

55. *Title*: Communication Intervention for Infants and Toddlers with Cochlear Implants
     Abstract: Discussion of communication intervention with very young children who have cochlear implants examines: (1) the developmental appropriateness of materials and procedures; (2) behavior and compliance issues; (3) the need for less didactic instruction and more incidental learning emphasis; and (4) recognition of the home as the primary venue for language learning. A communication assessment protocol....

56. *Title*: Early Language Stimulation of Down's Syndrome Babies: A Study on the Optimum Age to Begin
     Abstract: Examined the marked delay in language acquisition suffered by babies with Down's Syndrome and how early treatment affects the subsequent observed development among 36 subjects in Spain. Found statistically significant differences in language acquisitions in favor of newborns, compared with 90-day-old through 18-month-old infants who experienced early stimulation treatment.

57. *Title*: Measuring Early Language Development in Preschool Children with Autism Spectrum Disorder Using the MacArthur Communicative Development Inventory (Infant Form)
     Abstract: Collected data on early language development of preschool children with autism spectrum disorder, using the MacArthur Communicative Development Inventory. The pattern of development of understanding phrases, word comprehension and expression, and production of gestures, was compared to the typical pattern. Implications for assessment and intervention are discussed.

58. *Title*: The Development of Inversion in Wh-Questions: A Reply to Van Valin
     Abstract: Responds to a critique of an earlier article. Reexamines the pattern of inversion and universion in Adam's (1973) wh-question data and argues that the Role and Reference grammar explanation put forth cannot account for some of the developmental facts it was designed to explain.

59. *Title*: Genre and Evaluation in Narrative Development
     Abstract: Examined Venezuelan children's developing abilities to use evaluative language in fictional and personal narratives. Looks at whether the use of evaluative language varies in fictional and personal narratives, there is a relationship between the use of evaluative language in these two narrative genres, and the role children's age and socioeconomic status.

60. *Title*: Lexical Choice Can Lead to Problems: What False-Belief Tests Tell Us about Greek Alternative Verbs
     Abstract: Greek has two verbs of agency that can be used interchangeably to mean "to look for." Examined whether children will obey the principle of contrast to diagnose that one verb is mentalistic and the other is to be construed behaviorally. A study of mothers' verb use confirmed that the verb preferred in home use gave below chance performance on a false-belief test while the less-established verb....

61. *Title*: The Role of Modeling and Request Type on Symbolic Comprehension of Objects and Gestures in Young Children
     Abstract: Considered whether modeling and the type of an adult's request influenced children's ability at age 1 year and 8 months and 2 years and 2 months to comprehend gestures and replica objects as symbols for familiar objects. Evaluated whether modeling and type of request influenced children's ability at 1 year and 8 months to understand familiar objects as symbols. Suggests that symbolic....

62. *Title*: Chinese Children's Comprehension of Count-Classifiers and Mass-Classifiers
     Abstract: Two experiments were conducted to test Chinese children's comprehension of count-and mass-classifiers. Participants were Chinese-speaking children ages 3 thru 8, plus 16 adults. Results cohere with the linguistic analysis that the count-mass distinction is relevant in Chinese grammar. Results also cohere with the current theory in cognitive development that the ontological constraint reflected in....

63. *Title*: Effects of Lexical Factors on Lexical Access among Typical Language-Learning Children and Children with Word-Finding Difficulties
     Abstract: Studied the influence of lexical factors, known to impact lexical access in adults, on the word retrieval of children. Participants included 320 typical and atypical language-learning children, ranging from 7 to 12 years of age. Lexical factors examined included word frequency, age of acquisition, neighborhood density, neighborhood frequency, and stress pattern. Findings indicated that these fact....

64. *Title*: Form Is Easy, Meaning Is Hard: Resolving a Paradox in Early Child Language
     Abstract: Offers resolutions to the paradox of infants' ability to abstract patterns over specific items and toddlers' lack of ability to generalize patterns over specific English words/constructions. Argues that contradictions are rooted in differing methodologies and stimuli content. Suggests that the patterns infants extract from linguistic input are not tied to meaning; toddlers do not lose these....

65. *Title*: Why Do Children Learn to Say "Broke"? A Model of Learning the Past Tense without Feedback
     Abstract: Presents a hybrid ACT-R model that shows U-shaped learning of the English past tense without direct

feedback, changes in vocabulary, or unrealistically high rates of regular verbs. Illustrates that the model can learn the default rule, even if regular forms are infrequent. Shows that the model can explore the question of why there is a distinction between regular and irregular verbs by examining....

66. *Title*: Seeing the Invisible: Situating L2 Literacy Acquisition in Child–Teacher Interaction
Abstract: Revisits an earlier study on English-as-a Second-Language (ESL) children's emergence into literacy, which was conducted with 5- and 6-year olds at a multilingual K-12 school in Casablanca, Morocco. Discusses the notion of "synchronicity"—a dynamic oneness between teacher and child—as the distinguishing feature of three classrooms where children's literacy development was taking place at an....

67. *Title*: The Play and Language Behavior of Mothers with and without Dyslexia and Its Association to Their Toddlers' Language Development
Abstract: The play and language behavior of mothers with ($n = 49$) and without ($n = 49$) specific reading disabilities were investigated during play with their 14-month-old children. Typically, reading mothers produced significantly more symbolic play and language in play interactions with their children than did the mothers with reading disabilities.

68. *Title*: Normative Scripts for Object Labeling during a Play Activity: Mother–Child and Sibling Conversations in Mexican-Descent Families
Abstract: Patterns of mother and sibling object labeling were observed during play. Subjects were 40 Mexican-descent mothers, their children aged 2–3, and older siblings. Mothers provided names for objects (referential labeling) as often as they mentioned objects within the ongoing activity (labeling in action), while siblings more frequently used referential labeling. Results suggest diverse....

69. *Title*: Moving Beyond Linear Trajectories of Language Shift and Bilingual Language Socialization
Abstract: Mexican-descent families' language socialization experiences and the evolution of their bilingualism were examined through interviews with 63 third-graders and their parents of various immigrant generations and follow-up interviews with 38 families 4–7 years later. Interviews revealed extremely positive attitudes about English, Spanish, bilingualism, and native language maintenance; changing....

70. *Title*: Bibliography of Recent Scholarship in Second Language Writing
Abstract: This bibliography cites and summarizes books, essays, and research reports on second- and foreign-language writing and writing instruction that have become available to its compilers during the period of January 1, 2002 to March 31, 2002.

71. *Title*: Neurolinguistic Aspects of Bilingualism
Abstract: Discusses aphasia, the language deficit resulting from damage to the language centers of the brain, in order to evaluate how research on bilingual and polyglot aphasic individuals has contributed to our knowledge of the representation of language and languages in neurologically intact humans' brains. Examines the literature on treating lateral dominance for language in bilinguals and evaluates....

72. *Title*: /l/ Production in English–Arabic Bilingual Speakers
Abstract: Reports an analysis of /l/ production by English–Arabic bilingual children. Addresses the question of whether the bilingual develops one phonological system or two by calling for a refinement of the notion of system using insights from recent phonetic and sociolinguistic work on variability in speech. English–Arabic bilinguals were studied.

73. *Title*: Phonetic Evidence for Early Language Differentiation: Research Issues and Some Preliminary Data
Abstract: Highlights methodological issues that impact phonetic-phonological data collection and interpretation in studies of early language differentiation. Issues include language context, bilingual versus monolingual mode, and adult listening bias. Presents data from two bilingual children, aged 4 and 2, learning Japanese and English.

74. *Title*: Developing Vowel Systems As a Window to Bilingual Phonology
Abstract: Examines vowel systems of German–Spanish bilingual children to determine whether there is interaction between the two language systems. Given the differences in the vowel systems, which point to a more marked system in the case of German, two predictions are considered: 1) bilingual children will acquire the vowel length contrast in their German productions later than monolingual German-speaking....

75. *Title*: The Role of Markedness in the Acquisition of Complex Prosodic Structures by German–Spanish Bilinguals
Abstract: Addresses bilingual phonological development in the prosodic field by studying the transition from a single metrical foot to the production of one foot preceded by an unstressed syllable or to the production of two consecutive feet. Uses monolingual data to form a baseline comparison with the bilingual data. Establishment of two different constraint hierarchies for the two languages studied....

76. *Title*: Effects of Prelinguistic Milieu Teaching and Parent Responsivity Education on Dyads Involving Children with Intellectual Disabilities
Abstract: This study evaluated the effectiveness of Prelinguistic Milieu Teaching for toddlers ($n = 39$) with

intellectual disabilities and responsivity education for their parents as a means of facilitating children's communication and language production skills. Comparison of parent–child pairs receiving or not receiving the intervention found the intervention facilitated parental responsivity. Effects on....

77. *Title*: Evaluating Attributions of Delay and Confusion in Young Bilinguals: Special Insights from Infants Acquiring a Signed and a Spoken Language
Abstract: Examines whether early simultaneous bilingual language exposure causes children to be language delayed or confused. Cites research suggesting normal and parallel linguistic development occurs in each language in young children and young children's dual language developments are similar to monolingual language acquisition. Research on simultaneous acquisition of French oral and sign language is....

78. *Title*: Developmental Dyslexia as Developmental and Linguistic Variation: Editor's Commentary
Abstract: This commentary reviews forthcoming articles on the scientific study of dyslexia, genetic and neurophysiological aspects of dyslexia, cross-linguistic aspects of literacy development and dyslexia, and theory-based practice. It concludes that educators should continue to strive to promote theory-based research and evidence-based practice to achieve better prevention of and intervention for....

79. *Title*: The Speech and Language of Children Aged 25 Months: Descriptive Data from the Avon Longitudinal Study of Parents and Children
Abstract: The Avon Longitudinal Study of Parents and Children (ALSPAC) provided descriptive data on the speech and language of 25-month-olds. Findings indicated great range in the stage of expressive language development achieved. Girls showed more advanced skills than boys. A clear pattern was identified in use of sound classes. Child verbal comprehension and expressive stage related to pretend play, turn....

80. *Title*: It's Never Too Early
Abstract: Describes a statewide language-development program developed among Maryland's city, county, and regional library systems to help parents prepare their preschoolers for success in school. Discusses child development, the role of libraries, storytelling training, and preschool literacy efforts by the Public Library Association; and lists Web resources.

81. *Title*: Syllable Omission by Two-Year-Old Children
Abstract: A study examined the ability of 10 2-year-olds to produce minimal pairs of novel trisyllabic words with primary stress on the first or second syllables. The syllables contained dissimilar or similar vowel contrasts to determine if segments affected omission. Omission was more frequent for the first syllable of weak-strong-weak word pairs.

82. *Title*: From Ear to Cortex: A Perspective on What Clinicians Need to Understand about Speech Perception and Language Processing
Abstract: This article reviews experiments that have revealed developmental changes in speech perception that accompany improvements in access to phonetic structure. It explains how these perceptual changes appear to be related to other aspects of language development. Evidence is provided that these changes result from adequate language experience in naturalistic contexts.

83. *Title*: Factors Affecting the Development of Speech, Language, and Literacy in Children with Early Cochlear Implantation
Abstract: This study investigated factors contributing to auditory, speech, language, and reading outcomes in 136 children (ages 8–9) with prelingual deafness after 4–6 years of cochlear implants. While child and family characteristics accounted for 20% of outcome variance, the primary rehabilitative factor was educational emphasis on oral–aural communication.

84. *Title*: Changes in Speech Production in a Child with a Cochlear Implant: Acoustic and Kinematic Evidence
Abstract: A method is presented for examining change in motor patterns used to produce linguistic contrasts. In this case study, the method is applied to a child who experienced hearing loss at age 3 and received a multichannel cochlear implant at 7. Post-implant, acoustic durations showed a maturational change.

85. *Title*: In the Beginning Was the Rhyme? A Reflection on Hulme, Hatcher, Nation, Brown, Adams, and Stuart (2002)
Abstract: Describes phonological sensitivity at different grain sizes as a good predictor of reading acquisition in all languages. Presents information on development of phonological sensitivity for syllables, onsets, and rhymes. Illustrates that phoneme-level skills develop fastest in children acquiring orthographically consistent languages with simple syllabic structure. Maintains that for English, both....

86. *Title*: How Much Do We Know about the Importance of Play in Child Development? Review of Research
Abstract: Discusses children's play in conjunction with intellectual development, language, and social benefits. Suggests that play develops personality, encourages personal relations, stimulates creativity, adds to happiness,

and advances learning. Encourages parents and teachers to provide children with richly varied play experiences to promote cognition, language, social/emotional behavior, and....

87. *Title*: Literacy-Based Planning and Pedagogy That Supports Toddler Language Development
    Abstract: Provides an overview of early language and literacy development and influences. Details how teachers can use storybooks to plan toddler curricula, presents criteria for selecting toddler books for curriculum projects, and describes how one book served as the foundation for a curriculum project, focusing on representing ideas and concepts from the book and incorporating activities throughout the....

88. *Title*: The Lexicon and Phonology: Interactions in Language Acquisition
    Abstract: This article highlights the link between lexical and phonological acquisition by considering learning by children beyond the 50-word stage and by applying cognitive models of spoken word processing to development. The effects of lexical and phonological variables on perception, production, and learning are discussed in the context of a two-representation connectionist model.

89. *Title*: Whole-Word Phonology and Templates: Trap, Bootstrap, or Some of Each?
    Abstract: Cognitive mechanisms that may account for the phenomena of whole-word phonology and phonological templates in children are described and strategies for identifying whole-word phonological patterns in normal and disordered phonologies are proposed. Intervention strategies that draw on these same mechanisms as a way to overcome their inappropriate persistence are recommended.

90. *Title*: Facilitating First Language Development in Young Korean Children through Parent Training in Picture Book Interactions
    Abstract: Eleven native-Korean-speaking, Korean-American mothers of children aged 2–4 received 1 hour of training in specific language facilitation techniques around picture-book interactions. A control group received instruction in general emergent literacy development and first-language acquisition. Four weeks later, treatment-group children showed significantly increased language production and....

91. *Title*: The Relationship between Early Language Delay and Later Difficulties in Literacy
    Abstract: Presents diagnostic model of early language delay; examines four longitudinal studies exploring relationship between early language delay and later literacy development. Identifies findings providing strong evidence of continuity between language delay and later reading difficulties and the importance of severity and chronicity of the impairment. Asserts that early language delay is a key risk....

92. *Title*: Use of the Language Development Survey (LDS) in a National Probability Sample of Children 18 to 35 Months Old
    Abstract: Data from 278 children (ages 18–35 months) were used to norm the Language Development Survey (LDS) and the Child Behavioral Checklist. Vocabulary scores increased markedly with age, were higher in girls, and were modestly correlated with socioeconomic level. Correlations between LDS scores and checklist problem scores were low.

93. *Title*: Play and Language in Children with Autism
    Abstract: This article considers the relationship between play and language skills of typical children and children with autism. Evidence for a relationship is reviewed, and it is concluded that if there is a relationship between play and language in children with autism it is weak, if it exists at all.

94. *Title*: Tracking Preschoolers' Language and Preliteracy Development Using a General Outcome Measurement System: One Education District's Experience
    Abstract: This article describes an application of a general outcome measurement system, Individual Growth and Development Indicators, with 68 preschoolers (ages 3–6). Results indicate the measures were easy to use; efficient in administration, scoring, and data interpretation; and provided valuable information for making early childhood education and special education decisions.

95. *Title*: Child Education and Literacy Learning for Multicultural Societies: The Case of the Brazilian National Curricular References for Child Education (NCRs)
    Abstract: Discusses promotion of multicultural child education and literacy learning. Focuses on identity building and language development. Analyzes Brazilian government's "National Curricular References for Child Education." Argues that predominance of a monocultural, cognitive-based approach to child education is detrimental to children whose cultural and linguistic patterns are different from the....

96. *Title*: Is Chronic Otitis Media Associated with Differences in Parental Input at 12 Months of Age? An Analysis of Joint Attention and Directives
    Abstract: Argues that parental input is an important factor often neglected in research that may mediate language outcomes. Investigated how parents interact with their 12-month-old children who suffer from otitis media status. Results indicate that parents of chronically affected children direct attention more often and engage in fewer joint attentional episodes than parents of nonchronically affected....

97. *Title*: The Language Proficiency Profile-2: Assessment of the Global Communication Skills of Deaf Children across Languages and Modalities of Expression
Abstract: Two studies investigated the developmental trends and concurrent validity of the Language Proficiency Profile-2 (LPP-2), a measure of language and communication skills for deaf children. Results indicate that the LPP-2 has good utility not only as a measure of overall language development but also as a predictor of achievement for English language and early reading skills.

98. *Title*: Hearing Status, Language Modality, and Young Children's Communicative and Linguistic Behavior
Abstract: This study compared early pragmatic skill development in 76 children (ages 1–4) with severe or profound hearing loss enrolled in either a simultaneous communication (SC) or oral communication (OC) approach to language learning. Results indicated some advantages of the SC approach, although overall frequency of communication and breadth of vocabulary did not differ between SC and OC groups.

99. *Title*: Assessment of Language Skills in Young Children with Profound Hearing Loss under Two Years of Age
Abstract: The validity of the Diary of Early Language (Di-EL), a parent report technique, was evaluated with nine children with profound hearing loss using cochlear implants or hearing aids. Lexical data, reported by parents using the Di-EL, agreed with results of the MacArthur Communicative Development Inventories and the Rossetti Infant Toddler Language Scale, suggesting the Di-El's validity.

100. *Title*: Play as the Leading Activity of the Preschool Period: Insights from Vygotsky, Leont'ev, and Bakhtin
Abstract: Discusses ideas from Vygotsky, Leont'ev and Bakhtin to show how fantasy play acts as its own zone of proximal development that contributes to the development of symbolic mediation, the appropriation of social roles and symbols, and the preschool child's preparation for elementary school.

101. *Title*: Parental Identification of Early Behavioral Abnormalities in Children with Autistic Disorder
Abstract: Parents of 153 children with autism completed a questionnaire on early childhood behaviors of concern and age of onset. Parents identified the following concerns: gross motor difficulties; social awareness deficits; communication problems; and unusual preoccupations. There was a significant interval between parents first noticing abnormalities and definite diagnosis.

102. *Title*: Genetic Evidence for Bidirectional Effects of Early Lexical and Grammatical Development
Abstract: Two cohorts of same-sex twin pairs were assessed on grammar and vocabulary. Findings indicated that vocabulary and grammar correlated strongly at 2 and 3 years in both cohorts, with a consistently high genetic correlation between vocabulary and grammar at both ages. Findings suggest that the same genetic influences operate for vocabulary and grammar, a finding incompatible with traditional....

103. *Title*: Paradox Lost? No, Paradox Found! Reply to Tomasello and Akhtar (2003)
Abstract: Asserts that the posited paradox between infancy and toddlerhood language was not eliminated by Tomasello and Akhtar's appeal to infants' robust statistical learning abilities. Maintains that scrutiny of their studies supports the resolution that abstracting linguistic form is easy for infants and that toddlers find it difficult to integrate abstract forms with meaning. Claims that intermodal....

104. *Title*: What Paradox? A Response to Naigles (2002)
Abstract: Presents evidence that the supposed paradox in which infants find abstract patterns in speech-like stimuli whereas even some preschoolers struggle to find abstract syntactic patterns within meaningful language is no paradox. Asserts that all research evidence shows that young children's syntactic constructions become abstract in a piecemeal fashion, based on what children have heard in the input....

105. *Title*: Phonological Neighborhood Density Effects in a Rhyme Awareness Task in Five-Year-Old Children
Abstract: Investigates one plausible source of the emergence of phonological awareness—phonological neighborhood density in a group of 5-year-old children, most of whom were pre-readers. Subjects with a high vocabulary age showed neighborhood density effects in a rhyme oddity task, but 5-year-olds with lower vocabulary ages did not.

106. *Title*: Private Speech in Preschool Children: Developmental Stability and Change, Across-Task Constituency and Relations with Classroom Behavior
Abstract: Examined developmental stability and change in children's private speech during the preschool years across-task constituency in children's self-speech, and across-setting relations between private speech in the laboratory and behavior at home and in the classroom. Clear associations were found between children's private speech use in the laboratory and their behavior in the classroom and at home....

107. *Title*: Input and Word Learning: Caregivers' Sensitivity to Lexical Category Distinctions
Abstract: Twenty-four caregivers and their 2- to 4-year-old children took part in a storybook reading task in which caregivers taught children novel labels for familiar objects. Findings indicate parental speech could provide a rich source of information to children in learning how different lexical categories are expressed in their native language.

108. *Title*: The Ability to Learn New Word Meanings from Context by School-Age Children with and without Language Comprehension Difficulties
Abstract: Investigated young children's ability to use narrative contexts to infer the meanings of novel vocabulary terms. Two groups of 15 7- and 8-year-olds participated; children with normally developing reading comprehension skills and children with weak reading comprehension skills. Results are discussed.

109. *Title*: Relative Clause Comprehension Revisited: Commentary on Eisenberg (2002)
Abstract: Eisenberg (2002) presents data from an experiment investigating 3- and 4-year-old children's comprehension of restrictive relative clauses. From the results, she argues that children do not have discourse knowledge of the felicity conditions of relative clauses before acquiring the syntax of relativization. This article evaluates this conclusion on the basis of the methodology used.

110. *Title*: Adult Reformulations of Child Errors as Negative Evidence
Abstract: Examined whether there was negative evidence in adult reformulations of erroneous child utterances, and if so, whether children made use of that evidence. Findings show that adults reformulate erroneous utterances often enough for learning to occur. Children can detect differences between their own utterance and the adult reformulation and make use of that information.

111. *Title*: J's Rhymes: A Longitudinal Case Study of Language Play
Abstract: A longitudinal study of one child documents an invented language game consisting of suffixal reduplication and onset replacement. Argues that this game may more closely resemble adult rhyme.

112. *Title*: The Acquisition of Nuclei: A Longitudinal Analysis of Phonological Vowel Length in Three German-Speaking Children
Abstract: Studies of vowel length acquisition indicate an initial stage in which phonological vowel length is random followed by a stage in which either long vowels or short vowels and codas are produced. To determine whether this sequence of acquisition applies to a group of German-speaking children, monosyllabic and disyllabic words are transcribed and acoustically analyzed. Results are discussed.

113. *Title*: Brief Report: Developmental Change in Theory of Mind Abilities in Children with Autism
Abstract: A longitudinal study investigated developmental change in theory of mind among 57 children (ages 4–14) with autism. Theory of mind tests were administered on an initial visit and one year later. Data indicated significant developmental improvement in theory of mind ability, which was primarily related to the children's language ability.

114. *Title*: Strip Mining for Gold: Research and Policy in Educational Technology—A Response to "Fool's Gold"
Abstract: Responds to a recent critical report on computers in childhood. Highlights include computers, children, and research; social and emotional development; types of software; motivation; social and cognitive interactions; cognitive development; creativity; language and literacy; writing and word processing; mathematics and reasoning; and science and simulations.

115. *Title*: Developmental Profiles of Children Born to Mothers with Intellectual Disability
Abstract: The developmental status of 37 Australian preschool children (ages 5–78 months) born to mothers with intellectual disability was assessed. In all developmental domains, a substantial proportion of the children (between 35% and 57%) showed a delay of at least 3 months. Delays in physical and communication development were most prevalent.

116. *Title*: Do Children with Down's Syndrome Have Difficulty with Argument Structure?
Abstract: The language transcripts of seven children with Down's Syndrome (DS) and seven typically developing children with comparable mean length of utterance levels were compared for verb argument structure. Findings suggest that syntactic difficulties may delay children with DS in overcoming the optional subject phenomena and the lesser number of anomalous arguments shows their inadequate knowledge of….

117. *Title*: Preschoolers Are Sensitive to the Speaker's Knowledge When Learning Proper Names
Abstract: Two experiments examined young children's use of the familiarity principle when learning language. Found that even 2-year-olds successfully identified the referent of a proper name as the individual with whom the speaker was familiar. However, only 5-year-olds reliably succeeded at determining the individual with whom the speaker was familiar based on the speaker's knowledge of an individual's….

118. *Title*: How Children Use Input to Acquire a Lexicon
Abstract: Examined relation of social–pragmatic and data-providing features of input to productive vocabulary of 63 2-year-olds. Found benefits of data provided in mother–child conversation, but no effects of social aspects of those conversations. Properties that benefited lexical development were quantity, lexical richness, and syntactic complexity. Proposed integrated account of role of social and….

119. *Title*: "One Child, Two Languages: A Guide for Preschool Educators of Children Learning English as a Second Language," edited by Patton O. Tabors. Book Review

Abstract: Maintains that Tabor's edited work is the most comprehensive and practical book on the topic available and an essential part of the knowledge base for early care and education professionals. Highlights the book's practical suggestions, concrete examples to illustrate language principles, and recommendations for teachers. Asserts that the content is timely and of critical importance for early....

120.   *Title*: The Acquisition of Communication Skills by People with Brain Injury: Some Comparisons with Children with Autism
Abstract: This research identifies the extent to which different contexts modified the language of four people with brain injuries. The four contexts included: their own home, a residential camp, a post-camp period with support, followed by a return home with limited support. Measures demonstrate the success of the enriched camp facility.

121.   *Title*: Adjectives Really Do Modify Nouns: The Incremental and Restricted Nature of Early Adjective Acquisition
Abstract: Three experiments introduced 2- and 3-year-olds to novel adjectives either using full noun phrases and describing multiple familiar objects sharing a salient property or describing nouns of vague reference. Found that both groups mapped novel adjectives onto object properties when given taxonomically specific nouns with rich referential and syntactic information, but not when given more general....

122.   *Title*: Attention to Novel Objects during Verb Learning
Abstract: Three experiments investigated whether preschoolers attend to actions or objects when learning a novel verb. Findings showed that children learning nouns in the context of novel, moving objects attended exclusively to appearances of objects. Children learning verbs attended equally to appearances and motions. With familiar objects, children attended more to object motions than appearances, similar....

123.   *Title*: Children's Command of Quantification
Abstract: Two experiments investigated how child and adult speakers of English and Kannada (Dravidian) interpret scopally ambiguous sentences containing numerally quantified noun phrases and negation. Results showed that 4-year-olds' interpretations were constrained by the surface hierarchical relations (the c-command relations) between sentence elements and not by their linear order.

124.   *Title*: Helping Language Grow
Abstract: With early diagnosis and intervention, students with language delays can succeed. This paper presents warning signs and recommends seeking expert help, explaining that supporting such children involves such things as reading to them, using simple but grammatically correct sentences, and following their lead. A sidebar notes areas that may be connected to language delays (e.g., syntax, semantics,....

125.   *Title*: Gestural, Signed, and Spoken Modalities in Early Language Development: The Role of Linguistic Input
Abstract: Examined potential effects of early exposure to sign language on the use of communicative gestures by a bilingual hearing child of deaf parents. Data were analyzed to identify types and tokens of communicative gestures, words, signs, and the ways in which they were combined.

126.   *Title*: Children's Acquisition of the English Cardinal Number Words: A Special Case of Vocabulary Development
Abstract: To understand the development of number–word construction, students in grades 1, 3, 5, and 7 named and counted from a set of numbers into the billions in two studies. Findings are discussed both in relation to children's growing knowledge of the number system and to vocabulary development.

127.   *Title*: The Role of Abstract Syntactic Knowledge in Language Acquisition: A Reply to Tomasello (2000)
Abstract: Argues that Tomasello's (2000) interpretation of young children's conservatism in language production depends on questionable premises. Reviews evidence against the assumptions, showing that children learn item-specific facts about verbs and other lexical items. Asserts that researchers must explore the interactions of lexical and more abstract syntactic knowledge in language acquisition to....

128.   *Title*: Phonemic Awareness: A Complex Developmental Process
Abstract: This article uses a developmental model of language (Situational-Discourse-Semantics or SDS), along with a constellation or neuro-network model, to describe the developmental emergence of phonemic awareness. Ten sources of phonemic awareness are profiled along with developmental continuum, providing an integrated view of this complex development.